The Second Chance for God's People

The Second Chance for God's People
Messages from Hebrews

TIMOTHY W. SEID

WIPF & STOCK · Eugene, Oregon

THE SECOND CHANCE FOR GOD'S PEOPLE
Messages from Hebrews

Copyright © 2008 Timothy W. Seid. All rights reserved. Except for brief quotations in critical publications or reviews, no part of this book may be reproduced in any manner without prior written permission from the publisher. Write: Permissions, Wipf and Stock Publishers, 199 W. 8th Ave., Suite 3, Eugene, OR 97401.

Wipf & Stock
A Division of Wipf and Stock Publishers
199 W. 8th Ave., Suite 3
Eugene, OR 97401

ISBN 13: 978-1-55635-826-5

Manufactured in the U.S.A.

Unless otherwise noted, the Scripture quotations in this publication are from the New Revised Standard Version Bible, copyright 1989, Division of Christian Education of the National Council of the Churches of Christ in the United States of America. Used by permission. All rights reserved.

Bob Hartman, "It's All About Who You Know," Lyrics. *Jekyll & Hyde*, Inpop Records, 2003. Used with permission.

Elizabeth Mahr, "The Start is the Finish," Marathon Guide.com, Accessed March 26, 2008. Online: http://www.marathonguide.com/features/FMStories/ElizabethMahr.cfm. Excerpts used with permission.

For my parents,
Rev. William E. & Mary Jane Seid,
on the occasion of their 60th wedding anniversary

Contents

Acknowledgments xi

Introduction xiii

Section One: The Son Compared to Angels (1:1—2:18)

Jesus Is the One (1:1–4) • 3

Angels Worship the Son (1:5–13) • 9

Take a Closer Look (2:1–4) • 15

Who's in Charge Here? (2:5–9) • 21

Jesus Helps His Siblings (2:10–18) • 26

Section Two: Jesus Compared to Moses (3:1—4:16)

Building Houses, Servants and Sons (3:1–6) • 33

Arriving at the Destination (3:7–11) • 39

Distractions Along the Way (3:12–19) • 44

Rest Area Ahead (4:1–10) • 49

Traveling Together on the Journey (4:11–13) • 54

It's all About Who You Know (4:14–16) • 59

Section Three: Jesus Compared to the High Priesthood of Aaron (5:1—6:20)

Heroes of the Priesthood (5:1–10) • 67

Food for Thought (5:11–14) • 75

Growing Up, Not Falling Back (6:1–8) • 81

Signs of Life (6:9–12) • 89

Seize the Day (6:13–20) • 96

Section Four: The Melchizedek Priesthood of Jesus Compared to the Levites (7:1—8:13)

An Oldie but a Goodie (7:1–10) • 107

More Powerful, Longer-Lasting (7:11–17) • 114

God's Better Half (7:18–25) • 120

He's Just What We Need (7:26–28) • 127

Here a Tent, There a Tent (8:1–6) • 133

New Deal (8:7–13) • 139

Section Five: The Heavenly Sanctuary Compared to the Earthly (9:1—10:39)

The Ineffectiveness of Worship under the First Covenant (9:1–10) • 147

The Effectiveness of Worship under the New Covenant (9:11–17) • 154

Jesus' Single Treatment for the Cancer of Sin (9:18–28) • 160

Jesus Is the Key to Lasting Fulfillment (10:1–18) • 166

Time Is of the Essence (10:19–25) • 172

A Pep Talk for the Last Quarter (10:26–39) • 178

Section Six: Examples and Exhortations to Faithful Living (11:1—13:25)

Faith Is Made Evident in Faithful Lives (11:1–7) • 189

Abraham: Our Journey of Faith that Leads Home (11:8–16) • 197

Abraham to Joseph: The Blessings of Faithfulness (11:17–22) • 204

Moses: Faithful Leadership for the People of God (11:23–28) • 210

Israelites, Joshua & Rahab: Faith Brings Us Through (11:29–31) • 218

The Sordid and Unsorted People of Faith (11:32–40) • 226

The Race Is On (12:1–4) • 236

The Discipline of God and Its Benefits (12:5–11) • 246

Getting There Safely (12:12–17) • 256

Making It to the Top (12:18–24) • 266

Believing Is to "Be Living" at the Summit (12:25–29) • 273

The Christian Path Is a Lover's Lane (13:1–6) • 280

Follow the Leader on the Trail Leading to Life (13:7–9) • 287

The Outer Life of the Believer (13:10–16) • 295

An "Apple"cation a Day Keeps the Soul Doctor Away (13:17–25) • 304

Acknowledgments

I owe a debt of gratitude to the members of Salem Friends Meeting, Liberty, Indiana, for supporting me and working with me through the book of Hebrews. In addition, Earlham School of Religion provided me with the means to put this book together, including the helpful editing suggestions of ESR student Carrie Drees. The reader will find throughout this book references and stories about my wife, Suann, and our five daughters, Abby, Heidi, Emily, Lauren, and Tabitha. It's been my privilege to be a part of their lives and to have them share a part of themselves through my work.

Introduction

I GREW UP AS a preacher's kid. Both of my parents are graduates of Moody Bible Institute. My earliest memories are about attending church and hearing my father preach sermons. One of those memories is of a time when I was allowed to sit with a friend. I must have been about six or seven years old. I don't remember what I was doing, but I'm sure I was being noisy and disruptive. Dad stopped his sermon and told me to go sit with my mother. She was completely embarrassed and a bit angry. I think that was the time she tried to pinch my leg and couldn't get a good grip. She may not have been able to get my attention then, but I did come to her one day around that age and ask her what it meant to be a Christian. My recollection is that she led me down the "Romans Road" and had me pray a prayer of salvation. It must have worked, because most of my life has been lived in a relationship with God through Jesus Christ. Their faithfulness to God has made a lasting impact on me and countless of others who have been privileged to have had them minister to them in their churches.

It was during my junior year of high school in Michigan when I began to feel the call to serve God in the ministry. I decided to attend the Grand Rapids School of the Bible and Music. My eighth-grade sweetheart, Suann, joined me there and after graduation we were married. After that came several more schools. Our life was filled with books and babies.

Somewhere during those years I was aware that my father was preaching through Hebrews. It was the last sermon series of his that I was aware of. I became interested in Hebrews after graduating from Wheaton College Graduate School. We were house-sitting for some people during the summer prior to our moving to Providence, Rhode Island, where I had been accepted into the doctoral program in Early Christianity at Brown University. I knew that an eminent scholar of early Judaism taught in the program. I decided I was going to concentrate my studies on areas that would contribute directly to doing a dissertation on Hebrews. I planned

Introduction

to study Alexandrian Judaism in the works of Philo and Alexandrian Christianity through Clement and Origen. Before I arrived at Brown, however, Horst Moehring became ill and some months later passed away. Throughout the next five years of course work with Stanley Stowers and Susan Ashbrook Harvey, among others, I never thought about the book of Hebrews. It wasn't until the time I needed to submit a dissertation proposal that I discovered clues that suggested Hebrews made use of an ancient Greek form of rhetoric called comparison (*synkrisis*).

I spent the next two years researching and writing my dissertation. My five daughters only remember that I was the one getting them ready for school in the morning, since Suann was unselfishly working full-time to support us. Before tackling the Greek of Plutarch, Hermogenes, and Aphthonius, I was expertly tying hair into ponytails and desperately trying to find one more sock.

I don't know if I had experienced prophetic insight back when I thought about studying Hebrews. In any case, my life has become entwined with the text of a book that has eluded many and continues to be a book of great mystery. I've come back to Hebrews in an attempt to get at the primary message of the document for Christians today. God has led me on a journey that has made its way among the Religious Society of Friends (Quakers). After graduating from Brown University in 1996, I began to serve part-time at a Quaker church in So. Dartmouth, MA called Smith Neck Friends Meeting. After several years we became "convinced Friends." It was because of that opportunity I was led to my current position at Earlham School of Religion in 2001. I discovered a wonderful group of people at Salem Friends Meeting in Liberty, IN, who called me to be their pastor. They patiently listened to me as I began forming my thoughts about the meaning of Hebrews.

LANGUAGE AND LITERARY SETTING

Hebrews is one of the most enigmatic books of the New Testament. We've never known for sure who wrote it, because the document lacks any information about the author. Many in the early Church held that Paul wrote Hebrews. The earliest manuscripts of the Bible, for instance, place Hebrews with the letters of Paul. There have been many conjectures about the authorship, but one of the most enduring comments about the authorship of Hebrews is the statement attributed to Origen, "God knows."

Introduction

Not only do we not know who wrote Hebrews, we also don't know what kind of a document it is. The end of Hebrews is like a letter, but it doesn't begin like one. Other indications suggest that we are to read Hebrews as if it were a speech delivered to an audience. Hebrews even calls itself a "word of exhortation" (13:22), a phrase that could be translated as an "exhortation speech." The author refers to his action as speaking: "And what more should I say?" (11:32). By all accounts, Hebrews reads like a speech. The last chapter of Hebrews, however, looks like a typical ending of a letter. In fact, the same verse that seems to name Hebrews as a speech goes on to say, "for I have written (a verb meaning "to write a letter") to you briefly" (13:22). Scholars will disagree about how to interpret this verse, but all would agree that Hebrews certainly is not "brief."

Even the title is confusing. The book is clearly about Jewish history and the Old Testament, so it makes sense that it is "To the Hebrews." But the language of Hebrews is highly stylized Greek with evidence of Hellenistic rhetoric and philosophy. Also, the text of the Old Testament quoted in Hebrews seems to be from the tradition of the Greek translation (Septuagint or LXX) of the Old Testament.

The most important feature for interpreting the book of Hebrews is its rhetorical structure. As early as John Chrysostom in the fourth century, Hebrews has been described as containing comparison. In my doctoral dissertation, I pointed out the location of these comparisons and demonstrated how they function in Hebrews. Ancient Greco-Roman rhetorical handbooks and elementary exercises (*progymnasmata*) demonstrate how to write a comparison. Speeches from antiquity contain examples of formal comparisons. The second-century author Plutarch wrote comparisons of famous Greeks and Romans.

Hebrews is structured around a series of comparisons: Jesus is compared with angels (1–2), with Moses (3–4), and with the high priest (5–6); the Melchizedek priesthood of Jesus is compared with the Levitical priesthood (7), and the Tabernacle of the Old Testament is compared with the heavenly tabernacle (8–10). After each comparative section, the author draws the lessons for life and encourages the people to remain steadfast in the midst of suffering and persecution.

One of the clues when comparison occurs is that the Greek author would use a construction that is similar to our method of saying, "on the one hand," and "on the other hand." These Greek words, called particles,

Introduction

do not usually get translated in our Bibles. So when we encounter these comparisons, I will point out where this construction occurs.

The way these comparisons function is to take something that is agreed to be a great example or model of something. Then the rhetorician shows how the thing being praised is even better than the great thing. It looks something like this: On the one hand, Moe is a great leader, who rose to the challenge when times looked desperate. On the other hand, Joe is an even greater leader, since not only did he lead the people but he was successful in accomplishing the goal set before him. This is significant for the interpretation of Hebrews. For much of church history, Hebrews has been understood to be about the problem of Jewish Christians lapsing back into the legalism of Judaism in the face of mounting persecution. The rhetoric of Hebrews suggests rather that the author is seeking to encourage the people of God to continue to be faithful by persuading them that, while God was active in the past through people and institutions God enacted, God is now doing something even greater through God's Son. God's people weren't able to accomplish the goal of what God planned, but now they can be assured they will make it all the way together.

CIRCUMSTANCES THEN AND NOW

We really know very little about the circumstances of the community for whom Hebrews was written. We will find that they are not that different from us. We often take what we have for granted and tend to forget what is the central and guiding force in our lives. We face difficult times, and sometimes people fall away from the faith. We need the reminders and encouragement that Hebrews has to offer us. Our faith will be enriched by coming to know better who Jesus is and how we know Jesus is the fulfillment and embodiment of who God is and what the Bible teaches us.

Hebrews functions like an open letter. Although we get glimpses of the historical and social setting of the intended audience, Hebrews contains no explicit address. The closing of the document helps us little, since "those from Italy" (13:24) could mean residents or expatriates. So we don't know the location of the author or the audience. The assumption has been that they were Jewish Christians. But the title of the book, "To the Hebrews" is not considered part of the original writing and was added later to copies of the document. There is nothing explicit in the text to suggest the audience's ethnicity, and it is just as likely that they were

Introduction

primarily Gentile proselytes to a form of Jewish Christianity (for example, 6:1–2 is the language of Gentile conversion).

As to the date of writing, we are also at a loss. Scholars have assumed, since Hebrews fails to mention the Jerusalem temple, it must have been written after the temple's destruction in 70 CE. Again, it's just as likely that the author wrote in the 50s or 60s. The author's world is not that of a particular historical setting as much as it is a biblical worldview. He writes as though the tabernacle is still in place and priests continue to carry out their duties. In all these ways, Hebrews transcends place and time. Its message, therefore, is still speaking to us today.

MESSAGE OF HEBREWS

As you will see from my writing, I developed a habit early in my preaching days to arrange my messages with three points and to alliterate words. I can't tell you how many times two points of a message come to my mind alliterated and then I spend mind-wracking hours trying to come up with a third. That may happen in this section, because two fundamental aspects of Hebrews that come to mind for me are comparison and community.

Comparison, according to the ancient Greco-Roman texts, functions to show side-by-side how one object is greater than another object considered to be good in itself. One is not praised and the other denigrated. Rather, one is shown to have its merits, and then the other is shown to be even superior. The problem Hebrews surmounts is one of human failure. It's not that Christianity has superceded Judaism. Hebrews states the law of Israel, the Torah, was valid (2:2); Israelites were evangelized (4:2, 6); the roll-call of the faithful begins with the figures of biblical history. What God has done in Jesus is a Jewish response to a human dilemma. For that, we Gentiles must be eternally grateful.

That leads me to the second alliterative term, community. In the ancient world people thought of themselves as members of a community, which might be as small as a family unit or it might be as large as an ethnic group or nation. Our mentality in the post-enlightenment Western world has been to focus on our individual selves. The religious effect of this is often illustrated by the title words of the popular song, "I Come to the Garden Alone." That's not really the biblical view, nor is it the view of Hebrews. The Apostle Paul, for example, sees people relating to God as members of the ethnic/nationalistic groups of Jews/Judeans and Gentile

Introduction

nations. The author of Hebrews conceives of people as being members of the people of God, either as pre-Jesus members or post-Jesus members. The first group failed as they tried to reach the intended goal of the Promised Land. Hebrews claims that God has given God's people a second chance to remain faithful and enter God's rest.

You've been waiting to see if I would come up with a third alliterated point. I won't disappoint you—unless you don't like alliteration. The third is completion. I will spend a considerable amount of time discussing the word "perfect" and other related terms. The language of perfection has to do with attaining the goal (*telos*). Our English words "complete" and "mature" most clearly describe the concept of the Greek language regarding "perfection" (*teleiōsis*). Put simply, we as followers of Jesus—the one whom God made perfect (2:10; 5:9; 7:28)—must strive to complete God's work in us, so that together the people of God will complete the goal of entering God's rest. The author of Hebrews portrays Jesus as a human person who endured suffering and persevered through trials. Because of that God exalted Jesus, and Jesus inherited the position of Son of God. Through his experience he was appointed to be a heavenly high priest. All of this was for the purpose of bringing the people of God to its stage of completion in the heavenly realm. Within our communities we function to help each other achieve spiritual and moral maturity, to fulfill the grand design God has for each one of us together.

Section One

The Son Compared to Angels
(1:1—2:18)

Jesus Is the One (1:1–4)

A FATHER'S RELATIONSHIP TO a son is a special bond. But I wouldn't know about that—I have five daughters. I wouldn't trade any of them for a son, but I can't help feeling I've missed something other men have experienced with their sons.

While we were expecting our first child, we picked out boy names and girl names. I was elated to watch our first child being born. After discovering we had an Abby and not a little Timmy, I probably told myself, Maybe the next one will be a boy. In spite of what you may think, I did not keep trying to get my wife pregnant just to try for a boy. Over the next 11 years, we had four more children—all girls. I can honestly say, I was happy with each daughter being born. I do remember, however, watching one of them being born and looking for a tell-tale sign that it was a boy. Would this be the one? Would this one be the son I wanted? It was not to be. We eventually figured out what was causing us to keep having babies and fixed the problem. I still wonder what it would have been like to raise a son, but usually we're too busy—and proud, and fulfilled—with our five daughters to think of what might have been.

When we read the Old Testament, we understand how important bearing sons was to families. Because of the way society was structured, sons would bring greater prosperity to a family through the work they did. Daughters would tend to be a drain on the family's wealth, especially when it came to giving a dowry for her marriage. The sons in the family would, of course, bring in the dowries from their wives. As unfair as that system was, it is the cultural context for how people thought about sonship.

There was another connection between a father and a son. Daughters were thought to be more closely connected to their mothers, while sons were considered to have received more "maleness" and, therefore, to be more like their fathers. We still use the expression, "He's a spittin' image of his dad." In that patriarchal culture, being more like Papa gave sons greater respect and more power than daughters.

Section One: The Son Compared to Angels

That connection between fathers and sons came to be symbolized in one of the most important figures in Israelite society. The king was portrayed as God's son on earth. Psalm 2, the coronation psalm, depicts this relationship. In Ps 2:6 Yahweh states, "I have set my king on Zion, my holy hill." The king responds in vs. 7, "I will tell of the decree of the LORD: He said to me, 'You are my son; today I have begotten you.'"

Before Israel developed a monarchy, there was another group referred to as "sons of God." Angels were designated this way in Gen 6:4, "The Nephilim were on the earth in those days—and also afterward—when the sons of God went in to the daughters of humans, who bore children to them. These were the heroes that were of old, warriors of renown." The Psalms also speak of angels in this way. For instance, Psalm 89:6 asks, "For who in the skies can be compared to the LORD? Who among the heavenly beings (lit. "sons of God") is like the LORD?"

For the author of Hebrews, Jesus was the only one who fulfilled this role as God's son completely. That which was said of others was fulfilled in the person and work of Jesus. Everything pointed forward and had its culmination in Jesus, God's son. In this first section of Hebrews, the author begins to draw a comparison of the son to angels in the way God has communicated to people over the thousands of years. Jesus is God speaking to us (1:1–2), the radiant image of who God is (1:3a), and is the effective agent of God in the world (1:3b–4).

JESUS IS GOD'S SPEECH
FROM GOD'S OWN MOUTH (1:1–2)

In biblical antiquity, God spoke to God's people through a variety of emissaries. The author of Hebrews will come to focus more on the role of angels, but first he will mention the role of the prophets. The prophets talked about the future time as the last days or latter days. The author of Hebrews considers his own time as those last days. God now has spoken to us—not just to people a long time ago and in a far away place (1:1). In the past God spoke through angels and prophets in mysterious ways, but now God has spoken by God's own Son (1:2).

Remember that sonship in Jewish thought was not just a family relationship. It was also used metaphorically to represent other roles. We noted earlier the text in Genesis that mentions the "sons of God" procreating with the daughters of men (Gen 6:2, 4). Those "sons of God" came

Jesus Is the One (1:1–4)

to be viewed as angels, the angels that fell from God's favor (Job 1:6; 2:1; 38:7; cf. Matt 5:9; Luke 20:36). We also explained the way in which the king is called God's son. Sonship, therefore, came to be a messianic title (Messiah or Christ simply meaning the anointed one, the king). We'll also see how the role of messiah came to have two aspects. In the time after the Babylonian captivity and the return of the Jews to the land under the rule of the Persians, two figures came to power representing dual messianic roles. One was the king and the other was the high priest (Zech 6:11–13). In Hebrews, Jesus comes to fulfill both aspects. In fact, the role of high priest figures more prominently in Hebrews than that of the political ruler. Through his life and death, Jesus is named to be Son and is appointed to be God's heir over all (1:2–4). Yet, Jesus existed prior to birth, life and death, since it is through him that God created the world of time, space and matter (1:2).

People search all their lives for the one thing that will give meaning to their existence. Maybe it will be the career they choose that defines them and gives meaning to the time and energy they expend in life. Maybe it will be in collecting meaningful things: house, car, land, art, music, books. Maybe it will be in the selecting of a soul mate, the coming together of two whole people who become two parts of one life. Many people find that life only comes to have ultimate meaning when they discover the finality of God's voice in our world through the deep spiritual connection with Christ. God always has the last word, and God's last word to the world was Jesus. We continue to hear whispers of God in worship and meditation, but Jesus was the shout of God, "My son, this is Him; this is Me!"

George Fox, the founder of the Religious Society of Friends (Quakers), looked for the one who would speak to his condition. He sought out the priests of the Church, but he was not satisfied with what they had to say. He turned to the protestants—the dissenters—and sought help among their pastors. Their words were also found to be inadequate. Fox tells in his *Journal* of the only one he found to meet his need.

> And when all my hopes in them and in all men were gone, so that I had nothing outwardly to help me, nor could tell what to do; then, Oh! then I heard a voice which said, "There is one, even Christ Jesus, that can speak to thy condition." When I heard it, my heart did leap for joy. Then the Lord let me see why there was none upon

the earth that could speak to my condition, namely, that I might give him all the glory.[1]

We are missing out if we have not heard God speaking in the person of Christ, if Christ has not come to be in the center of who we are. Our lives will be poorer for not defining our own existence in relationship to the person of Christ, the one whom the Scriptures identify as God's Son.

JESUS IS THE RADIANT IMAGE OF GOD'S GLORY AND ESSENCE (1:3A)

The author of Hebrews attempts to tell us what kind of a being the Son is, what sort of nature he has. He explains the relationship of the Son to God with two terms that refer to copies or emanations from an original. The first term is "reflection." You might say that, if you could hold a mirror up to God, what you would see in the mirror is the image of God's Son. This same term appears in the Greek Bible to personify Wisdom: "For she is a reflection of eternal light, a spotless mirror of the working of God, and an image of his goodness" (Wisdom 7:26). The second term is synonymous with the first. In the same way a reflection is a copy of the original object, so an "imprint" or "stamp" is the copy of an original object. God's Son is the physical instantiation of the divine essence of God's being. God not only created the worlds through Jesus (1:2) but holds the material universe together through "his powerful word" (1:3), the pronouncement of "Let there be ..." (Gen 1:3, 6, 14).

Quakers often talk of Jesus as the Light or Inner Light. I think the author of Hebrews would say that God is the lamp, but Jesus is the light. It is hard for us to conceive of what the real difference is. The point is that Jesus is the expression of God's presence, actions and power in the world: The doing of God is Jesus, the speaking of God is Jesus, the presence of God in our lives is Jesus. The mystery of God in our world is brought to life for us through the Son who shows us the will and work of God all around us.

---

1. George Fox, "A Journal or Historical Account of the Life, Travels, Sufferings of George Fox: In Two Volumes," vol. 1 in *Works of George Fox* (Philadelphia; New York: Marcus T. C. Gould, 1831), 74. Accessed: March 14, 2008. Online: http://dqc.esr.earlham.edu/toc/E12877488A-000.

Jesus Is the One (1:1-4)

JESUS IS THE EFFECTIVE AGENT OF GOD (1:3B-4)

The angels of God and the prophets could bring messages from God and act on God's behalf, but what they could not do was make a once-and-for-all cleansing of sins. Jesus was both high priest and sacrifice, who made the purification of sins—and then he sat down (1:3). His status as Son exceeded that of angels, and his inheritance was more distinguished than theirs (1:4). He had accomplished what others were not able to do for over a thousand years. The work was finished and Jesus sat down next to God at God's right hand.

Remember blackboards? I don't know why we went from blackboards to green boards and now to whiteboards. Sometimes the writing on chalkboards sort of stays there, even after it's been worked over with an eraser. Sometimes the chalk just gets smudged around on the board. The worst situation with a blackboard is when in school your name gets on the board. Maybe you were talking, cut in line, or just forgot your homework—maybe worse. You can see your name on the board, maybe a few marks next to it. Even after the board is erased, there's still a faint reminder of your wrongdoing.

It doesn't matter what your spouse or your closest friend may tell you, you have not always been perfect—you have not yet arrived. I'm sure you are wonderful in every way, but you're not perfect. You also may be great at forgiving others, making restitution, finding ways to make things better, but you can't make up for the failures of others and especially for yourself. If we had the power to wipe our slate clean, we would have to keep using the magical eraser until we wore it out.

That's not true of Jesus. What we couldn't do, Jesus has done. He's not standing at the chalkboard continually erasing the marks against us. He finished erasing the board, washed it clean of all the chalk dust so there's not even the hint of writing against us, and then he went and sat down—next to the principal, if we continue the metaphor. So now we have a chance to live life the right way. We know who this one is and we've become his followers. There have been great teachers, prophets, and world leaders, but Jesus is the one who did it all. The message of Hebrews will be, So don't you dare neglect, forget, grow tired, become weak, or turn away from this one. He is the one on whom we are pinning our hopes and we must continue on so that we may arrive at our final destination.

Section One: The Son Compared to Angels

∽

In this first section, the author started to draw a comparison of the Son to angels in the way God has communicated to us over the thousands of years. Put succinctly, Jesus is God speaking to us, the radiant image of who God is, and he is the effective agent of God in the world.

Every so often I will watch the Matrix movies again. Do you remember the question, Is Neo the one? They had been waiting for the One, looking for the One. We learn that there had been others, but the cycle of the Matrix had continued. Neo became the One and stopped the cycle. He broke through and freed everyone. But people still had to accept reality, they had to make choices, they had to persevere.

No, Neo is not the one (and certainly Keanu Reeves is not the one). Jesus is the One, not the angels of God. Jesus is the One who has spoken God's message to us. Jesus is the One who radiates the very essence of God's being. Jesus is the One who set us free. Jesus, God's Son, is the One.

Angels Worship the Son (1:5–13)

SOME OF THE MOST intriguing religious figures for people are angels. Back in the 90's we seemed to have been going through an angel craze. My family and I were living in southeastern Massachusetts at the time. A newspaper photographer took a photo of the sky and in that photo people saw the image of an angel. For many people that was a meaningful revelation of the presence of the angelic world. Some people think they have a guardian angel that is always with them. One tradition about angels is that when people die they become angels. For some religious groups, the angelic world is a very real presence and is part of their everyday experience.

In the pre-scientific world of antiquity, people were even more fascinated by the spirit world. For the Hebrew people, angels were God's messengers and often accompanied the great acts of God among the Israelite people. God was called Lord Sabaoth, the Lord of Hosts—the hosts referring to the angelic army of God. Worship in the temple was often characterized by the presence of angels, particularly the creatures known as cherubim and seraphim.

After the time when much of the Judean nation was exiled in Babylon and then returned to the land under the domination of the Persians, the literature of the Jews, particularly apocalyptic writings, came to be filled with stories of angels. Angels are involved in creation, the Fall, the Flood, the Patriarchs, Moses and the exodus, the giving of the law, the institution of the tabernacle and sacrificial system, and the settlement in Judea. Most of all they are connected to the heavenly realm, and in the future will be involved in the final battle.

When the author of Hebrews decided to write about the superiority and finality of Jesus, he first selected the greatest personages of biblical history in order to compare Jesus to them and show that Jesus has surpassed them. The author of Hebrews will present a chain of quotations to show that Jesus has a greater status than the angels. In fact, he will show

Section One: The Son Compared to Angels

that the angels bow to the authority of Jesus (1:5–6), and that angels are even the servants of those who will inherit salvation (1:7–12). The Son has been chosen above all others; all others serve the Son, the Son being the only one who reigns on the throne next to God (1:13).

ANGELS ARE NOT CHOSEN BUT ARE WORSHIPPERS OF THE SON (1:5–6)

The author of Hebrews writes, "For to which of the angels did God ever say." The expected answer is, none of them. The first quotation is from the enthronement or coronation Psalm 2, "You are my Son; today I have begotten you." Remember that in the Old Testament, the anointed king of Israel is referred to as God's son. The author of Hebrews most likely knew Psalm 2 as a unit. From all indications in Hebrews, the author most likely was reading and quoting from a Greek translation of the Bible, one not too dissimilar from the manuscripts still in existence. This Psalm describes the installation or inauguration of Israel's king, the messiah, the "anointed one." In the Greek Bible, the word is "Christ." The rulers of the Gentile nations are in opposition to Israel—to Yahweh and his Christ. In verses 6–9 the king is speaking about his inauguration as king. It's as if God says to the one to be anointed, "This day is like the day of your birth, when you become my son. It is your inheritance day, and I will give you the Gentile nations (in battle) if you only ask."

The next quotation in 1:5 ("I will be his Father, and he will be my Son") comes from 2 Sam 7:14. Again, the king is described as God's son. In this text God is speaking to David through Samuel. After David dies, God will raise up another king from David's line (2 Sam 7:12). This descendant will build God's house, and his throne will be established eternally (2 Sam 7:13). God will have a father and son relationship with this messianic figure (2 Sam 7:14). This messiah will experience punishment at the hands of humans, but his reign will continue eternally (2 Sam 7:16).

Verse six cites another biblical text ("he brings the firstborn into the world"), this one from Psalm 89. The author of Hebrews, reading this psalm in Greek, would certainly understand 89:6 as referring to Jesus, "For who in the heavens shall be compared to the Lord (Jesus) and who shall be likened to the Lord (Jesus) among the sons of God (angels)?" This understanding of "sons of God" is made stronger by recognizing that the Greek Bible of Job 1:6 and 2:1 translate the Hebrew "sons of God"

Angels Worship the Son (1:5–13)

as "angels of God." Psalm 89 goes on to describe a vision of David, who calls upon God saying, "You are my Father, my God, and the helper of my salvation" (Ps 89:26; LXX 88:26). The next verse identifies the person in question as the pre-eminent son, the firstborn. The psalm goes on to talk of the enduring character of the reign of this messiah who is God's firstborn son (Ps 89:28–29).

The next quotation in Hebrews ("Let all God's angels worship him") probably comes from Deut 32:43. Again, this is a quotation dependent on the Greek Bible, which reads, "Rejoice, O heavens with him and let all the sons of God worship him. Rejoice, O gentiles, with his people and let all the angels of God be strengthened by him" (trans. mine). The author of Hebrews takes the object of this worship to be God's messiah.

These quotations substantiate the assertion that God places greater value in the one who is the anointed ruler than the angels. This one is actually called God's Son and God is a Father to the Messiah. Not only that, the angels are destined to be the worshippers of God's Son, the Messiah.

This makes sense, doesn't it? Could you imagine someone in the legends of Camelot holding great reverence for a knight or maybe even for a herald, the messenger of the king? The crowds give great acclaim and applause for these individuals of the court. Then someone stands up and begins to speak about Arthur. The knights are important in the protection of the kingdom and the heralds bring the important messages, but most important of all is the king, King Arthur. To him has been given Excalibur, he is the chosen King of Camelot. These others are merely the servants of the King.

The author of Hebrews wants to be sure people understand that even the angelic "sons of God" do not equal the "firstborn" son, the one who is God's king par excellence. Angels are, according to Scripture, beings who worship the one who is God's messiah.

COMPARISON OF ANGELS TO THE SON (1:7–12)

The author of Hebrew begins here the formal language of comparison (*synkrisis*). Verse seven begins with the untranslated particle *men* introducing the comparative exchange. Verse eight makes the transition to the better half of the comparison with the conjunction *de*. The grammar of the Greek reads, "On the one hand, about the angels he says, . . . On the other hand, about the Son he says, . . ." The author continues to draw the comparison by quoting from the Bible.

The quotation in verse seven ("He makes his angels winds, and his servants flames of fire") comes from Psalm 104. The context of the passage in the psalm is God's power over natural forces. Most modern English translations render the Hebrew of the psalm similar to the New Revised Standard Version, "You make the winds your messengers, fire and flame your ministers." In Hebrew the same word is commonly translated either "wind," "spirit," or "breath." The same can be said for the Greek word, but there is a more common term for "wind" in Greek. The literal translation of the Hebrew into Greek and the natural implication of the Greek leads to the interpretation Hebrews brings to the psalm, "He makes his angels spirits, and his ministers a flaming fire."

Think of those two concepts together, the wind and flame. Both wind and flame are able to go anywhere, penetrate anywhere. They can have such devastating and awesome power. Yet there is something temporary and fleeting, such vulnerability. That's how Hebrews understands the nature of angels in comparison to God's Son.

Verse eight begins the second half of the comparative exchange. Instead of a vulnerable and fleeting presence, the Son has an everlasting kingdom. An important grammatical point must be made here. In 1:5 the author of Hebrews used a particular grammatical construction without a preposition for the direct address of God to angels, "For to which of the angels did God ever say." In verse seven, God is not addressing the angels. Hebrews begins with the statement, "Of the angels he says." The following quotation is about or concerning the angels. Verse eight has the same construction, "But of the Son." The next quotation, then, is about the son, but not a direct address to the son, in spite of the fact it is often taken that way. The first part of the psalm quoted from Psalm 45:6 contains the statement addressed to Yahweh, "Your throne, O God, endures forever and ever. Your royal scepter is a scepter of equity." In the next line the psalmist addresses the king, the messiah, "You love righteousness and hate wickedness. Therefore God, your God, has anointed you with the oil of gladness beyond your companions." In this comparison, the angels are ministering spirits, but God's anointed is exalted above all others.

The next quotation in Hebrews 1:10–12 is nearly identical to the Greek Bible (Ps 102:25–27; LXX Ps 101:26–28). It tells us, though the material world is impermanent and temporary, the divine quality is perma-

Angels Worship the Son (1:5–13)

nence and eternity. Everything around is wearing out. Our clothes wear out. Our cars wear out. We wear out. Even our earth is wearing out; the sun is wearing out. It's just the nature of things. The divine is what lasts forever. Our future in this world is limited. Our future with Christ is eternal. It's not through angels that we share in that eternity.

PROPER PLACE FOR ANGELS (1:13)

In verse 13 the author asks a rhetorical question with an expectation that the answer is in the negative. The words of this psalm were never said about any angel. Psalm 110 is another messianic psalm and a very important text for the author of Hebrews. The quotation Hebrews gives begins in the psalm with this phrase, "The LORD said to my Lord." The capitalization of the first instance of Lord means that it translates the divine name, Yahweh. In other words, "Yahweh says to my lord (the king)." The Israelites imagined their king to be enthroned next to God in power. This psalm looked forward to the time when God would defeat Israel's enemies. This psalm goes on to identify the eternal priesthood of the messiah as that of Melchizedek (Ps 110:4), a theme Hebrews will continue to work toward until chapter seven.

The proper place for angels is not next to God on the throne. That is reserved for God's anointed, God's son. In fact, Hebrews tells us, angels are divine servants (a conflation of terms from Ps 104:4) and serve humans. As great as angels are, the Son is due greater reverence.

I'm something of an Anglophile—I like all things British. Many Americans are fascinated with the role of the Queen in Great Britain. Think of how court cases are represented as being prosecuted on behalf of R, *Regina*, the Queen. A rank of barrister is QC, Queen's Counsel. James Bond is a member of HMSS: Her Majesty's Secret Service. All those who are servants or ministers in the British government function on behalf of the Queen.

Similarly, all that the angels do are on behalf of the Son, God's anointed one. When we pray, the angels of God may be called into action, but it is through the authority of the one who sits next to God's throne in heaven. No angel achieved that status, only a human, the one called Jesus, the one appointed as Son of God, the Messiah, who is both King and High Priest.

Section One: The Son Compared to Angels

∽

It is the Son, therefore, who has been chosen above all others. All others serve the Son. It is only the Son who reigns on the throne next to God.

Whom do we call on in prayer? Some of us Protestants are confused about the practice of Catholics. It seems like they can't decide whom to worship. Do they say a prayer to Mary? Maybe they do something to St. Jude, or some other saint, depending on who is the patron saint of what they need. I remember listening to a friend talk about when he first learned about Jesus. Someone told him to pray to Jesus, the Son of God. He couldn't understand why he would pray to God's Son. His comment was, "Why talk to the kid? Why not talk directly to the Father?"

We do pray to God, but we come to God through the Kid. Jesus has earned the right to be God's Son. We join with the angels to recognize the rightful place of Jesus. It is through him that we are among those who are to inherit salvation.

Take a Closer Look (2:1–4)

SCHOOL IS TOUGH, BUT just wait until you get into the real world. In the movie *The Librarian*, the main character, Flynn Carsen (played by Noah Wyle), had never been out of school. He had 22 advanced degrees and his graduate school mentor signed off on Flyn's latest doctorate in Egyptology mid-semester, forcing him to leave the world of academia and go into the real world. Flynn Carsen finally begins to make practical use of his knowledge and also begins to learn some things he hadn't learned in school.

School is meant to prepare us for real life, but there are greater responsibilities and greater rewards in the real world. There are also greater trials and greater consequences in the real world. If we miss class or get a bad grade, we might get detention or probation. In the real world, if we miss too much work or fail at a project, we might get demoted or even fired. If we misbehave in school, we might get expelled. In the real world, if we misbehave, we might get arrested, fined, or even go to prison. Neglecting the rules and doing whatever we want when we're young may mess up the rest of our lives, but if we live wild and careless in the real world, it can lead to an early death.

The followers of Jesus in the mid to late first-century knew their Bibles. They knew that the people of God had often made bad choices as God sought to lead them out of Egypt to the Promised Land and give them instructions for how to be God's people. The generation that entered the wilderness was not the generation that made it out and into the Land. Those who transgressed God's law and disobeyed God's instructions received judgment. The tabernacle was a busy place as the priests continually offered sacrifices for the sins of the people.

Now that we have experienced the beginning of the end of the age through Jesus, along with the outpouring of God's Spirit on all people, shouldn't we take even greater care about how we maintain our allegiance to God? In this section of Hebrews, we are admonished to persevere (2:1), warned about being neglectful (2:2–3a), and we are reminded exactly what this salvation is that we have received (2:3b–4).

ADMONITION TO PERSEVERANCE (2:1)

Since what God has spoken recently at this end of the age is through the Son, it is necessary that we give a greater degree of attention and concern to that message, otherwise we might be drawn away from it (2:1). This idea is reiterated later in Hebrews 13:9: "Do not be carried away by all kinds of strange teachings; for it is well for the heart to be strengthened by grace, not by regulations about food, which have not benefited those who observe them." If we aren't careful about what we're doing, we might drift away from where we meant to go.

Driving a car is that way. I sometimes think I ought to just open up a driver's training school. I trained my two oldest daughters to drive, and now I need to begin training the next two. I like to give pointers about driving, sort of the Zen of driving. For instance, we should learn to drive defensively, always looking ahead to what's happening a distance in front of us. Not everyone knows before they learn to drive that people have a tendency to drive in the direction they look. I learned that riding a bicycle. When riding a ten-speed bike twenty miles per hour down a highway with only a few inches of roadway, it's crucial that you keep going straight even when you turn your head to look behind you. The tendency is to veer to the left a little when you turn your head around to the left. It could be a deadly mistake. Even driving a car, if we turn our attention to the left to check traffic behind us when changing lanes, we have a tendency to drift in the direction we are looking.

The same holds true when steering our lives. We get distracted in life by those things around us. When we watch too much TV or the wrong kinds of TV, our values begin to be shaped by what attracts our attention. We may hang around with people that don't have the same worldview we do. We want to get along with people and be liked, so we begin to talk and act like they do. Fellow travelers in life are sometimes driving toward places that emphasize selfishness and pleasure, and we are drawn into that flow of traffic. Before we know it, our spirituality and our morality has been left to the side and we are heading for a collision. We can't lose site of what God has done in this dawn of the kingdom brought about by Jesus and the presence of God's Spirit.

Take a Closer Look (2:1-4)

WARNING AGAINST NEGLECTING SALVATION (2:2-3a)

The author of Hebrews warns about the dire consequences of ignoring this salvation. The author wants us to consider two things about what people experienced in the Old Testament. First (2:2a), we shouldn't forget God gave the Israelites the law. In fact, Jewish teaching was that angels were involved in the giving of the law. The book of Acts mentions this: "You are the ones that received the law as ordained by angels, and yet you have not kept it" (Acts 7:53). Second (2:2b), the record of the books of Moses is that the Israelites always received a just punishment for transgression of the law and disobedience of God.

Since these two things were true about what we read in the Bible, how can we expect to escape from due judgment if we neglect such a great salvation that has been offered to us (2:3)? This same message is repeated in 12:25: "See that you do not refuse the one who is speaking; for if they did not escape when they refused the one who warned them on earth, how much less will we escape if we reject the one who warns from heaven!" The author of Hebrews wants them to understand the real danger inherent in disobeying God and being led astray.

This danger does not seem real to us. Nowadays kids have video games that simulate exciting adventures. When I was a kid, the most exciting kind of a game was to play cops and robbers or play war games. I remember one time I was playing cops and robbers with this girl. We were visiting her family in another town, so I was making the best of the day. She and I were on the same side and we were pretending to be in a gun fight. We were huddled down behind some furniture in the family room. There we were, pinned down. I'm sure I was deep into the game and my little heart was pounding. I was going to make a run for it. As I began to make my move, I told her, "Cover me!" Instead of a hail of gun fire from her, she picked up a blanket and put it over me. That completely spoiled my ability to imagine any real danger.

The story goes that there was a boot camp that was having trouble getting proper weapons for war games. Instead of real rifles they had toy guns. The guns didn't have bayonets, so they cut off broom stick handles and strapped them to the end of the gun barrels. A soldier asked the drill sergeant, "How are we supposed to use these things."

The sergeant replied, "For now, just go 'bangety, bangety' when you're firing your weapon."

Section One: The Son Compared to Angels

"But what about the bayonet," the soldier asked.

"Well, just say 'stabby, stabby,'" were the instructions. The time for training arrived and the two teams faced off in their bunkers. As the one team was advancing, the soldier noticed a man on the opposing group coming towards him without any weapon. He fired at him with his toy rifle, "Bangety, bangety." The man kept coming closer to him. He wasn't falling down as though shot. When he got close enough, the soldier used his bayonet, "Stabby, stabby," he yelled. No effect on him. The other soldier kept walking straight toward him, stepped on his toes, ran right in to him, knocking him down. As the soldier lay on the ground, his enemy walked over the top of him. As the man stepped off his chest, the soldier could hear him muttering in a low voice, "Tankety, tankety, tank."

The experience of the Israelites was real enough. God promised to bring them out of Egypt, through the Red Sea, across the desert, and into the Promised Land. Moses had gone up the mountain at Sinai to listen to God's instructions, to give the new people of God a constitution, a set of laws for how to live together and how to be God's people. When Moses returns to the people, he finds that they have abandoned the worship of the one God and are having a wild party worshipping a golden calf. In the ensuing years, time after time, they are led astray. "We're too hungry; we're too thirsty. We'll never make it. Moses, are we there yet?" God had told them what to do. When they transgressed and disobeyed, the consequences were real. But now, the author of Hebrews is saying, we're not just talking about obtaining rest from a long journey. We're talking about our ultimate destiny, the very immortality of our souls. This isn't your father's or your grandfather's school of life, this is life that schools us for eternity.

REMINDER OF THE VALIDITY OF THE GOSPEL (2:3b-4)

Jesus preached the saving gospel, according to the second part of verse three. The first generation of Jesus' followers confirmed the validity of the gospel (2:3b). The audience of Hebrews were people who heard the apostles talk about what Jesus had said and done. The apostles and others attested to it. The author of Hebrews is saying in 2:2, the law had been valid (Gk. *bebaios*) and, similarly, in 2:3 the gospel had been validated (Gk. *bebaioō*) by the apostles and other witnesses.

The language of verse four is reminiscent of the Acts of the Apostles. In Acts the message of the gospel is confirmed by the presence of supernatural phenomena. It was the same signs of God's breaking into the world with the coming of the end of the age in the ministry of Jesus. The beginning of Hebrews 2:4 reads, "God added his testimony by signs (Gk. *sēmeion*) and wonders (Gk. *teras*) and various miracles (Gk. *dunamis*)." Compare this to Acts 2:22: "You that are Israelites, listen to what I have to say: Jesus of Nazareth, a man attested to you by God with deeds of power (Gk. *dunamis*), wonders (Gk. *teras*), and signs (Gk. *sēmeion*) that God did through him among you, as you yourselves know." Hebrews says the Holy Spirit was distributed (Gk. *merismos*) among those who were the first witnesses. The narrative of Acts deals with the sign of God's acceptance of Gentiles by the giving of the Holy Spirit. It is first signified at Pentecost with the image of the lightning that forked like tongues of fire and spread itself to each of the apostles. Acts 2:3 says, "Divided (Gk. *diamerizō*) tongues, as of fire, appeared among them, and a tongue rested on each of them." The wording of this text and Acts 2 clearly shows a connection between these texts. For the author of Hebrews, there should be no doubt what has happened is the real thing. Jesus said it, the apostles confirmed it, and God corroborated it with supernatural signs.

When new things happen to us, we sometimes become disoriented and wonder if it can be true. When my wife and I traveled to England, it just didn't seem real. You wake up in the morning, and you have to remind yourself, I'm really here. You walk outside, and the signs are everywhere. Cars—mainly small cars—are driving on the left side of the street. Double-decker buses are swinging their way through round-abouts. There's no mistaking the signs that this is not just a fairy-tale land, but it's a real place, with real people, living real lives.

We need reminders sometime that our lives are not just an illusion. Christian faith is not just religious practice intended to give life added significance and a way to cope with the pressures of life. If we do not pay attention to Christian teaching and practice, we can be distracted into thinking that this mortal life is all there is. We might tell ourselves, if we have one chance, only a limited time to experience life, why shouldn't we take the greatest advantage of it for ourselves: Seek the greatest pleasure, the least suffering and effort, and get as much as we can from life?

Take a closer look. This world still remains the only sign of life in the universe. As violent as our earth seems to be at times, as weak and prone to illness as our bodies are, as evil as some people can act, there's no escaping the conclusion that this is an immensely complex and ordered world guided by physical laws that the most intelligent people still can't quite fathom. And this world is not a permanent place: Our lives, even the existence of our world, is a whisper of time, a tick of the universe's clock. It's all designed with a beginning and an end, and we have been given the capacity to try to understand its meaning.

Two thousand years ago Jesus changed the course of human history. Real people in a real place said that Jesus really rose from the dead, providing a way to experience the reality of eternity with God. Millions of people have had their lives changed, become much more than they would have been, and have experienced a life filled with love, joy, peace, and hope. It doesn't get much more real than that.

We are admonished to persevere, warned about being neglectful, and reminded exactly what this salvation is that we have received. Our school teachers have tried to get us to pay attention. Suann and I were in a class in high school with a substitute teacher. It was geometry, as I remember. I don't remember any of the geometry, but I remember that teacher. When we would begin to get noisy, she would bark out the same order as if the two words were one, "Quiet please." Every time, it was the same thing, "Quiet please." It became fun just to get rowdy so she would say, "Quiet please." We had another teacher who liked to use the same corny phrase, "Be Alert. America needs more 'lerts.'" It could have been worse. Funny and corny is better than loud and mean.

Our faith deserves our attention. As nice as we want church to feel and as positive as we want people to feel about their Christian faith, there are real consequences to our failure to take seriously the very real demands of a righteous God. The message of Hebrews contains the promise of a second chance for God's people, but with it comes the responsibility to live up to the challenge of faithfulness to God.

Who's in Charge Here? (2:5-9)

IN TIMES OF CRISIS, we want to know who's in charge. That's what people in New Orleans were wondering after Hurricane Katrina blew threw and left such devastation: "Who's in charge here?" When the levees collapsed and parts of the city began to flood, people sat on roof-tops or wherever they could find to be out of the water, and they waited for help to come. Their signs and their screams were asking, "Who's in charge here?" As rescue workers began to gather and try to coordinate their tasks, they were asking, "Who's in charge here?" A month later and two more hurricanes, Rita and Stan, and a devastating earthquake, people of Earth are wondering, "Who's in charge here?"

Some scientists blame the increased hurricane activity on human action in the production of carbon gases that are thought to be raising the earth's temperature. Some Christians want to insist that in spite of the terrible and evil things that happen in our world, God is in control, God is on the throne, and we have to accept what happens—at least those things beyond our control. But the New Testament repeatedly teaches that the world has not yet been brought under complete control.

The audience of the book of Hebrews includes people who have experienced subjection under the Roman empire. Each day brings another crisis, another upheaval in the order of life; another blow to their ability to cope with the rigors of work and the struggle to survive; another moment of exasperation when they ask themselves, "Is God really in control, is Jesus really reigning with God in heaven? Why is the world like this if Jesus is God's Son, the appointed heir to rule with God, who has been exalted to the heavens beyond the angels."

Who's in charge? Scripture says it's not the angels (2:5-8). In fact it doesn't look like anyone is in charge right now (2:9), but it does look like Jesus is taking charge (2:9).

Section One: The Son Compared to Angels

SCRIPTURE SAYS IT'S NOT THE ANGELS WHO ARE IN CHARGE (2:5–8)

The author of Hebrews has been comparing Jesus to the angels. They have not been appointed and exalted (1:2, 4); they are wisps of wind and fire (1:7, 14); they minister on behalf of God for the benefit of humans (1:14). The angels have had a significant role to play in God's redemptive work in the world. They even took part in the greatest moment of Israelite history, when God gave them the instructions for civic and religious life of their new nation under God (2:1). Now God has done something even greater by appointing and exalting Jesus as God's Son (1:2–4). We would be foolish to ignore this great thing God is doing, because with greater reward comes greater responsibility (2:1–3).

In the rest of chapter two, the author is drawing a connection a step at a time between the concept of Jesus as Son, who has a familial relationship with humans as a brother, to Jesus as High Priest, who performs that function well because of his empathy with humans. Although Jesus shares human experience for a time, he is ultimately exalted above them (2:9). Jesus functions as a pioneer of human experience and will bring sisters and brothers along with him in this victory over death (2:10–16). Because of his sharing in human experience, Jesus is able to serve as an effective high priest (2:17–18). In this way the rest of chapter two is a transition to the next comparison.

In verses 6–8a, the author quotes from Psalm 8. But he introduces the quotation as though he doesn't know who said it or where: "someone has testified somewhere." Perhaps the quotation was part of a collection of quotations from the Old Testament which describe the coming messiah. In any case, the quotation in Hebrews is nearly word for word what we find in the Greek Bible, except for the omission of the phrase "and you have set him over the works of your hands" (LXX Ps 8:7). In the Hebrew Bible, Psalm 8 describes the high status God accorded to humans. We could paraphrase the psalmist's words in this way: "God, I can't believe you would care about humans or the children of humans. You caused humans to be a little less than divinity by showing them such honor and giving them dominion over the world." The Greek translation has allowed for a different way of interpreting the psalm. This messianic reading can be paraphrased in this way: "What is a human being that you are concerned about him, or the messianic "son of man," that you take notice of him? You diminished him a little bit lower than the angels, you have crowned him as messiah with glory and honor, putting everything in subjection under his feet."

For the author of Hebrews, the idiom "a little lower" does not mean "lower rank" but is understood in a temporal sense, "a little while." Psalm 8 then indicates that the messiah is temporarily lower than angels but then crowned with glory and honor, enthroned with everything in subjection to him. Put succinctly, Hebrews concludes the angels are not in charge.

New forms of religion and spirituality come along as people continue to try to find who or what's in charge. Some forms of feminist spirituality say that it's the mother goddess, Gaia, who is in charge. Elizabeth Clare Prophet talks about Jesus as one of many Ascended Masters who come to guide humanity. Tom Cruise is a follower of Dianetics founded by L. Ron Hubbard. Wherever you go, you are sure to find people who are searching for who's in charge. And then they will do whatever they can to influence that entity so that life will be well for them.

Christians act the same way sometimes. We treat prayer and religious observance as a talisman. We act with superstition when we say and do—or don't say and do—particular things because we think unless we say and do—or don't say and do—those things, God will not give us what we want or even punish us by bringing misfortune to us or our loved ones. The answer to the question, Who's in charge?, is not answered by angelic beings, spirit guides, pagan deities, or even a God who is controlled by superstitious acts in the guise of Christian living.

DOESN'T LOOK LIKE ANYONE IS IN CHARGE (2:9)

The author of Hebrews proceeds to comment on two aspects of the Psalm 8 quotation. He wants the audience to know that God did not leave out something. The problem of evil and calamity is not due to God forgetting something and allowing the world to be independent or unrestrained. The reality is, it's too early to see everything being in subjection to Jesus. We just don't see it yet.

We may complain every four years when we have to go through the whole process of electioneering and voting, but we really don't have that much to complain about. Remember how kingdoms and empires used to be. Even if they were fortunate enough to have a clear successor to the throne, the king or queen could be embroiled in war for decades trying to get the various parts of the empire under subjection. The average people on the street may not even know who the current king was—or even if there were one. All they would know is the chaos and confusion that keeps life in constant turmoil. Imagine them saying, "I thought King John was on the throne. Why are there still bandits on the road, crooked tax collectors always increasing rates, and the quality of life spiraling down. Who's in charge?" The answer comes back, "King John is on the throne, but it takes time to get everything under control. Just wait until he comes again, then he'll set everything right."

Granted, it's now been awhile. For the author of Hebrews, it possibly had only been a few decades. Just give it time, he could say. Now it's been several millennia and, as a pastor, I am obligated to tell you, just keep holding on. Not yet, but soon you will see everything under subjection. It may not look like anyone's in charge, but you need to look a little closer.

BUT IT DOES LOOK LIKE JESUS IS TAKING CHARGE (2:9)

We don't see everything in subjection, but we do see Jesus crowned with glory and honor. For about thirty years he was lower than angels, but now he has been exalted. Why was he exalted? Because he suffered in death. It was by God's grace that Jesus would taste death for the benefit of everyone.

Imagine in our make-believe kingdom that the soon-to-be-King John has discovered a plot to overthrow the kingdom. Let's say it's suspected that someone has poisoned all the wine to be used at the inaugural ceremony the following day. If the people are allowed to drink the wine, they might all die. In an act of selfless bravery, King John himself tastes the wine. The next day he rises from bed unharmed, the wine is safe, the people are saved. After the ceremony, a man is returning home and is stopped along the way. The question is asked, "Who's in charge?" The traveler replies, "King John."

"How do you know," asks the townsperson.

"Because I saw him crowned," he responds.

What makes the difference between Christians committed to God and people who are without spiritual and religious commitment? They question, they blame, and sometimes they seek revenge. Why are we able, they might ask us, to live in peace and tranquility, to have love in our hearts, to experience joy, to worship and honor Almighty God, when all around us is tragedy, violence, and loss of life? Three words make the difference for us—or at least they should: We see Jesus. The circumstances of

Who's in Charge Here? (2:5-9)

life are the same for us. We too are stunned by the destruction and loss of life that comes from a tsunami, a hurricane, or an earthquake. We too are disgusted by the many who die each day in a war nearly half-way around the world. We too are brought to tears when we hear of the astounding numbers who are dying in areas of Africa. We are able to live in peace and tranquility, to have love in our hearts, to experience joy, to worship and honor Almighty God, because . . . we see Jesus. Jesus has come to the throne. We don't see everything in subjection yet, but we will.

Who's in charge? Scripture says it's not the angels, in fact it doesn't look like anyone is in charge, but it does look like Jesus is taking charge. One of my favorite series of books of all time has been *The Chronicles of Narnia*. I love the way C. S. Lewis portrayed Jesus as the lion Aslan in *The Lion, the Witch and the Wardrobe*. Under the rule of the white witch, it's always winter and never spring. When her reign is broken and Aslan has come to power, the children first see Father Christmas. Then the snow begins to melt, the stream begins to flow again. The world begins to come alive. Aslan is coming!

How do you see the world? Do you see the world under the domination of evil? Or do you see the glimpses of life that bring hope? Do you see Jesus? Jesus on the throne at the right hand of God? Jesus crowned with glory and honor? The one who tasted death for you? It may not look like it at times, but God has set Jesus in charge and he is coming.

Jesus Helps His Siblings (2:10–18)

THERE ARE WAYS IN which life is easier when you have an older sibling. Older siblings are good to have, because they experience life a few years before you do. Older siblings learn how to do things, and they can teach you, or you can learn from watching them. When you get in a predicament or someone is trying to hurt you, an older sibling might be able to stand up for you, help you, or protect you. You might be less fearful than you would have been otherwise. Sometimes older siblings even take the blame for you.

In chapter one of Hebrews, Jesus is described as one who is appointed to be God's Son. These verses in Hebrews build on that theme in order to relate Jesus' role as Son with his function as High Priest. We might think of this as Jesus being our big brother, for Hebrews shows how Jesus has led the way for his siblings. He is intimately acquainted with all the experiences that his siblings have. It's because of this that Jesus can be the High Priest *par excellence*. Jesus, our big brother, is willing to have us for his siblings (2:10-13), he handles the biggest problems we face (2:14-16), and he is able to help us by putting everything right (2:17-18).

OUR BIG BROTHER HAS US FOR HIS SIBLINGS (2:10-13)

According to Hebrews, God, the one who is in charge of this entire universe, wants to lead his children home to heaven. To do that, God chose Jesus to be the pioneer—the point person, the big brother—in this work of saving God's children (2:10). Jesus had to grow up like anyone else, experience the temptations of life, suffer the same kind of pain we have to experience. God made Jesus into the perfect big brother, for he and we have the same Father. Jesus claims us as his brothers and sisters (2:11). The Old Testament quotations (Ps 22:22; Isa 8:17, 18) confirm for the author of Hebrews that Jesus chose us and willingly became our big brother (2:12-13).

The difference is, kids don't usually have a choice who their siblings are. At the beginning of every school year, I hear my younger kids tell sto-

Jesus Helps His Siblings (2:10-18)

ries about a teacher who says, "Are you Emily's sister," or "Are you Lauren's sister?" The way siblings feel about each other, they usually want to say, "No, we're not related." The teacher might not believe that there are two families with the last name of Seid in the same school and they are unrelated!

When God looked at us and saw what a problem we were, Jesus said, "That's my kid brother; that's my little sister." Jesus acted the part of big brother to lead the way. He claimed you and me and went through life and death ahead of us, so that he could bring us home.

OUR BIG BROTHER HANDLES OUR BIGGEST PROBLEMS (2:14-16)

The biggest problem we face in life is death. These bodies of flesh and blood are prone to disease and injury, they need constant care and nourishment, and they seem to demand all sorts of things that aren't good for us. In order for Jesus to be our big brother, he had to share in the same human experience. If he had intended to be the leader of the angels, he wouldn't have needed a body. But as an embodied and incarnate person, he was here to help humans. Jesus does battle with the biggest bully of the universe, the devil. The devil is depicted as having the power of death and humans are held captive to the fear of death. Jesus is to destroy the devil and set us free from the fear of death.

My brother was too much older than me to have been any help on the school playground. If you had a sibling only a few years older, you might have been able to tell bullies that your big brother or sister would stand up for you. My brother did help me out once, unknowingly. It was spring time and for some crazy reason I went out for cross country. We hit the road after school and ran out into the country. We were joking around and trying to make the best out of running miles in the cold and wet. We saw a car driving down a rode parallel to us. I thought I would be a tough guy for my friends, so I made an obscene gesture to the car. Everyone laughed and I got a little rep' for being so bold. A few minutes later the car drove up to us, stopped, and several big guys got out. I was immediately identified as the one who—let's be honest—flipped them off. Under that pressure, I became the world's greatest actor and liar. I made up a story about how I thought it was my brother, that he drove a car exactly like that. I convinced them that I wouldn't make that gesture to people I didn't know. I was so calm and acted so surprised that it wasn't my brother, that they had no choice but to give me a warning and leave. The fact is, I did have a brother, he was living at home in those days, and if I had seen him driving in a car down the road while I had to run in the cold and the melting snow, I probably would've given him a gesture. The difference is, he would have beaten me up for it.

When we face the inevitable conclusion of our lives, we should remember that our big brother faced the same experience. When pain racks our body and we feel there's no way we can face the end, we know that Jesus experienced the worst that life has to offer. The greatest foe we have in life is a beaten bully; there's no reason to fear death, because Jesus went first and defeated that foe for us.

OUR BIG BROTHER HELPS US BY PUTTING EVERYTHING RIGHT (2:17–18)

Jesus became like us in every way: he cried, he hungered, he thirsted, he became weary and slept, he became angry, he felt sorrow, he bled, he felt pain, he felt abandoned, he gave up his life and died. What more could you ask of someone who is to be your representative, who is to intercede for you in heaven, who is to make your pardon for sin? Like no one else, Jesus is the one who is able to help us.

Pastors and priests are individuals who are meant to help us in life. But many Protestants think that pastors are a different sort of person. People will change how they talk or say something like, "Pardon my French." My father tells of walking up to someone who quickly hid his cigarette behind him. My Dad just kept talking to the guy until finally the cigarette burnt down to his fingers and he had to let go. For Catholics, they have even more reason to feel like their priests might not understand what the regular person goes through. Some might say that a priest can't understand marriage and parenthood. Some may think that a priest couldn't understand the day-to-day struggles of working in a factory or a business, the responsibilities of one's own household, the worry about job security and advancement in order to meet the needs of a growing family. It was undoubtedly the same way with the Israelites. The High Priest of Israel could also be viewed as disconnected to the everyday life of the people. What is most impressive about people called to this ministry is when they are the sort who know how to help people and can get the job done.

Jesus Helps His Siblings (2:10–18)

Jesus is that sort of High Priest. The Gospels report that Jesus grew in wisdom and stature, in favor with God and people (Luke 2:52). Hebrews says Jesus learned obedience by the things he suffered (5:8). According to Hebrews, Jesus achieved the ultimate completeness of life—God perfected him through the things he experienced (2:10). That's why Jesus is able to help us (2:18).

∽

Jesus, our divine big brother, is willing to have us for his siblings. He handles the biggest problems we face, and he is able to help us by putting everything right. Many of us might not be able to remember how our older siblings helped us, because what we remember from childhood tends to be the shocking kinds of things. For instance, I can remember when we were little kids, when my brother was going to examine my throat, pretending to be a doctor. For some strange reason he stuck a Cocoa Puff on the end of a pencil. He touched the back of my throat and made me throw up. Again, I can remember when we were playing softball. I was the catcher, and my brother was up to bat. I must have been too close to the plate, because he swung at a pitch and clobbered me in the head. I've never forgotten that, though I can't quite remember what happened afterwards.

Maybe if we think hard enough we can remember the times when we felt accepted by our older sibling. We felt a sense of confidence about life, because we were following in someone else's footsteps: They had faced challenges and had succeeded, so we knew that we could too. We might even remember that an older sibling was there to help fix things, to smooth things over, to be there for support.

We have that kind of big brother in Jesus. He's proud to call you and me his sibling. He was willing to face the greatest challenge for our benefit. He knows all about what we face and is present with God to intercede for us. That's why Jesus is far greater than the angels and will be shown to be the most excellent heavenly high priest.

Section Two

Jesus Compared to Moses
(3:1—4:16)

Building Houses, Servants, and Sons (3:1–6)

It takes a lot of people and a lot of hard work to build a house. If you watch a show like *This Old House*, you get to see what it takes to build or remodel a house. About the only person you can do without on the *TOH* job site is the guy that's the host—no offense. You need Norm to be the general contractor to oversee the whole project. You need Tom as the carpenter to build the structure of the house. You need Richard to put in all the plumbing and heating. You need Roger to landscape around the house.

Did you see the show with the biblical theme where they had a contractor named Moses? Moses was a hard worker but a bit of the quiet type. People didn't think he could hack the job, but he faithfully showed up each day and rose to each new challenge. They worked like slaves on that job, but when it got too bad he led them out for some rest and refreshment. They went across to Starbucks for milk and honey; it flowed there. Moses seemed really important for that house, until we were introduced to the owner's son. Behind the scenes the owner had been guiding the building of the house along with his son, Joshua. Joshua had been a carpenter's son, but because he had put so much into that house, so much suffering, so much sweat, so much blood, that the owner had adopted him and elevated him to lead architect and designer. The son was preparing the house for his family, and it is a large one.

The author of Hebrews has been narrating the story of Jesus' place in God's salvation history. God has worked in a variety of ways in history. Along with the privileges he has given to humankind have come responsibilities. Through the mediation of angels God had worked in the earliest history of humanity in the formation of the Israelite nation. God's instructions for living in that ancient society were often ignored by the people, and they suffered the consequences. God worked through Moses, the great leader and prophet of the people, to bring them out of enslavement to a land he promised them, a land flowing with milk and honey. Hebrews wants us to understand that the role and status of Jesus as God's son takes the work that God had done in the past to another level. And with that greater level comes even greater responsibilities and consequences. But because this work is carried out through God's Son, it will achieve its purpose among humans and will bring us to our destination.

When we, as residents of a heavenly home, think about the role of Jesus being like Moses', God's faithful prophet, we realize that Jesus is to be honored even greater than Moses (3:1–2). Jesus is like the architect of the heavenly house and is more than a servant like Moses (3:3–4). He is, in fact, the Owner's son and heir to the heavenly estate (3:5–6).

JESUS IS CHARACTERIZED BY FAITHFULNESS TO GOD (3:1–2)

Hebrews describes our relationship with God as a holy partnership in this building company (3:1). God's work among us is not the building of a Christian society or nation like he did among the Israelites. Ours is a heavenly calling (2 Cor 5:2; Phil 3:14; Eph 2:4–7). We are called to give careful consideration to the role of Jesus in God's salvation history. Part of our shared commitment about Jesus is that he is like Moses (3:2). Like Moses, Jesus was sent by God, he functions as high priest, and he is most notable for his faithfulness to God in every respect. The words of Hebrews allude to a verse from Num 12:7. Here the text is describing the way God would speak to other prophets by visions and dreams, but Moses is different than them: "My servant Moses is not so; he is faithful in all my house." Therefore, God will speak face-to-face with Moses. Jesus is faithful just like Moses "was faithful in all God's house."

It wasn't until we were over forty that Suann and I owned our first house. It may take another forty years before we actually get the house furnished the way we would want it. Most of the time our house is just the building we live in. It has that lived-in look. I was talking with a woman who never watches TV. I asked her, "Then where do you eat your meals?" Once in awhile we clear off the place where the clothes are stacked, papers are piled, and the remnants of last month's homework project still sit, and we eat together. Fall is approaching quickly and I need to give the lawn one last mow so that raking leaves isn't like combing the grass. I caught myself thinking the other day, "Soon I need to brush the grass," when I meant "mow the grass." Currently I'm locked out of my garage. So until I

Building Houses, Servants, and Sons (3:1–6)

get a locksmith to let me into the garage or a good wind blows it over, I won't be able to get to the mower and take care of the outside of the house. All of that is to say, it takes a lot more to own a house than to pay the mortgage. A good homeowner is one who faithfully cares for the house.

We can rely on Jesus as the faithful landlord who manages the home in which we reside. This world is a place ideally suited for the kinds of creatures we are. There's no reason to doubt that our experience of life goes on after our death in a home that is also designed by our creator to suit the kind of creatures God has made us to be.

JESUS IS CLAIMED TO BE FABRICATOR AND FURNISHER (3:3–4)

In early Jewish teaching, Moses was highly praised and honored. The following text from the extra-biblical book titled Wisdom of Jesus ben Sirach (or Ecclesiasticus) is typical of the great acclaim accorded to Moses.

> From his descendants the Lord brought forth a godly man, who found favor in the sight of all and was beloved by God and people, Moses, whose memory is blessed. He made him equal in glory to the holy ones, and made him great, to the terror of his enemies. By his words he performed swift miracles; the Lord glorified him in the presence of kings. He gave him commandments for his people, and revealed to him his glory. For his faithfulness and meekness he consecrated him, choosing him out of all humankind. He allowed him to hear his voice, and led him into the dark cloud, and gave him the commandments face to face, the law of life and knowledge, so that he might teach Jacob the covenant, and Israel his decrees. (Sirach 44:23b—45:5)

Hebrews claims that Jesus is worthy of more glory than Moses (3:3). There are several senses of the word "house" in this passage. The word house could refer to the structure in which someone lived, even if that is a tent, perhaps equivalent to our terms "house" and "home." It could also refer to a family group, a tribe of people, as in the expression, "the house of Jacob," or "the house of David." There's also the expression "house of God," which was a way to refer, first, to the tabernacle—the portable tent for worshipping God as nomads—and, secondly, to the temple in Jerusalem. Finally, it could refer to the church (1 Tim 3:15; 1 Pet 2:5 ; 4:17). Jesus is worth more glory than Moses to the same extent that the builder of a house is honored over the house.

Section Two: Jesus Compared to Moses

A few years ago I listened in on a discussion about the basketball abilities of Michael Jordan. These two older guys were talking about the superhuman feats Jordan could accomplish, for which he rightly has been called Air Jordan. But what they were saying was that Jordan was able to run down the basketball court, jump, hang in the air, and do a slam-dunk—and make that leap from half-court line. The younger kids in the room were trying to correct them that Jordan jumped from the free-throw line, but they insisted it was from half-court. Moses was like Michael Jordan for the Jews. His feats became legendary and came to be glorified as superhuman. Yet, you could have Michael Jordan and Moses in the gym, but when Jesus enters, it's Jesus' "house". Hebrews is saying, as great as Moses was, Jesus is worthy of even greater glory and honor.

JESUS IS COMPARATIVELY GREATER AS THE SON OF THE FOUNDER (3:5-6)

Once again in these verses we have the grammatical construction that signals comparison: "Moses, on the one hand, was faithful as a servant. Christ, on the other hand, as a son." Notice that comparison functions by praising the person or object to be compared. Then the comparison is made by showing how the other person or object is even greater. What that means is, Hebrews doesn't denigrate what God did through Moses. But the author does praise Jesus by saying, as great as Moses was, Jesus is even greater. Hebrews makes the comparison that Moses is described as a servant, someone who is a mere attendant to religious ceremony. Jesus is also faithful like Moses, but he is faithful as God's son.

Here the analogy subtly changes and the followers of Jesus become the house. Notice the conditional statement: "We are his house, if we should hold firm." The main idea in Hebrews is that the early people of salvation history often did not hold fast, they did not possess the inheritance they were given, they did not enter the rest promised to them—because of unfaithfulness and disobedience. Hebrews says, there's no guarantee here for you. Don't be like them. You need to hold tight, give firm allegiance to Christ, don't give up.

Suann used to work for a family business. It was a business started by a woman who was passing the business on to her very capable daughter. The son in the family was a nice guy, probably quite intelligent, but he wasn't the front office person. He handled the finances and payroll

Building Houses, Servants, and Sons (3:1–6)

behind the scenes. I got the benefit of going along with Suann to the annual Christmas party, which was always at a posh restaurant around Providence, RI. It was interesting to watch the family interact with the employees. Even though the son had what seems to have been a minor role in the family business and perhaps a lower spot on the organizational chart, you knew that he enjoyed a higher status than heads of departments. I enjoyed talking with him about the interests we shared. But the point is this. A son, who has a small part in the family business, has greater influence than the hired employees. In the same way, Jesus, God's son, has a greater role in God's unfolding of salvation history than God's servants.

We miss the point, however, if we only think of Hebrews as elevating Christianity above Judaism. That's not the point at all. The point is, humans have a poor track record for living faithfully to God. That includes religious people of past centuries. Now we have our own generation to think about. Will future generations look at us and think, "They really dropped the ball in their generation. That was the time when Christians became a minority, when the Bible became an antiquarian curiosity, when people of faith allowed or contributed to violence in the world, when people searched inwardly for meaning and only found an imperfect self." We must hold tight not just to tradition for the sake of tradition but to the reality of God's work in the world, that work that brings hope to the human heart.

※

When we, as residents of a heavenly home, think about the role of Jesus being like that of Moses, God's faithful prophet, we realize that Jesus is to be honored even greater than Moses. Jesus is like the architect of the heavenly house and is more than a servant like Moses. Jesus is the Owner's son and heir to the heavenly estate.

Building houses for poor people is a noble cause. Each one of us, however, works everyday building a house. It could truly by called a habitat for humanity. George Fox, in now famous words, described how we are to live in this world, as people who are leading the way to the heavenly call.

> This is the word of the Lord God to you all, a charge to you all in the presence of the living God; be patterns, be examples in all countries, places, islands, nations, wherever you come; that your life and conduct may preach among all sorts of people, and to them. Then you will come to walk cheerfully over the world, answering that of

Section Two: Jesus Compared to Moses

God in every one; whereby in them ye may be a blessing, and make the witness of God in them to bless you: then to the Lord God you shall be a sweet savour, and a blessing.[1]

---

1. Fox, "Journal," vol. 1 in *Works*, 289. Accessed: March 14, 2008. Online: http://dqc.esr.earlham.edu/toc/E12877488A-000.

Arriving at the Destination (3:7–11)

In any type of mission, voyage, or quest, loyalty to leadership is crucial if there is to be success. We've heard stories of sea voyages to distant lands. Day after day, the sailors get farther from their homes without knowing if they are getting closer to their destination. When supplies begin to run low and members of the crew begin to grow sick and even die, there begins the talk of mutiny. The crew loses confidence in the captain, and they want to turn back. The day finally comes when they can't take it any more. They take over the ship, kill the captain, and turn to head for home. The tragedy is, of course, that the destination was within reach, and they aren't able to survive the return trip home.

We can imagine the wagon trains that made their way west in those days of the American frontier. It must have been grueling, day after day, rattling across the prairie, winding through mountain passes, fording streams. In the morning, pack up the wagons and begin the day's travel. Travel for a few hours, and then have to stop to fix a wheel. At night, circle up the wagons, care for the animals, prepare a meal, and try to get a night's sleep. It's understandable that along the way people would want to give up. Every valley with trees, grass, and a river would look like a promising place to make a home. Why continue traveling for months and months to reach the west, just because it seemed like a new frontier and held out such promise. People may begin to doubt their leaders. Maybe the trail boss doesn't know the way or maybe the destination won't be as good as they say. Why not leave the group and go your own way? Those who did leave often ended up starving, freezing, or being killed by animals.

The ultimate travel story in the Bible is the moving of the Israelite people in the Exodus to return to the area where Abraham had been promised a home-land in Canaan. Moses got the people out of Egypt, across the Red Sea, and to Mt. Sinai. There they formed the laws and rituals upon which Israelite society was to be based. As they slowly moved northward through the desert, from one oasis to the next, the people continually rebelled against Moses and against God. The result was that the generation of people who left Egypt were to die in the wilderness, and it was the next generation who entered the Promised Land. That wilderness journey came to typify the experience of the Jewish people as they often found themselves oppressed, exiled, and dispersed on the journey back to inherit God's promises. It has also represented the spiritual journey of people who find themselves captivated by the world and who must learn to follow the path back to enjoy the fullness of what God offers.

The words of God and the works of God should lead us to obedience rather than rebellion (3:7–9). Straying from God's plan results in us not arriving at the final destination (3:10–11).

THE WORDS OF GOD AND THE WORKS OF GOD SHOULD LEAD US TO OBEDIENCE RATHER THAN REBELLION (3:7–9)

The author of Hebrews attributes the words of Psalm 95:7–8 to the Holy Spirit (3:7). The first part of Psalm 95 is a beautiful call to worship the God of creation. The end of verse seven marks a transition to a rehearsal of Israel's disobedience and rebellion, a group of verses the author of Hebrews will reflect on again and again.

> O that today you would listen to his voice! Do not harden your hearts, as at Meribah, as on the day at Massah in the wilderness, when your ancestors tested me, and put me to the proof, though they had seen my work. For forty years I loathed that generation and said, "They are a people whose hearts go astray, and they do not regard my ways." Therefore in my anger I swore, "They shall not enter my rest." (Ps 95:7b–11)

In the Old Testament, stubbornness and rebelliousness is described metaphorically as a "hard heart" or "stiff neck." The Old Testament book of Numbers describes the times when the children of Israel complained and rebelled against Moses.

> Now when the people complained in the hearing of the LORD about their misfortunes, the LORD heard it and his anger was kindled. Then the fire of the LORD burned against them, and consumed some outlying parts of the camp. But the people cried out to Moses; and Moses prayed to the LORD, and the fire abated. So that place was called Taberah, because the fire of the LORD burned against them. The rabble among them had a strong craving; and the Israelites also wept again, and said, "If only we had

Arriving at the Destination (3:7-11)

> meat to eat! We remember the fish we used to eat in Egypt for nothing, the cucumbers, the melons, the leeks, the onions, and the garlic; but now our strength is dried up, and there is nothing at all but this manna to look at." (Num 11:1-6)

Psalm 78 describes the wilderness wanderings, the rebellion of the people, and the judgment of God against that generation.

> Yet they tested the Most High God, and rebelled against him. They did not observe his decrees, but turned away and were faithless like their ancestors; they twisted like a treacherous bow. For they provoked him to anger with their high places; they moved him to jealousy with their idols. When God heard, he was full of wrath, and he utterly rejected Israel. (Ps 78:56-59)

It's a bit cliché, but the road of life is littered with broken dreams. People set out with a goal in life, but along the way they get sidetracked. Maybe the way gets too tough and people give up on their dream. It makes some people angry and bitter. They had a different vision of what they wanted to do in life, but they've had to settle for something else.

Each one of us has a spiritual path in life with an ultimate destination. We also have a goal within our own community of faith. We work together to help each other on this journey, to do the work of ministry together, and to form a deep relationship as brothers and sisters in Christ. We also share a goal as the people of God in this generation. How each person and each group lives up to their potential will determine how well our generation lives up to its spiritual destiny.

STRAYING FROM GOD'S PLAN RESULTS IN US NOT ARRIVING AT THE FINAL DESTINATION (3:10-11)

Verses 10-11 continue the quotation from Psalm 95. God responds to Israel's disobedience in anger and judgment. The context for these verses is Numbers 14. When the Israelites hear the report of the spies concerning the great size and strength of those dwelling in the land (Num 13:27-33), they respond with great fear and acrimony (Num 14:1-2). They question the wisdom of having left Egypt and decide to choose a new leader to help them make the return trip (Num 14:3-4). At first Yahweh wishes to destroy them, disinherit them, and form a new nation in their place (Num 14:11-12). Moses, however, intercedes for the people and Yahweh relents (Num 14:20). Nevertheless, Yahweh announces their punishment: "None of the people who have seen my glory and the signs that I did in Egypt and in the wilderness, and yet have tested me these 10 times and have not obeyed my voice, shall see the land that I swore to give to their ancestors; none of those who despised me shall see it" (Num 14:22–23). When Moses told the people the bad news, "the people mourned greatly" (Num 14:39).

We can get this sense with athletic teams. It's exciting to follow a sports team through a season. Each game that's won is one step closer to the final victory. Each loss is a test of a team's resolve. Maybe you can remember a time when you've cheered for your team in a championship game. There comes the moment at the end when you realize they're going to make it. The end comes and all those months of supporting your team pays off. You let out a cheer or jump up and down. Then there are those other times when your team is just not up to it. As the clock ticks down you get a sinking feeling, they're not going to make it. Your mind is numb, you feel sadness and emptiness. The story of the Exodus is that way. The Israelites who left Egypt weren't going to make it back home. It would be up to their children to reach the final destination.

Our own efforts in life may not reach a successful conclusion. A hardness of heart, a stubbornness of will might prevent us from remaining loyal to God and committed to following the ways of God. It's sad to meet people who are angry and bitter with God and who have turned their back on the church and their Christian faith. It is so much better to experience a life of victory and accomplishment, a life which grows in spiritual maturity each year. That's the life of blessing, that's the life of promise.

∽

Hebrews tells us the words of God and the works of God should lead us to obedience rather than rebellion. Straying from God's plan results in us not arriving at the final destination

Arriving at the final destination can be tricky. My parents came to visit us when we were living in Rhode Island. It was probably for my graduation from Brown University. I gave my father specific directions on how to go from the freeway straight across to a secondary road. I had one statement then in the directions: "Stay on that Road until you come to the street. It's a winding road, but just stay on it." He didn't trust my directions and turned around to go back to the main road. He then traveled around

Arriving at the Destination (3:7–11)

a big loop around the city and back almost to where he had been. If he had just trusted me a little bit more, he would have found his way.

We must trust the directions God has given us for life. The path sometimes seems winding and may take us through difficult places. But we must stick to God's directions for life and trust that in the end, God will bring us home.

Distractions Along the Way (3:12–19)

There are two kinds of travelers, those who travel to arrive at the intended destination and those who visit a succession of diversions until they finally arrive at a destination, not necessarily the one they originally had planned. I can remember as a boy taking family vacations. Ours were always car trips that usually ended at a relative's house or at the home of some preacher or missionary family somewhere. I can remember only once that we stopped to see a sight along the way. Usually we were lucky if our dad stopped the car for a bathroom break.

Can you imagine how long it would take to get somewhere if we abandoned our planned trip and took a detour at every interesting place along the way? You could imagine what would happen if you were traveling and stopped for every diversion. The trip is supposed to take just one hour. But you haven't had breakfast, so you stop at a restaurant to eat. Further down the road, you see a gourmet coffee shop, so you stop to get some good coffee. Then there's an antique store that you've heard about, and you stop for an hour of browsing. A few miles further you run across a specialty candle store, and you have to stop. The trip goes on like that, an excursion of diversions. Some travelers not only get diverted by distractions that waste time but that waste a person's character and a sidetrack becomes a dead-end.

For the author of Hebrews, the situation of this group of people to whom he was writing was dire. He was afraid of them getting sidetracked, losing their way. The paradigmatic story of redemption from bondage to sin as illustrated in the Exodus contained a failure of the people to complete the journey God had provided. They left home in Egypt but never arrived at their destination. It's a classic example of what it means to lose your way, and it happens all the time to Christians and to churches. The author of Hebrews wants us to know, we can be sure of arriving at our destination if each of us is heart-conscious toward God (3:12), if we

Distractions Along the Way (3:12-19)

encourage each other to stay faithful (3:13-14), and we remember what happens to those who fail through unbelief (3:15-19).

EACH BEWARE OF TURNING FROM GOD IN UNBELIEF (3:12)

Individually, we should be careful about our own attitudes to God. The author describes it as having an "evil, unbelieving heart" (3:12). The expression "turn away from the living God" implies following false gods and idols. God was distinguished from pagan gods because they were represented by a physical object. God was the *elohim hayyim*, the living God. Deut 13 has a dire warning about false prophets that distract the Israelites from God to worship idols. Deut 13:10 states that the one should be stoned who seduces others "to turn you away from the LORD your God."

How are people drawn away these days? One of the most powerful forms of persuasion is the media. Television shows are not written just to entertain or educate. They are frequently created to manipulate society. I often get the sense, when I'm watching a sitcom that's really funny or clever—but the life situation or the philosophical message is not one I would have agreed with—that the writers and producers were really smart to affect my way of thinking through entertainment. People get the message that, those who appear as models for behavior and beliefs are people we should want to imitate. If we don't, then we are outmoded and irrelevant—or just plain boring. That happens whenever someone charismatic or glamorous is put in front of us. If we want to be like them, we should believe like them.

We should not, of course, follow the instructions of Deuteronomy 13:10 in a literal way. Rather, we are to keep watch on ourselves to see how we are being affected. We should find ways to balance the influences in our lives. Our minds and character are continually being molded by what we see and hear. Why would we want to set a bad example for ourselves to follow?

TOGETHER ENCOURAGE EACH OTHER TO FAITHFULNESS (3:13-14)

Not only should we watch out for ourselves, we should be watching out for each other. It's not just on Sunday that we should encourage each other, but we should be doing it every day. It's like the old line about doing something tomorrow: every day you can put something off, because every day always has a tomorrow. Our instruction is about what we should do "today." Each day it is "today," so each day is the day in which we should not harden our hearts.

What is distracting us from God is deceptive and deceitful; it lures us away with false promises and empty pleasures. We can give each other encouragement because we are not alone on this trip. Remember that we have a tour guide. Christ is our companion on this trip.

Notice that here again we have one of those conditional statements in verse 14. We belong to Christ as long as we stick to what we started until the end. Hebrews continues to point out that we can't rely on some initial spiritual experience that would allow us to go on and live life any way we want to.

What if we could perform an autopsy on someone and determine their spiritual condition? The coroner makes a slit down the man's chest, cracks the ribcage open, and removes the heart. When the spiritual detective comes for a briefing, the coroner takes the heart and hits it with a hammer. "Clang," it goes. It's a hard heart. The detective deduces that this man had stopped listening to God. The ears were intact; the man could hear the words, but there was no obedience. His vision was okay, but he would not see what God wanted to show him. He could walk but was unwilling to follow the path God set before him. His arms were strong and healthy, but he would not put his hands to the task God gave him. All symptoms lead back to the condition that had developed in the major organ, his firm determination to do what he wanted to do and ignore, even detest, what God wanted.

It could go a different way. The coroner pulls from a woman's chest a heart that is soft and malleable. It's obvious that she had allowed God to direct her life. She was open to hearing God, seeing what God laid before her, walking in God's Spirit, and accepting life with open and willing hands.

Not everyone needs an autopsy to determine the cause of death. For many people, it's obvious what's killing them—spiritually speaking. They're cold and indifferent to people around them, they freeze from the inside out. Or they are always angry, and they burn with antagonistic fever. Bitterness, despondency, selfishness, narcissism, lust, and domination choke the spiritual life from a person. Spiritual health is visible in people who have a positive outlook in spite of circumstances, whose power displays itself in focused energy toward the good of others, whether it's happy encouragement or righteous indignation to right a wrong. The spiritually vital person is open to listen, willing to change for the better, soft and gentle toward the misguided or the unfortunate.

We spend so much time talking about physical health. What would we be if we spent just as much time talking about our spiritual health. Give yourself a spiritual check-up; do it every day. Today is the day to keep your heart tender toward God.

DON'T BE LIKE THOSE WHO FAILED THE TEST BECAUSE OF UNBELIEF (3:15-19)

Hebrews again quotes the Psalm 95 passage. Then three times the author asks a question about the identity of those spoken of in the quotation. Those who were rebellious were the Israelites who left Egypt with Moses. Who were those with whom God was angry? It was the Israelites who sinned against God, and their carcasses were left along the way. Who were those who would not enter God's rest? They were the disobedient. The conclusion, then, is that the Israelites from ancient time did not arrive at their destination because they disobeyed God along the way. We in the present time as Christians are not any better than they, but we have a better guide than Moses in Christ. That's the message of Hebrews.

I've been getting where I need to drive to lately thanks to map web sites. I can remember when I used to do pulpit supply in Rhode Island and southeastern Massachusetts. Once I was having a terrible time with someone's directions to their church. After a few wrong turns we discovered that the directions they had given us were turned around and we had to do the opposite of what was written. There were many times when I arrived at a church just in time or maybe even a little late.

Tony Campolo tells of such a time. He was driving around trying to find the church. He finally located the church and, since he was late, walked to the platform while the congregation was singing the first hymn. He soon discovered that it was not the right church and had to excuse himself. I may get lost along the way and I might be late, but I've always gotten to the right church.

Not everyone gets where they're going. Highways are dotted by crosses marking the places where people failed to reach their destination. Church cemeteries don't have as many corpses of past members as church rolls have lists of those who have died out along the way. We set up monuments to remember the one, but the others are lost to memory and perhaps simply lost.

～

We can be sure of arriving at our destination, if each of us is heart-conscious toward God, if we encourage each other to stay faithful, and we remember what happens to those who fail through unbelief.

Suann and I don't go shopping together any more. It probably has saved our marriage; at least it saved our sanity. Shopping for me is like a quest or a hunt; for Suann the pleasure of shopping is the journey. We would go to a store for the purpose of buying something we needed. I figure out how long it will take us to walk to the right section of the store, pick up the merchandise, find a cashier, pay, and then exit. As soon as we enter the store, Suann is pulled away to look at something totally unrelated to what we are doing. If our walk through a store could be plotted, it would look like one of those *Family Circus* cartoons. It's a wonder we actually end our journey at the exit. We could end up lost somewhere in the store and have to set up camp in the sporting goods section. We would be the WalMart couple, roaming the store at night looking at pretty colors, feeling fabrics, and smelling candles, perfume and potpourri.

The spiritual journey is in itself exciting. It is filled with satisfying experiences; it is intellectually stimulating. But it is not just about the journey. It is about not being diverted from the ultimate goal. We want to reach that destination together: no stragglers, no one left behind. We're on our way together with Christ as our companion on the journey.

Rest Area Ahead (4:1–10)

Humans, like all animals, need rest, a cessation of activity, an undisturbed and secure time of quiet and solitude. One of the nicest things that transportation departments have done is create rest areas. Many rest areas are like little parks. They often have picnic areas with shade trees and sometimes have scenic views. I must admit, most of the time for me the beauty of a rest area is that it gives another kind of relief. There have been only a few times when we have planned a stop along the way and have had a picnic meal prepared to enjoy a rest area.

One of my favorite dumb jokes is about rest areas. I have no idea where I heard it, so I'm telling it in my own way. This guy was traveling from Kentucky to Indianapolis. When it began to grow late, people began to worry what could have delayed him. He finally arrived and someone asked him, "What happened? How come it took you so long to get here? Did you have car problems or was there a traffic jam?"

"No, sir," he began to explain, "It was my first time driving on the freeway. I saw a sign that said 'Clean Restrooms.' It took a bit a doin' but I cleaned five before I left the freeway."

When taking a trip, people are on the lookout for rest areas. Many times a sign for a rest area will say how much further it is to the next rest area. The ultimate rest area is, of course, when we finally reach our destination. We reach the comfort and security of home.

Hebrews is making a connection between the rest that the Israelites were to have at the end of their escape from Egypt to the Promised Land and the heavenly rest available for the people of God at the end of their escape from this world. Because the generation of Israelites that left Egypt disobeyed through faithlessness, they were to die in the wilderness leaving their children to settle in the new land. Since the rest that was promised was not fulfilled, Hebrews argues that the promised rest is still available, as long as the present generation is faithful to God and doesn't falter in the midst of persecution. We are told in these verses that the heavenly rest area is still open and still ahead for us (4:1–2). It's a rest from the labors of life (4:3–8). To enter we must remain faithful and obedient to God (4:9–10).

REST AREA STILL OPEN (4:1–2)

The NRSV translates the main verb in verse one as "take care." Doesn't that sound nice? Actually, the term used there is the word commonly translated "fear." Modern translations have tamed the language to have it read, "take care." In other texts, the word "fear" is translated as "reverence." Modern pastors and theologians don't want to scare people. That's something for revival preachers. We miss the gravity of the situation, however, if we mask the language. The author of Hebrews is afraid that some of the church members have fallen along the way, just like the Israelites did in the wilderness.

It's interesting that in this text Hebrews says the Israelites were evangelized just like we are now. Verse two literally reads, "Indeed we have had the gospel preached to us just like them." The good news of God's salvation was declared to them, but they didn't follow through on what God expected of them. The reason the message didn't benefit them is that faith was not part of the mix in their conduct.

There's nothing worse than being on a trip and being on a stretch of road without a rest area. I had a horrific experience traveling through Boston. We were going to visit the campus of Gordon College, north of Boston. I began to desire the facilities of a rest area somewhere south of Boston. The further I drove, the more I wanted a rest area, and the faster I went. By the time we found an exit with some hope of a gas station, my body was completely straightened out so that about the only contact I had with the car was my head touching the roof of the car and my foot on the accelerator. To this day, I can't think of Boston without thinking of needing a restroom. Even worse, I suppose, is anticipating an upcoming rest area, only to arrive at the destination and find the sign says, Closed.

As long as we are still on this journey of life, there's a sign that says, Rest Area Ahead. God has promised that rest and refreshment is still an open possibility for us. What we should fear, according to Hebrews, is that some of us might lose faith along the way, and for those people the sign will say, Rest Area Closed.

Rest Area Ahead (4:1-10)

WHAT KIND OF REST? (4:3-8)

The entrance requirement for the final rest area is faithfulness and obedience. The concept of rest in the Bible is complex. The Israelites were slaves in Egypt where their existence was characterized by labor. The Exodus itself was a release from bondage and the beginning of that search for rest. The journey through the wilderness and their entrance into the Promised Land was another kind of rest: It was intended to be a rest from the surrounding nations, a rest from war.

But the concept of rest had a larger symbolic meaning. The practice of working six days and then resting on the seventh, the Sabbath, was based on the belief that God created the world in six days, and then God rested from work on the seventh day. God's rest has been going on ever since. God worked six days and then retired, so to speak. The people of God will also rest from their work and join God in rest.

For many people, their lives are defined by what they do on the weekend. You could imagine that people's idea of heaven in some ways matches what they do at the end of the day or on the weekends. Some people will be experiencing in heaven their extreme sports from planet to planet, galaxy to galaxy. Others will be sitting in easy chairs, laying on hammocks, or, for the more active people, rocking on heaven's front porch. I know one person who will be taking a long nap at the beginning of eternity. Whatever heaven turns out to be, it is a rest from labor and an eternal peace and safety from conflict, fighting, and war.

Perhaps many of us rest so much and enjoy such peace and security that we have lost the appreciation for what an eternal rest is. Others are such workaholics that they don't like the idea of vacations or retirement, not to mention the inactivity of death. We should think about those people in parts of the world for whom life is constant work just to stay alive and for whom violence and war prevents them from having a moment's peace. For those people, for people like those to whom Hebrews was written, an eternal rest is a glorious concept and is not something a person would want to miss.

FAITH AND OBEDIENCE ARE REQUIRED
TO ENTER THE REST (4:9-10)

The conclusion to the argument is that there still exists this promise for the people of God to enter God's rest. The former group did not enter because of disobedience: They were not persuaded that God really was going to give them what God promised. They complained when things got tough and they rebelled when they didn't get what they wanted in life. However, they were no better or worse than we are now. If we pay attention to what happened to them, we will not make the same mistake but will be able to enter God's Sabbath rest.

For many people the greatest motivation in life is their retirement. It seems these days a career has become what one does to prepare for the retirement years. People work hard, do without some things, scrimp and save, so that they have what they'll need when they retire. People are health-conscious so they'll be in good shape to live it up during retirement.

A few years ago I put all of our finances into a software program for budgeting and keeping financial records. I spent a week entering a year's worth of check registers so that I could have a pattern of income and expenses. After I had it all set up, I was playing around with its different functions for long-range planning. I had just started a retirement plan, but we had no savings toward retirement. I pressed a button asking the program to show me what retirement would be for us. The message came back that after just a few months I would run out of money. I was so depressed by that I quit the program and never looked at it again.

We devote so much attention to weekends and to our retirement years. There's something far more important that should guide our lives. How are we living each day as a preparation for the final retirement? What are we doing to get ready for the eternal rest. Are we taking care of our spiritual health, so that we are fit to experience the best that life has to offer, eternal life in the presence of God?

༄

We have learned in these verses that the heavenly rest area is still open and still ahead for us. It's a rest from the labors of life. To enter we must remain faithful and obedient to God.

I was officiating at a funeral this past year when something happened that made me suddenly aware of which state I was living in. Children had been walking—and sometimes running—around the funeral home. I heard a man talking to one of the boys. I assume he was trying to settle him down. There we were in the presence of death and the occasion for reflecting on the meaning of life. The question I heard was, "So who's your favor-

Rest Area Ahead (4:1-10)

ite NASCAR driver?" I was reminded how close we live to Indianapolis. I suppose the conversation had some relevance in the funeral home. In some ways, NASCAR racing is the symbol of life, the circle of life. Maybe heaven for some Hoosiers is turning into the final pit stop.

However we look at it, we must realize—even fear—that our participation in God's rest is dependent on how we live life. Faith is not a one time exercise of belief in Jesus. Christian life is not just a matter of attending church, saying some prayers, and reading the Bible. It's about living in faithfulness to God and being obedient to the voice of God. God rested from the work of creation and waits for you and me to join with God in our rest.

Traveling Together on the Journey (4:11–13)

I**F YOU WERE TO** win a group trip to visit a far off country, whom would you choose to go with you? Your first choice would probably be your family members. Maybe you would choose some friends, friends you've known from school or people you've worked with. How many church-going people would say their first choice would be to take their church group with them? Yet, this is the group we have chosen to go through life with, the group that is to make sure we not only get through life but that we also make it to heaven.

There are countless TV shows, movies, and computer games in which the hero is given a mission and he or she has to choose a team to help achieve the goals of the mission. People are chosen for their personal qualities of loyalty, sense of responsibility, ability to work as a team; their courage, strength, and endurance. One person is gifted with the wisdom of strategy, another with technical skills, someone else knows transportation and logistics, yet another has strength and agility. The hand-picked team is confident they can trust each other, that they have what it takes to go the distance, and that in spite of their personal quirks and eccentricities they have a bond that means they stick together, accomplish the mission, and everyone gets home safe.

The author of Hebrews pictures the group of believers to whom he writes as fellow-travelers in life. The great example from their religious history is the exodus group, living a nomadic existence, slowly making their way to the promised resting place. That's the way of life for the followers of Jesus: they are traveling together, working their way through the obstacles and pitfalls, helping each other along the journey, so that in the end they all get the rest they deserve—the spiritual rest God provides, the same rest when God rested from God's creative work.

The Israelites became disobedient to God and rebelled against God's appointed leaders. They did not trust the God who revealed God's nature to them through the signs displayed to Pharaoh, the dividing of the Red

Traveling Together on the Journey (4:11–13)

Sea, and the provision of food and water in the wilderness. They did not trust the God who gave them God's word in commandment and instruction on Mt. Sinai, who promised in God's covenant with Abraham to be their God. Consequently, that generation did not enter their place of rest but wandered and fell in the wilderness.

The author of Hebrews uses that negative example to encourage, exhort, and warn his fellow-travelers that they must not make the same mistakes if they want to get to their heavenly place of rest together. The message is as important now as it was then.

The church in many ways has separated itself from the task of living life as a community of faith. Instead, the church has settled for being a place outside of regular living, to meet with people for an hour or two once a week. It has settled for those people to have nothing to do with the rest of how the members live life. Instead, church people want to simply go through motions of religiosity on Sunday mornings in hopes of feeling better about themselves and of warding off some divine retribution for how they act the rest of their week.

This portion of Hebrews talks of our work of achieving rest (4:11), of God's word that analyzes who we really are (4:12), and of our own word of accountability (4:13).

OUR WORK OF ACHIEVING REST (4:11)

Pop Christian culture says just accept Jesus and you've got it made. Just walk the aisle, have a salvation experience, then go to church, attend bible study, and witness to your friends until Jesus comes. That's not bad, but it misses so much of what the New Testament teaches about the Christian life. Here the author of Hebrews says, "Make every effort to get to heaven!" Strive for it, work hard for it, be diligent to get there! Notice that WE are to work at it together, so that "not a single one of us" should fail. It's not me being concerned about me so that I achieve something. It's all of us together making sure that we don't lose anyone along the way.

How many times have we heard stories of a group traveling through the forest or jungle. Single-file they make their way through the underbrush. The slowest, weakest person is a straggler at the end of the line. Sure enough, one by one, silently and swiftly, the last one is picked off. The group continues on, oblivious to their loss.

Section Two: Jesus Compared to Moses

The Church is filled with stragglers and continues to be depleted of those stragglers who fade away little by little. Along the way of life, one by one, people have lost their way. They've been picked off by worldly cares and concerns. Someone becomes more concerned with career and doesn't have time for faith and spiritual disciplines. Another becomes disillusioned and no longer considers it reasonable to trust in God or rely on the church. Yet another chooses a different lifestyle, what they think is fun, exciting, and pleasurable. For whatever the reason, the church has barely noticed that one by one their fellow-travelers have been lost along the way, lost and forgotten. If we are susceptible to being stragglers, God is able to detect our inner motives, even though others can't tell who we really are.

GOD'S WORD THAT ANALYZES THE CORE OF WHO WE ARE (4:12)

The phrase "word of God" is complex. It refers collectively to the being of God who is characterized by speaking truth with authority, of knowing all things, of cutting right to the heart of the matter with a prophetic voice through God's chosen messengers. It's contained in the Bible, but it's more than the Bible itself. It's the message brought by God's messengers, a message of command and precept, of prophetic exhortation and warning, of wisdom and philosophy for life. It's not a dusty Bible on a shelf, but a vital and vibrant message incarnated in the lives of people. It penetrates and separates like a laser beam. The division becomes apparent, the division between good and evil, wise and foolish, right and wrong, virtue and vice, godliness and sin, justice and iniquity, peace and violence. What something looks like on the outside is cut through to get at the core motives and commitments.

What would we find if we did soul surgery? What if we could dissect the one person you are into its constituent parts? Imagine a diagnostic machine connected to the brain and heart, which could display on a monitor your core being, the essence of who you are? The soul doctor turns the dial and the machine displays your ambitions and motives. Your deepest passions show up in a contrasting color. Compare it to what you say it is you want in life, the way you act, the way you appear to people. Turn the dial again and you see what motivates your choices and behaviors, what makes the difference for you, how you judge what to do and what not

Traveling Together on the Journey (4:11-13)

to do. Perhaps we could detach your ethereal self from the material, the spiritual from the carnal. To what extent is your character and behavior controlled by the physical nature of your body; biology and psychology ruling over theology, philosophy, and spirituality? We are all affected by the biological makeup of our bodies due to thousands and thousands of years of human adaptation to environments. We are the products of years of psychological and mental development through stages of life that go into who we are and who we will become. God knows all of what makes us who we are—nature and nurture—and judges that for which we are morally responsible.

OUR WORD OF ACCOUNTING RESPONSIBILITY (4:13)

From other people we can hide who we are and dress up our particular natures. We cannot hide from God. God sees all and through all. God does not judge a book by its cover, let alone its pretty dust jacket; we are all an open book before God. The last phrase of verse 13 could be put this way, "to God a word (Gk. *logos*) must be given for us." The *logos* of God discerns what we should be and who we are and it is through our *logos* that we explain why.

We place a great deal of importance on judges and the legal system. We may not be able to know the truth about people, but we've developed a justice system to determine what we'll accept as fair and reasonable. A person comes before a judge and claims he is innocent. As best it can, the judicial system analyzes all of the relevant information. The defendant is caught in inconsistencies to his story. He is not what he appears to be. The evidence shows beyond a reasonable doubt that he did the deed and is the kind of person who could do such a thing.

The only judge who is 100% accurate and knows all the facts is God. But just as a leopard can't hide his spots, who we are comes out in ways that cause us to fall behind in the spiritual journey of life. The baggage of materialism and selfishness weighs us down and we become stragglers. More important than being left behind in some future rapture is being left behind, having fallen by the wayside, wasting away in a lifeless desert, never making it to the spiritual place of rest, that culmination of a life lived well.

Section Two: Jesus Compared to Moses

∽

There is work to do for us to achieve our rest together. But we need to be open to hear God's word that tells us who we are. We need to be aware that we will give to God our own word of accountability.

The people around you at church are the people with whom you've chosen to be on this journey. Their gifts are there to help you on the way. They depend on your gifts to help them. Together we are committed to working together to achieve the goal, to experience together the entering into God's rest. The Church's motto should be, "No Child of God Left Behind."

It's All about Who You Know (4:14–16)

It's all about who you know. We normally say that when we're being cynical. Someone doesn't get a job and they tell their friends, "It's all about who you know." At a banquet, someone sees a person they know sitting at the head table with the leaders of the organization or with the guest speaker, while they are sitting at a crummy table in the back with their view partially blocked by a pillar. To make himself feel better, he comments to his friends, "It's all about who you know."

I'll bet more than one person in New Orleans has said, "It's all about who you know," when they didn't get help cleaning up and rebuilding in their neighborhood and people somewhere else did. If the tables are turned, and we are the ones who have received the benefit, we might explain our good fortune to others, "I guess it's all about who you know."

While I was in graduate school at Brown University, I met a guy named Allen who was working on his dissertation in the philosophy department and working in computer services. He and a few others organized a Computing in the Humanities Users Group, affectionately called CHUG (although I was never a witness to any chugging; maybe they just didn't invite me). I became interested and spent a great deal of time learning about computers, some programming, and how to format text documents properly. Allen began to get me freelance work, such as doing the typesetting for the phone listings in the campus directory, creating camera-ready copy for a few professors' books, and working on some unique jobs that involved some programming in order to create documents. Time after time I was given opportunities because I knew Allen. There was even one time at a conference in Chicago that, because of my connections with Allen and the others, I was invited to go to dinner with the people at the conference who were working on the application of technology to biblical studies—even getting to sit next to the person who was the foremost person in the field in those days. Allen is now at the University of Illinois, a leading expert in the field of digital libraries and has been interviewed on Fox television. A few years ago I contacted him and he responded with, "Look at us now. We've graduated and gone on to get positions in higher education, doing significant work." My response to him for my part was, in essence, "it's all about who you know."

In the situation of the people to whom the book of Hebrews is addressed, there was little about their circumstances that was what they had come to know. Every week in the synagogue they would hear about the house of God where the priests would intercede for the people through prayers and sacrifices. The High Priest would represent all of the people once a year by entering into the Holy of Holies, into the very presence of God in that inner sanctuary behind the purple curtain. For these people, little was left of the former glory. Even if Hebrews were written in the 50s or 60s, many of the people had come to view the temple as a source of religious and political corruption. After the destruction of Jerusalem in the early 70s, when Hebrews was probably written, the people no longer had a temple or a priesthood. No one to intercede for them. No one to enter the presence of God. No one to offer the sacrifices. The only blood being shed in Jerusalem was the blood of the martyrs.

For some Jews and Gentile god-fearers, all hope was not lost. They believed that a sacrifice had taken place back in the 30s that once-and-for-all achieved God's forgiveness for the sins of the people. There was no longer a need for a High Priest to make sacrifices in the Jerusalem temple. There was no reason to lament the absence on the throne of a king who is a descendant of David. All hope was not lost, even though the Romans had squashed rebellion and wrested control from the religious and political authorities in Judea.

Some people had been loyal to the Herodians. Some supported the Sanhedrin. Others had been part of various rebellions and followed this or that messiah. A number of people had fled to the wilderness and joined the Jewish monastic community by the Dead Sea. A few had come to know a man from Galilee named Jesus; they were confident that after his stellar leadership of their group, his endurance through suffering and martyrdom, that God had raised him from the dead. They were empowered by God's spirit because of whom it was they knew.

Life for us often seems out of control. The dominant voices in our society are those that promote materialism, advocate the use of power to get what you need, and getting ahead in life is based on who you know. We feel insignificant in the big scheme of things. Who's going to help us? How

It's All about Who You Know (4:14–16)

can we get anyone to listen to us? Who knows what I'm going through enough to show me a little sympathy? When am I going to get a break? Hebrews has two words of encouragement at this point: First, we need to do our best to stay committed (4:14–15); second, we need to go to God when we need help (4:16).

DO OUR BEST TO STAY COMMITTED (4:14–15)

The main clause in verse 14 is "let us hold fast to our confession." Followers of Jesus commit their allegiance to him and with it hold to a particular way of life and ways of thinking about God. The most important part of being a member of the group of Jesus followers is to maintain one's allegiance, to "hold fast."

The opening clause is subordinate and gives the basis for why we should be doing our best to stay committed. Verse 15 will give a second reason. First of all, we should stay committed because of what Jesus has accomplished and, secondly, because Jesus acts on our behalf.

In chapters 1–4 Jesus is compared to the angels who have been active with God in creating the world and bringing God's message to humanity through the words of law and prophecy. People failed to respond to God's leading and were found to be faithless and disobedient. Consequently, God allowed them to lose their way and even lose their lives. Their experience becomes our example.

Hebrews is leading into the next way of comparing Jesus and demonstrating the way in which what God has done in his Son has surpassed what God has done in the past. The next comparison beginning in chapter five will be the priesthood. Not only can Jesus be described as priestly, but in this heavenly typology Jesus is a High Priest, in fact a "great high priest"—an expression applied to those high priests of previous centuries who not only served as religious functionaries but also held political power. Jesus' rise to power was exaltation to heaven.

Frequently in Jewish writings, heaven is described as being multi-layered—three or even seven stories of heaven. Jesus passed through the heavens, penetrated to the highest heaven, the dwelling place of God, where God is described as seated on a throne. The one to whom we claim allegiance is the one who has risen to ultimate power in the universe.

In the tragic love story of *Tristan and Isolde*, we learn the lesson of heeding our allegiance. Without giving away too much of the story for those who might want to see the movie, Tristan grows up to become second to the king, King Marke. Tristan faces the moral dilemma, does he give in to his passions and be with Isolde, his true love, or does he stay committed to his allegiance to the king, someone who has been like a father to him. Tristan becomes distant from the king to King Marke's utter amazement. Together they had dreamed of the day when the tribes of Britannia would be united against the Irish, when their tribe would be supreme and rule with strength and equity. And when it finally becomes a reality, Tristan is reluctant to be a part and lends no support to his king. In the end, Tristan pays dearly for his divided loyalty.

God must be utterly amazed at our behavior at times. God chose a people, rescued them from oppression, protected and fed them in the wilderness, gave them a means for relationship with God, and in return God gets complaints and faithlessness. God gives to the people leaders in the forms of judges, priests, prophets, and kings and they are not listened to; they are abandoned and even killed. The Messiah, Jesus, endures the antagonism and assaults of the enemies of God's people, faithfully suffers a martyr's death, and is raised to the heavens to sit next to God's throne. Still the people of God falter and flounder in their commitment to God in the world. How often must God come to us as King Marke does so tragically to Tristan and just want to know why. What more could we want? What more could we ask for? In the end we could also pay dearly for our divided loyalty.

Jesus has two qualities that make him the best sort of mediator. One is the divine aspect, that he has entered the heavenly temple as a great high priest. The second relates to where he got his start. Since he was one of us, he is able to intercede for us in heaven with sympathy for our human weaknesses. But even though he experienced the testing of human existence, he was not tainted by it.

We like to hold up as an example people who have achieved something but started out like us. We feel a special affinity to those people. The politician who now serves in state or federal government but who came from our home town is one we feel can represent us, because he or she was one of us. The pastor who came from the same kind of town as us, went to the same sort of schools, but through it all was well-liked and well-thought of, we may feel is someone who could understand us. That's why we should maintain our allegiance, remain committed, "hold fast to our confession."

It's All about Who You Know (4:14–16)

Jesus was one like us and now he is our representative, our intercessor, our advocate before God. Surely that's a good reason for us to be devoted followers of Jesus. It is our effort that's called for, but it's not the only thing. When we come to the difficult times and our strength and conviction falters, we are able to get the help we need.

HELP'S AVAILABLE WHEN NEEDED (4:16)

Approach is what someone does when they come to God. Moses approached the burning bush (Acts 7:31). The children of Israel approached the foot of Mt. Sinai where God's presence was seen and heard (Exod 16:9; 34:32; Lev 9:5; Deut 4:11; 5:23). The priests approached the altar with sacrifices (Lev 9:7, 8). In prayer to God we are transported to the highest heaven, to the throne room of God, and we approach God's presence.

Rather than a throne of judgment, it is a throne of grace. We are to be in fearful reverence and awe, but, because of the one who sits next to the throne of God, we are able to come with boldness and confidence. At the right time, when we need help, we experience the mercy and grace of God.

Remember the story of Joseph at the end of the book of Genesis? Nearly the baby of the family, one of Daddy's favorites and apparently a bit pretentious, Joseph was always having visions of grandeur. Just when the boys think Joseph is long-dead and they are in peril of losing everything, whom do they end up bowing in front of other than Joseph, now the Pharaoh's right-hand man? They are oblivious to the identity of this one who is the answer to all their needs, one who is in fact one of them, their own brother, who loves them still and is ready to show them mercy and grace.

When life comes at us hard, knocks us off our feet, what's our response? Most of the time most of us turn away from the help that's right in front of us. "No one knows what we're going through," we think, "No one can help me with this." That's not true. Our brother, one of the guys, someone who's been through it all, is the one who stands ready to help. We are oblivious to the one who has the power of the universe at his disposal, the one who loves us, gave his life for us, penetrated through to the highest heaven, and is now the Great High Priest of the universe. His help is there just when we need it.

Section Two: Jesus Compared to Moses

∽

The final exhortations in this first section of Hebrews is we need to do our best to stay committed and we need to go to God when we need help. The Christian band Petra has a song called "It's All About Who You Know."

> You are tied-in and networked
> You've got people to see
> You have friends in high places
> You've got places to be
> You've got plenty of time to make your mark
> You've been able to get things done
> And all the white shirts will take your calls
> You've really had quite a run
>
> Who can you turn to
> When your life is behind you?
>
> You have learned how to pull strings
> And call in a favor or two
> You have found some ways to spend your time
> Instead of with "you-know-who"
> There's only one name
> You can call on without blame
>
> Some may wonder where, when if not how
> There's no worry, if you know Him now
> Nothing we do here below
> Is gonna save us 'cause
> It's all about who you know
>
> (Chorus)
> When you get to the end and you've got nothing to show
> It's all about who you know[1]

Do you know him? Are you staying committed to him? Do you turn to him for help in your time of need? If it's all about who you know, then we are very well connected.

---

1. Bob Hartman, "It's All About Who You Know," Lyrics. *Jekyll and Hyde*, Inpop Records, 2003. Accessed March 14, 2008. Online: http://www.petrarocksmyworld.com/jah.html.

Section Three

Jesus Compared to the High Priesthood of Aaron (5:1—6:20)

Heroes of the Priesthood (5:1–10)

MY HERO CAN BEAT up your hero. Did you ever get into an argument like that when you were a kid? We love our heroes, don't we? By admiring a hero or heroine, we claim something for ourselves. The virtues, strengths, and accomplishments of that person represent who I am or who I aspire to be. That hero or heroine could represent my family, like an uncle or aunt who became a leader in local government. The hero or heroine could be a model for my country, like a war hero or someone who gave great service to the country by fighting against a disease or working toward justice for an oppressed segment of the population. A hero or heroine could also be an icon of a religion. He or she embodies the best of what that religion has to offer. To extol the virtues of that person, is to extol the virtues of the religion.

I had a long line of heroes as I was growing up. I had a Batman phase. I remember getting a Batman disguise, it was sort of a hard plastic helmet. But I couldn't really be Batman without the cape. I went to the neighbor lady and asked her about what I could use for a cape. She gave me a long, black, silky piece of material for a cape. For days I went around with this old lady's slip tied around my neck. I had other heroes too, most of them ones you would recognize: Superman, Green Hornet, John Glenn (my space phase), and Hercules (my Classic Comic book phase in third grade).

I can't say that Jesus was ever my hero. I didn't act like the Ned Flanders twins on *The Simpsons* and act out scenes from the gospels as a child. "No, I want to play Jesus this time, you played him last time." Imagine your sister complaining, "I don't want to be the woman caught in adultery again. You throw too hard."

Jesus is a hero, even though we may think that designation is too mortal to apply to the divinity of Jesus. Jesus has been compared to other religious figures, like the Buddha, Moses or Mohammed, or to people like Gandhi. The more we can say about our religious representative in

Section Three: Jesus Compared to the High Priesthood of Aaron

comparison to others, the more we can say about our own religion and its ability to raise us up to be like that person.

The Greco-Roman world loved its heroes—the super-human, semi-human, or simply human figures that represent the character and virtues of the city or nation. Poems and plays depict their stories with their great feats of prowess and wisdom. Praise speeches extol the nobility, upbringing, education, offices, and service to the city-state. One way to amplify the virtues of a person was to draw a comparison between him and some other figure from popular culture. Teachers of Greek rhetoric left behind for us instructions on how to write a comparison and gave models for its composition. As we've been seeing, the author of Hebrews is familiar with the writing of comparisons and uses them throughout the book of Hebrews.

Remember what we've said about the writing of comparisons. The goal of a comparison is to show how your subject is equal to or better than some other good subject for the purpose of praising your subject and exhorting others to model themselves after the virtues of the subject. One wouldn't choose an inferior subject for comparison. It does little good to compare the virtue of loyalty with that of laziness. Of course loyalty excels laziness; that would be a weak comparison. The form of the comparison is also important. A more forceful comparison is one that treats one topic at a time in a series of comparative exchanges. Another form of comparison practiced in Greek literature is one in which the topics for comparison are treated for one subject and then the topics are covered for the second subject under comparison. This latter type is what we find in this comparison in Hebrews.

In the comparison in chapter five, Hebrews is going to treat each topic for one character, the High Priesthood and then those same topics beginning at verse five in reverse order for the other character, Jesus. The ordering of topics creates what's called a chiasm. Chiastic structures occur when an author deals with several topics and then returns to the same topics but in reverse order. The outline below illustrates the chiastic structure. Not only are the topics in the comparisons similar, but the author uses key terms that are either linguistically related or are synonymous words in Greek.

Heroes of the Priesthood (5:1–10)

POINTS OF COMPARISON: HIGH PRIEST (5:1–4)

1A Appointment (*kathistatai*) to High Priesthood (5:1)
  1B Ability to have empathy (*metriopathein*) with weak (5:2)
    1C Makes offerings (*prospherein*) (5:3)
      1D Honor (*timēn*) of High Priesthood Not Taken (5:4)

POINTS OF COMPARISON: CHRIST (5:5–10)

      2D Christ did not glorify (*edoxasen*) Himself (5:5–6)
    2C Offers prayers (*prosenegkas*) (5:7)
  2B Learned obedience through experiences (*epathen*) (5:8)
2A Designated (*prosagoreutheis*) a High Priest (5:9–10)

The goal of the comparison is not simply to reinterpret Old Testament texts for a new context. It is rather to persuade the audience to value the excellency of God's work in Christ and encourage the audience to remain committed to God and to the community of faith in spite of persecution and suffering. This comparison actually does not assert Jesus as more excellent than the high priest, but simply attempts to show equality. Jesus deserves our loyalty by being everything that a high priest should be: someone appointed to the role (5:1 and 5:9–10), who feels for people (5:2 and 5:8), makes offerings for them (5:3 and 5:7), and who is divinely appointed rather than self-seeking (5:4 and 5:5–6).

APPOINTMENT TO PRIESTHOOD (5:1 AND 5:9–10)

First on the list for comparison is the appointment of the high priest. In 5:1 Hebrews describes the high priest as "put in charge." Then in verse 9 and 10, Jesus is also described as "having been designated" by God as a high priest. Both terms refer to the appointment of a high priest.

The language of verse nine may be surprising to us. It says of Jesus, "having been made perfect." We typically think of Jesus as the perfect Son of God made incarnate in the world and then slowly revealing his true nature. We don't tend to think in terms of Jesus as a young man who handled life in a way that caused him to become a complete, mature, perfect human and by means of that perfection to become the source of salvation. But that's what Hebrews says. In Jesus' early years, according to Luke 2:52, "Jesus increased in wisdom and in years, and in divine and human favor." In Jesus' final years, according to Hebrews, Jesus matured in the fullest sense and God exalted him.

Section Three: Jesus Compared to the High Priesthood of Aaron

The culmination of this section is the reference to Melchizedek. With this reference, the author of Hebrews will begin a parenthetical section that comes back around again to the topic of Melchizedek at the end of chapter six. Chapter 7 contains a comparison focused on the character of the Melchizedek priesthood. The primary lineage of high priests comes through the line of Aaron, which we begin to read about in the book of Exodus. Before that priesthood, however, we find in Genesis a person that Abram meets: "King Melchizedek of Salem brought out bread and wine; he was priest of God Most High" (Gen 14:18). Nothing much is known of this prototype of the priesthood. Notice that he is both a king and a priest. His name means "my king is righteous." The city is named Salem (a term related to *shalom*, "peace"), which is considered the area later known as Jerusalem. You can see that "salem" remained in the name of the city of Jerusalem.

The point of the comparison is Jesus' equality with the high priest. Just as high priests were appointed to the role, so also was Jesus appointed by God to the role of high priest. In Hebrews chapter seven, the author will argue that Jesus' priesthood is greater, since it is an eternal priesthood.

How might we think about this aspect of the priesthood? For most of us, when we think about priests, we think about the Roman Catholic Church. For the sake of illustration, let's imagine two young men, good Italian Catholics. They live in the same city but are from different parishes. Antonio is from the Saint Dominic's parish; his friend Marco is from Saint Sophia's. Saint Sophia's has a new priest, Father Jesús. Marco admires his new priest and thinks that wonderful things are happening at Saint Sophia's. Antonio is skeptical of the new priest at Saint Sophia's and considers their priest at Saint Dominic's to be a regular guy, someone who really is in touch with the people. Antonio claims that this Father Jesús bought his way into the priesthood. Marco defends his priest, "Not only was Father Jesús appointed by the bishop, he was clearly appointed to be our priest by God because of what he has been able to do in our parish."

Jesus wasn't from a priestly line, and he did not serve as a priest in the temple. Nevertheless, Jesus has shown himself to be a high priest in that God has appointed him in the way that God appoints high priests. By realizing this, Hebrews expects us to respond more faithfully toward God. Even though there is not an earthly high priest any longer, there is a high priest in heaven appointed by God.

Heroes of the Priesthood (5:1–10)

FEELING FOR OTHERS (5:2 AND 5:8)

The second comparison relates to the relationship of the priest to those whom he serves, and it is found in verse two and then in verse eight. Hebrews says that the high priest is able to "deal gently." It's an unusual verb in Greek, *metriopatheō*, a compound of two words the second of which is *patheō*, which means "to experience extreme emotion, suffer." This word *metriopatheō* is frequently used in contexts where it means "to moderate the passions," an idea attributed to Aristotle to describe his position that one does not completely remove bad desires, but one must learn to moderate them. In the context of verse two, Hebrews is saying that the high priest is able to moderate his anger with people because he has the same failings as they do.

The comparison in verse eight says that Jesus "learned obedience through what he suffered." Here is the verb *patheo* in verse eight which we saw within the compound word in verse two. The high priest of Israel is *metriopathetic* with people's weaknesses, while Jesus also functioned as a high priest by being empathetic. Here again Jesus is described as "learning obedience." Hebrews pictures Jesus as someone who grows and matures. Through his actions he attains a particular stature in the eyes of God and as a consequence becomes the high priest in the heavens.

Back to our illustration. Antonio tells Marco one day how good their priest is at Saint Dominic's. His priest has compassion on people. He loves them, he doesn't get angry with them when they miss church or confession. Antonio challenges Marco about his priest, Father Jesás.

"You want to talk about passion for his people," Marco asks, "let me tell you about passion." He goes on to describe the pain and suffering Father Jesús has experienced with the people at Saint Sophia's. "Your priest may be compassionate," Marco says, "but our priest knows the passion of Christ, who feels the pain of his people and experiences the suffering for himself."

That's our great high priest. That's the one to whom we owe our allegiance. His priesthood is based on his own sufferings for us. What else should we do than to claim Christ as our great high priest and remain loyal to him?

Section Three: Jesus Compared to the High Priesthood of Aaron

MAKING AN OFFERING FOR THE PEOPLE (5:3 AND 5:7)

In the third comparison, the high priest is said in verse three to "offer" sacrifices. Notice in verse seven that Jesus "offered up" prayers and supplications. The same verb is used in both cases. The high priest offers a sacrifice; that's what a high priest does. Jesus is also a high priest because he also made an offering to God. That offering was his prayers and supplications along with his loud cries and tears. His offering was to the one able to save him from death. That much we understand, but Hebrews says Jesus was heard on account of his reverent submission. In other words, Jesus earned the right to be heard as a high priest.

Once again Antonio is boasting of his priest at Saint Dominic's. He describes how the priest makes a point of acknowledging his own sinfulness, his own need for divine forgiveness. Antonio likes that humbleness of his priest. Marco is surprised by that attitude. What they have noticed at Saint Sophia's is how Father Jesús prays to God for strength both for him and for the people. He nearly cries out to God for Saint Sophia's to be a place where people are committed to God in all aspects of their lives. For Marco, that makes Father Jesús a better priest than any other, and someone he will continue to support.

Jesus wasn't a priest in the temple in Jerusalem and didn't carry out the daily, weekly, or yearly function of the high priest in making offerings to God. He did, however, fulfill the priestly role by offering up prayers to God, and God heard his prayers. No stronger claim can be made for priests than to see evidence of God hearing their prayers. We can be sure that Jesus fulfills that aspect of being a high priest, and he does it in a way that challenges us to stay faithful to God.

NOT SEEKING HONOR FOR ONESELF (5:4 AND 5:5–6)

Finally, in the fourth comparison, the high priest in verse four does not "take the honor on himself." One would not be so presumptuous as to run for the office of high priest. Rather, one is called to it. Christ, by comparison in verse five, "did not glorify himself." Instead, God appointed him by choosing him to be the Son. Remember that the anointed king in Israel is called the son of God. The royal installation psalm, Psalm 2, says of the newly anointed king through the voice of Yahweh, "You are my son, today I have begotten you," meaning, "on this day of your coronation as king, it is like I have given birth to my divine designate." Because of Jesus' endur-

Heroes of the Priesthood (5:1–10)

ance, faithfulness and obedience, God exalted him after death which signified that Jesus Christ was the appointed king-priest, God's right-hand man in heaven.

The same psalm that begins with Psalm 110:1, "The LORD says to my lord, 'Sit at my right hand until I make your enemies your footstool'" is the one that goes on to say, "The LORD has sworn and will not change his mind, 'You are a priest forever according to the order of Melchizedek'" (Ps 110:4).

The most damaging claim that Antonio makes is that Father Jesús was an opportunist who pulled strings in order to get what he wanted from the church. Antonio claims that Father Jesús was practically moved in before the bishop recognized his appointment to that parish. Marco defends his priest. He tells how Father Jesús grew up in a Catholic home, attending a Catholic school. He decided at an early age to take his vows. Not only was he a good student in seminary, he also was active in mission work in the city and in developing countries. Father Jesús had sensed a calling to come to Saint Sophia's. He was obedient to that calling, even to the point of staying in the rectory while he waited to hear from the bishop. If being called by God to the priesthood is what makes a good priest, then Father Jesús is an excellent priest.

The divine calling of Jesus to his high priestly role is evident from all aspects of his life. Whatever can be claimed about the priesthood, it can be claimed of Christ—and then some. Knowing that God selected this one and has exalted him after raising him from the dead should encourage us to remain faithful people of God.

⸺

Jesus, therefore, deserves our loyalty by being everything that a high priest should be: someone appointed to the role, who feels for people, makes offerings for them, and who is divinely appointed rather than self-seeking.

In recent years we've seen a resurgence of interest in comic book heroes. Major movies have depicted for a new audience such heroes as Superman, Batman, Spiderman, X-Men, and Fantastic Four. Although the entertainment industry has been built on remaking old stories into new TV shows and movies, we might wonder why so many people in this time are enamored with superheroes.

The early 80s brought us the song sung by Bonnie Tyler, "Holding Out for a Hero" (lyrics by Jim Steinman and Dean Pitchford). The first verse nostalgically asks where have all the good men, the gods, and the heroes gone? Who's taking up the challenge against all odds? I imagine the author of Hebrews was asking the same question. I'm sure he knew the stories of the gods and of Hercules. For him, the people of the Bible, as he apparently read it in Greek, came alive as the same sort of larger-than-life characters. Within this context, Jesus came along. Jesus fulfilled all of these hopes and dreams. The chorus of the song not only reverberates with the message of Hebrews but also speaks to our own need. We are continuing to hold out for a hero, one who lives up to the qualifications of a hero, and one who will come to our rescue before the evils that lurk within the darkness destroy us.

I'm sure the author of Hebrews wanted his audience to be as excited about his message concerning Jesus as people are when they hear "Holding Out for a Hero." Jesus was that sort of person and exists as the hero of faith for us. That's all the more reason for us to claim our hero and diligently follow him.

Food for Thought (5:11–14)

YOU ARE WHAT YOU eat—or drink. Tea-drinkers claim that tea-drinkers are more peaceful people. To their way of thinking, the progress of coffee drinking in the western world has been thought to precede conflicts and wars. Tea-drinkers think of coffee-drinkers as more prone to violence. Of course, when coffee-drinkers hear that it makes them want to punch the tea-drinker in the nose.

In seventeenth century England, coffee-houses were becoming fashionable. A pamphlet was printed that purported to be from women in London who felt that their husbands were becoming less virile because of their coffee-drinking. The following excerpt contains the exact wording.

> Certainly our Countrymens pallates are become as Fanatical as their Brains; how else is't possible they should apostatise from the good old primitive way of Ale-drinking, to run a whoring after such variety of distructive Forraign Liquors, to trifle away their time, scald their chops, and spend their money, all for a little base, black, thick, nasty, bitter, stinking, nauseous Puddle-water.[1]

Their petition argued that only men over sixty should be allowed to drink coffee. Younger men of child-producing years should stick to ale. The men object that this is certainly not the case. Rather, coffee is a "harmless and healing Liquor, which Indulgent Providence first sent amongst us . . . to make us Sober and Merry."[2]

If it's true that "you are what you drink" it is even more the case, you are what you think. If you continually let yourself think negatively about

---

1. Well-Willer, *The Women's Petition against Coffee Representing to Public Consideration the Grand Inconveniencies Accruing to Their Sex from the Excessive Use of That Drying, Enfeebling Liquor: Presented to the Right Honorable the Keepers of the Liberty of Venus*, Variation: Early English Books, 1641–1700; 829:44 (London: [s.n.], 1674).

2. *The Mens Answer to the Womens Petition against Coffee Vindicating Their Own Performances and the Virtues of That Liquor from the Undeserved Aspersions Lately Cast Upon Them by Their Scandalous Pamphlet*, Variation: Early English Books, 1641–1700; 1466:11 (London: [s.n.], 1674).

each circumstance of life, you will be a wreck. You would be worried that the air you breathe has germs, so you would wear a mask all the time. Every palpitation of your heart would make you think your heart's going to stop and you'll die. You would be scared to death to be in a car or fly on a plane, for fear there would be a freak accident and that would be the end of you. Cognitive therapists would tell you, you are what you think.

The author of Hebrews interrupts his speech at 5:11 to scold his audience about their diet of thinking. It's as though the author of Hebrews sensed that his rhetorical analysis of the comparison between the priesthood of Aaron and the priesthood of Christ as it relates to Melchizedek was going to be too much for his audience to handle. He will leave off his discussion of Melchizedek for now, but he will pick it back up again at the end of this digression.

The author of Hebrews wants his audience to understand the integral connection between the maturity of our thinking with the maturity of our actions. First of all, sloppy thinking inhibits progress (5:11–12a). Secondly, immaturity leads to poor decisions (5:12b–13). And, finally, it is the mature person who has a developed appetite for what's right (5:14).

SLOPPY THINKING INHIBITS PROGRESS (5:11–12a)

It's as though the author of Hebrews has become exasperated. He senses that he has lost his audience. They're not going to get the point about the high priesthood and Melchizedek. It's not so much that it is complicated and too theological for their intellectual capabilities. The real issue is their ability to understand the situation in a way that will help them to act in the right ways. When they are tempted to abandon Christian faith and practice, will they be able to make the right decision based on their understanding of what God has done in Christ? If suffering and persecution comes, will they remember that Christ endured suffering, and the heroes and heroines of the Bible remained faithful to God in spite of their circumstances? It's all very difficult to take in, and the author of Hebrews is afraid they have become sloppy in the way they think about these things.

The same word—here translated "dull," other times as "sluggish"—is used by the Stoic philosopher Epictetus (ca. 55–ca. 135 CE). Stoic philosophers used argumentation as a way of training themselves to make right decisions about how to think and act, to choose what is virtuous and avoid what is vice.

Food for Thought (5:11-14)

> But what other man than the man of sense can use argumentation and is skillful in questioning and answering, and incapable of being cheated and deceived by false reasoning? And shall he enter into the contest, and yet not take care whether he shall engage in argument not rashly and not carelessly? And if he does not take care, how can he be such a man as we conceive him to be? But without some such exercise and preparation, can he maintain a continuous and consistent argument? Let them show this; and all these speculations become superfluous, and are absurd and inconsistent with our notion of a good and serious man. Why are we still indolent and negligent and sluggish, and why do we seek pretences for not labouring and not being watchful in cultivating our reason? (Epictetus, *Diss.*, 1.7.30)

Take as an example the popularity of state lotteries. What goes on in a person's mind when they're standing at a check-out counter and they decide, rather than just buy milk and bread, they'll also spend twice or three times as much on gambling? It may be that they no longer think about it at all. Force of habit has brought them to the place where they just do it without thinking. That's very sloppy thinking. Maybe they do have a little argument in their head.

"Think about how much money we could win."

"But the chances of winning is about the same as being struck by lightning, twice.

"But all I need to do is win once, then it would make up for the hundreds and thousands of dollars I've spent on gambling."

"But if you had saved that money instead, just think about how much money you would have. You had the money already; you just gave it away."

"But think of what we could do with all that money."

"You could buy things, but things don't last; things can't bring you lasting happiness. There's more to life than having money."

The person puts down the money anyway, duped by the fantasy of getting rich quick and easy and then living happily ever after. Most of the time the person walks out the door, throwing into the garbage a very expensive piece of cardboard.

We've become sloppy in our thinking, and most often we don't even listen to the rational arguments going on in our head, urging us to do the right thing. We don't want to listen. We don't want to think. We don't want to be bothered with the facts. We just want to do what makes us feel good now.

IMMATURITY LEADS TO POOR DECISIONS (5:12b–13)

The metaphor of age-appropriate food was typical in the ancient Greco-Roman world. Hebrews says, "By this age you should be grown-up teachers." Epictetus says, "Are you not willing, at this late date, like children, to be weaned and to partake of more solid food?" (*Diss*. 2.16.39). The Roman Stoic Seneca (ca. 4 BCE–CE 65) says, "How long shall you be a learner? From now on be a teacher as well" (Seneca, *Epistle* 33.9).

Instead of being teachers, the author of Hebrews chides his audience for needing to go back to kindergarten and re-learn the ABCs, "You don't have the chops for solid food, you need to be spoon-fed a bland, liquid diet!" The point is not that the people don't know things, it's that they don't use what they know to make right decisions. They don't have the capability to form right judgments. This is the same point that the Jewish philosopher Philo (20 BCE–50 CE) made.

> But seeing that for babes milk is food, but for grown men wheaten bread, there must also be soul-nourishment, such as is milk-like, suited to the time of childhood, in the shape of the preliminary stages of school learning and, such as is adapted to grown men, in the shape of instructions leading the way through wisdom and temperance and virtue. (Philo, *On Husbandry*, 9)

Imagine how odd it would be to have a twenty- or thirty-year-old in grade school. Or how ridiculous it would be for a forty- or fifty-year-old in kindergarten—a sixty- or seventy-year-old in pre-school. The youngsters are drinking milk; he's drinking milk of magnesia. The kids are talking about "Fitty Cent" and the old guy is remembering when you could buy a whole gallon of milk for fifty cents.

Mature Christians in the church should not only be disciples, they should be teachers. Instead of struggling with elementary Bible class, you should be teaching Advanced Christian Living. The church should be filled with Masters of the Art of Living. The more mature have attained the Ph.D. level, the "Practical-How-Do" of Christian character and conduct.

Food for Thought (5:11–14)

THE MATURE PERSON HAS A DEVELOPED APPETITE FOR WHAT'S RIGHT (5:14)

Who is the mature person? The word "mature" in Greek is that word we translate with English terms like "perfect" or "complete." The mature person is one who has attained the goal of complete personhood, the epitome of what it is to be human, a creature made in the image of God and formed over time to be like Jesus. The Apostle Paul says in 1 Corinthians 14:20, "Brothers and sisters, do not be children in your thinking; rather, be infants in evil, but in thinking be adults (mature, complete, perfect)."

What is the goal of maturity? Is it the memorization of Bible verses? Is it a knowledge of Hebrew and Greek? Is it a perfect attendance record at church? The goal of maturity, according to Hebrews, is that your mind has been trained to tell the difference between good and evil, between virtue and vice.

Life-changing decisions are often made in a split-second. We face a circumstance that could be an opportunity or an obstacle. We have to make a decision about what's the right thing to do. If we have not gained knowledge, practiced right-thinking, trained ourselves to do what's right, how do we expect to be mature, responsible people who make the right choice? We make moral decisions every day that have a direct impact on our spiritual condition. The right choices reinforce our progress in faith. The more right choices, the more progress we make, the stronger and more mature we become. The promise is the mature person will be the person who can withstand trials and suffering without losing faith. The promise is that's the person who will know what God's rest is.

Let me repeat: sloppy thinking inhibits progress; immaturity leads to poor decisions; and it is the mature person who has a developed appetite for what's right. I think this joke, available in hundreds of places on the Internet, puts it in perspective.

> A Doctor was addressing a large audience in Tampa.
>
> "The material we put into our stomachs is enough to have killed most of us sitting here, years ago. Red meat is awful. Soft drinks corrode your stomach lining. Chinese food is loaded with MSG. High fat diets can be disastrous, and none of us realizes the long-term harm caused by the germs in our drinking water. But there is

Section Three: Jesus Compared to the High Priesthood of Aaron

one thing that is the most dangerous of all and we all have, or will, eat it. Can anyone here tell me what food it is that causes the most grief and suffering for years after eating it?"

After several seconds of quiet, a 75-year-old man in the front row raised his hand, and softly said, "Wedding Cake."[3]

There are plenty of other potential bad choices in life that can upset our system for years to come. Those bad choices lead back to bad decisions. Hebrews has given us some food for thought: you are what you think.

---

3. Instant Humour: Wedding Cake. Accessed April 9, 2008. Online: http://www.instanthumour.com/wedding-cake/

Growing Up, Not Falling Back (6:1–8)

SOME PEOPLE NEVER WANT to grow up. Some young people—and even some adults—have the Peter Pan complex. They never want to grow up and face the maturity of adulthood.

Since 2001 my main job has been to oversee the distance learning program at Earlham School of Religion. Since the Masters of Divinity degree was designed as a five year program, we expected we would have graduated some students after five years. Instead, those who were on track for graduation held themselves back a year in order to graduate with their cohort. Sometimes students are hesitant about completing their program and to begin the process of beginning their ministries.

Education in the ancient Greco-Roman world was a graduated series of instruction in basic subjects leading to an advanced level of studying rhetoric to prepare for a career in law or politics. One option at that higher level was to join a philosophical school. The goal was not just to learn about philosophical or metaphysical concepts and the use of logic and argument. It was most of all to develop and progress in maturity, to be formed into someone who was a stable, virtuous, and productive member of society. During most of the adolescent years, being a certain age meant being at a certain level of education. One didn't decide to give up the study with the *rhētor* in graduate school and return to the *grammaticus* to begin studying the alphabet again, or to go back to an earlier phase of learning how to read Aesop's *Fables*.

If someone doesn't make the grade in school, the result is the person flunks out. A misbehaving student gets expelled. The student who doesn't make progress may be held back, but it's not possible to back up a few grades. There's no option to go back and start all over again. You can't become an adolescent and have another try.

Hebrews is making this point to his audience: As a Christian community, it is in danger of repeating the errors of the people of God in biblical history, a failing that could mean the removal of God's blessing and favor in this new age. Each member of the community must continue to mature in a way that leads to productive and virtuous Christian living, a life characterized by faithfulness and obedience to God.

The message for us is that not only can we not simply stay at the same grade all our lives, we must go on to graduate to maturity (6:1–3) because there's no chance for us to turn back time and start it all over again (6:4–6). Failure as the people of God can mean expulsion from the blessings of God (6:7–8).

GRADUATE TO MATURITY (6:1–3)

The exhortation to the people is for them to move on together toward perfection, to graduate, as it were, to maturity. The cohort needs to move ahead to advanced levels and leave behind the beginning phases of Christian education.

Philo, the Jewish philosopher from Alexandria, writing about the same time as Hebrews, describes a similar goal using the same language from Greek philosophy.

> But we must not be ignorant that repentance occupies the second place only, next after perfection, just as the change from sickness to convalescence is inferior to perfect uninterrupted health. Therefore, that which is continuous and perfect in virtues is very near divine power, but that condition which is improvement advancing in process of time is the peculiar blessing of a well-disposed soul, which does not continue in its childish pursuits, but by more vigorous thoughts and inclinations, such as really become a man, seeks a tranquil steadiness of soul, and which attains to it by its conception of what is good. (Philo, *On Abraham*, 1:26)

The topics that Hebrews lists reflect the circumstance of a group heavily influenced by Jewish practices. "Repentance from dead works" refers to the beginning stages in which a pagan convert to Judaism or to Christianity would turn from idolatry. This is not a reference to human effort toward salvation, as is commonly thought. Idols were thought of as works of human hands, objects that were dead in contrast to the living God. Consider this text from the Wisdom of Solomon.

> But miserable, with their hopes set on *dead* things, are those who give the name "gods" to the *works* of human hands, gold and silver

Growing Up, Not Falling Back (6:1–8)

fashioned with skill, and likenesses of animals, or a useless stone, the *work* of an ancient hand. (Wis 13:10 emphasis mine)

Along with the renunciation of idols is the worship of the one God, here described as "faith toward God." Compare this with how Paul described the conversion of gentiles: "For the people of those regions report about us what kind of welcome we had among you, and how you turned to God from idols, to serve a living and true God" (1 Thess 1:9). Hebrews repeats this concept further on: "how much more will the blood of Christ, who through the eternal Spirit offered himself without blemish to God, purify our conscience from dead works to worship the living God!" (9:14).

The instruction about "baptisms"—notice the plural—most likely refers to the Jewish practice of ritual washings, either in the washing of the hands and/or feet, or the regular practice of descending the steps of a *mikveh* until the body is completely immersed as a form of ritual washing. The "laying on of hands" probably refers to the rites of passage in which a young convert is given a blessing and an appointment to new levels of responsibility. The doctrines of Pharisaic Judaism included teachings about the "resurrection of the dead" and about the "future judgment." In all of this, Hebrews expresses the desire that God may permit them to move on to the later stages of mature living and leave the fundamentals behind.

That's not to say the fundamentals aren't important. There are times when we return to the basics and relearn the fundamentals. A violinist, for instance, might start learning to play the violin with some bad habits and poor technique. At some point the instructor might say to that person, "you need to begin again and learn to play correctly. You'll never progress without knowing how to do it right."

Sports teams often begin a new season, particularly after having had a poor season, with relearning the fundamentals. Get back to basics: dribbling, passing, shooting. The coach makes them play defense with their hands always up in the air to mold new habits and break old ones.

School teachers might start a new year by going back over the basics before moving on to new material. Some kids might forget over the summer and need a refresher. In these sorts of cases, it makes sense to go back a little bit and review the basics.

But there comes a time when, if you haven't got the basics down and you're not making progress, you risk being cut from the team. The team that doesn't improve can't expect to have a winning season and make it to the playoffs. They are out of the competition. It's like the expression, "fish or cut bait." You have to begin to excel in what you're doing, or you are going to be sidelined.

The same holds true in the life of faith. Individual Christians and whole churches can become stagnant. As a matter of fact, most churches exist in a continuous state of stagnation, which inevitably leads to decline. People don't improve. From one year to the next, there can be no marked change in their understanding of the Christian life or in their growth in Christian maturity. They remain the same year after year, not learning anything new, not becoming more mature in their practice of virtuous and faithful living in fellowship with God. Each church must learn how to graduate people from year-to-year to new levels of maturity. If we don't, we are all failing. The reality is we might as well close the doors and go somewhere else.

NO CHANCE TO START OVER (6:4-6)

Hebrews puts it in no uncertain terms, "It is impossible to restore again to repentance" (6:4). There's no chance to start over again. These verses have been taken to mean Christians who fall away from the faith are doomed. We have to remember that Hebrews is talking about the experience of one group of people—the Israelites who disobeyed and fell in the wilderness—and the other group, the followers of Jesus who, if they are not careful, could repeat the situation and fall away. As a group of people, they have been enlightened, they have experienced the power and goodness of God's new work. There's no chance for them to start over again. What Hebrews means is that they can't go back to the earthly life of Jesus and go through the historical experience of Christ's death, resurrection, exaltation, and the presence of God's Spirit in the world. It would mean crucifying Jesus again, putting Jesus on the cross again, all because they didn't get it right the first time. You can't go back and do it all over again.

I've been out of graduate school now for ten years. In the last two or three years I've been doing a great deal of reading in philosophical texts from around the first century. This had been the kind of study my professor, Stan Stowers, had expected us to do in our program at Brown University. But I wasn't getting it, and I dropped several courses because I wasn't understanding Greek philosophy. It's only recently that I've started to understand what my professor had been trying to teach us. I've been

Growing Up, Not Falling Back (6:1–8)

doing my best to catch up to where I should have been about ten years ago. In 2004, when I attended the Society of Biblical Literature conference in San Antonio, I had a chance to talk to Stan. I told him, "I'm finally getting it." I related how excited I was by the implications of the study of the philosophical schools as it relates to early Christianity. Then I said, "I really wish I could go back now and start over, knowing what I know now." He tactfully replied, "I wish I could too." But, of course, we can't. I can't get Brown to reinstate me as a student and give me my scholarship again. I can't get my colleagues to return to school with me. I certainly can't make myself younger so I can tolerate writing term papers for twenty-four hours straight. I can't go back and change the type of education I had, so I would be better prepared. I can't turn back the clock and start over again.

Jesus came into this world 2000 years ago to give people another chance. The history of the Old Testament, though it contains some success stories of individuals who excelled in faith, is a recitation of failure on the part of the people of God. From a Christian view, that cycle culminates in the Roman occupation and with a leadership largely controlled by people who lined their own pockets and who oppressed large portions of the Jewish population. For us as heirs of those who watched the life of Jesus, who were witnesses of the resurrection, and who experienced heaven breaking into the world through the presence of the Holy Spirit coming to reside within people, we are obligated to build on that, to continue to progress, to move ourselves forward in God's mission in the world. We can't expect that God will say, "Once, twice, three times a charm," and then start over again with some new work in the world. This is our time, this is our opportunity to move forward. There is no chance to go back and start again.

AN UNPRODUCTIVE LIFE IS A LIFE LIVED IN VAIN (6:7–8)

This simple agricultural analogy is meant to illustrate the point Hebrews is making. Various authors in the Greco-Roman world made such an analogy between education and agriculture. Quintilian (ca. 35–ca. 100 CE), a Roman rhetorician and author of *The Orator's Education* (*Institutio Oratoria*), describes education in similar terms.

> If you should say that the mind ought to be cultivated, you would compare it with land, which, if neglected, produces briars and thorns, but when tilled, supplies us with fruit. (Quintilian, *Institutio Oratoria*, 5.11.24)

Section Three: Jesus Compared to the High Priesthood of Aaron

Philo develops the metaphor of the mind as a field, which, when harvested, yields the fruit of virtue. Vice is represented as growth in the field which is unproductive and must be gotten rid of.

> For these when sown and planted in the mind will produce most beneficial fruits, namely fair and praiseworthy conduct. By means of this husbandry whatever trees of passions or vices have sprung up and grown tall, bearing mischief-dealing fruits, are cut down and cleared away, no minute portion even being allowed to survive, as the germ of new growths of sins to spring up later on. And should there be any trees capable of bearing neither wholesome nor harmful fruits, these it will cut down indeed, but not allow them to be made away with, but assign them to a use for which they are suited, setting them as pales and stakes to surround an encampment or to fence in a city in place of a wall. (Philo, *On Husbandry*, 9–11)

In agricultural terms, soil that absorbs the frequent rainfall produces a crop for the farmer. That's considered a blessing from God. Soil that fails to produce a crop but instead yields weeds—the worst of which are thorns and thistles—is unprofitable and, instead of a blessing from God, it is cursed. The only option, then, is to give up the possibility of producing any crop in that field and to burn off the weeds, or as Philo says, use the sticks to make a fence row. In another place, Philo develops the analogy further.

> These then are the professions and promises made by the husbandry of the soul, "I will cut down all the trees of folly, and intemperance, and injustice, and cowardice; and I will eradicate all the plants of pleasure, and appetite, and anger, and passion, and of all similar affections, even if they have raised their heads as high as heaven. And I will burn out their roots, darting down the attack of flame to the very foundations of the earth, so that no portion, nay, no trace, or shadow whatever, of such things shall be left; and I will destroy these things, and I will implant in those souls which are of a childlike age, young shoots, whose fruit shall nourish them. And in those souls which have arrived at the age of puberty or of manhood, I will implant things which are even better and more perfect, namely, the tree of prudence, the tree of courage, the tree of temperance, the tree of justice, the tree of every respective virtue. (Philo, *On Husbandry*, 1:17–19)

In education, the student who fails to soak up the knowledge and become a creative user of that knowledge is not going to graduate. There is

Growing Up, Not Falling Back (6:1–8)

no other option than dismissal and expulsion. Someone whose conduct in school is characterized by misbehavior and who never shows any hint of being a productive member of society will not be helped toward the next level of education or recommendations for placement and advancement.

At Earlham School of Religion we evaluate students periodically to gauge whether they are making progress. There are some who might pass their courses but whose character and conduct raises red flags. Before they participate in supervised ministry and allowed to graduate, they must demonstrate that they are making progress, maturing in character and spirit, becoming responsible people who are fit for ministry. Not everyone makes it.

The formation of Christian maturity is the same way. But I don't think the author has in mind primarily the experience of individuals. It is the cohort of students, it is the community of faith who either receive the blessing of God and continue on to experience God's rest or end with a curse from God and fall by the wayside in the wilderness of unfaithfulness and disobedience.

It can be seen in the life of a church as symbolized in church buildings. The vitality of a church lessens to the point of an inability to keep the doors open. The building then begins to crumble, and the remaining few struggle to keep the church alive. The building becomes no longer fit for habitation and is demolished to make way for another convenience store.

Let me repeat: Not only can we not simply stay at the same grade all our lives, but we must go on to graduate to maturity. There's no chance for us to turn back time and start it all over again. Failure as the people of God can mean expulsion from the blessings of God.

This is work that takes constant attention, just like many other areas of life. I'm slowly coming to the conclusion that I shouldn't be a home owner. In spite of the example of my father, who was a jack-of-all-trades and could do about anything around the house, in the yard, or in the garage, I have very little desire and even less know-how to keep up house, yard, and automobile. I can get up enough energy to mow the lawn and even do some trimming and edging. A week later I have to do it all again. There's no end to it. I love to see winter come, because it means I no longer have to mow the grass and hopefully there will be just enough snow to

Section Three: Jesus Compared to the High Priesthood of Aaron

cover the overgrown grass and the last bit of leaves I didn't take care of without there being so much snow that I have to shovel every day or so. I didn't trim the shrubs for a year, and the next summer received a notice that I was in violation of a city ordinance along the back alley. Little flags marked my yard in the back telling everyone how delinquent I was. The yard needs to be mowed, the shrubs need to be trimmed, the trees need to be cut back from power lines, the trim around the house needs painting, and I have my doubts whether the wild flowers in the front will ever look like anything more than weeds.

Our spiritual lives are like that. Our faith community is like that. If we don't tend to our lives, we begin to deteriorate, our vitality begins to decline, the red flags go up informing everyone that we are not fit for ministering to others, that we ourselves are in danger of losing the privilege of serving God and representing God in this world. It takes work. It takes cooperation. It means being devoted to God and the community of faith. But we must move on and we must move on together. We cannot stay spiritual adolescents. We must grow up.

Signs of Life (6:9–12)

Anyone who has been in the hospital knows the routine of nurses checking vital signs. From my experience in the hospital it is obvious to me that the ability to sleep through the night is not one of the vital signs they check or nurses wouldn't have been waking me up every few hours to check my vitals. I wasn't always sure what was being tested. Was it my ability to hold an object under my tongue? Was it how long I could endure my arm being squeezed by an air compressor? Was it whether the nurse holding my hand made my heart race, how red my face would get when she poked around my lower abdomen, and then whether my feet were ticklish?

We're all pretty familiar with the medical vital signs: temperature, blood pressure, heart rate; the sounds that a doctor listens for related to our heart, lungs, and other vital organs. Doctors can look at us, poke and prod us, and ask us how we're feeling. From all this they are able to diagnose problems and recommend treatments.

We often go through our day without thinking much about our physical health—except for those of us who are neurotic or hypochondriacs. But about every six months we take ourselves in to see the doctor and once again have an examination. The goal is that the doctor will not see any deterioration in our health. If we are recovering from a sickness, we hope to hear that the doctor sees signs of improvement. What happens if we don't have regular checkups? We run the risk of finding out one day that some disease or ailment has gone undiagnosed and that we are then so far gone there's nothing the doctors can do.

Although many of us don't work enough at being healthy, we become greatly concerned when we have problems, either through illnesses or injuries. I'm always struck by how much emphasis Christians place on their physical condition. Anytime Christians are asked for prayer concerns, 90% of the requests seem to have to do with medical conditions. Our physical condition is certainly an important part of our daily living, but in the big scheme of things, how important is it really?

Section Three: Jesus Compared to the High Priesthood of Aaron

Many of us have experienced the practice of someone saying they have an "unspoken" request. These tend to be issues of morality and spiritual problems. Somehow Christians need to get to the place where we feel comfortable and safe enough within our faith community to share what's really going on in our spiritual and moral development. Individuals need to practice daily self-examination. Small groups should meet weekly to checkup with each other and then encourage and pray for each other. If there's evidence of spiritual and moral deterioration, then be open to admonishing each other. The local church should have some way of assessing its spiritual vitality at least on a yearly basis. However, there's no way to do that when we only see the surface of people's lives and only meet for an hour or so a week in a formal setting.

The author of Hebrews is giving his audience a spiritual checkup. In the previous text, the author has given a rather harsh warning. If the church isn't making progress it risks losing the blessings of God. We can't make any improvement by taking a step forward and two steps back. God's people must be moving toward the goal of godly maturity.

Having given that warning, the author softens his approach. He has reason for hope that his audience is a group that gives evidence of spiritual and moral development. The author of Hebrews is confident in the signs of good things (6:9). There's a certainty of service for God (6:10), and hope of their completion of the supreme goal (6:11–12).

CONFIDENT IN THE SIGNS OF GOOD THINGS (6:9)

In spite of the dire warning about the dangers of an unfruitful condition of life, the author thinks that his audience is not at that point. He has confidence in the signs of good things. Not only has he softened his approach, he makes up to them, calling them "beloved."

It's like that thing they say about Southerners. In the American south people can say harsh things about people as long as they add one little phrase. You can say, "That Luella May, she is such a gossip—bless her heart." "Jim Bob won't ever find a wife—bless his heart." The author of Hebrews says, "You people are such juveniles, beloved—bless your heart."

He is persuaded that there are good things happening in the church. He is confident that these are signs of good health. Their conduct is having a salutary effect on the congregation's spiritual life.

Signs of Life (6:9–12)

I frequently read some article or hear someone lamenting the negative impact technology has had on the education and formation of young people. They cite statistics that show an increase in the amount of television viewing among teenagers. They talk about kids who sit for hours watching TV or being on a computer, who instead need to go for a walk outside in nature. Given these sorts of characteristics, we might generalize and say that kids who act in this way are not going to do well in school and aren't going to be properly socialized.

About mid-way through my daughter Lauren's first year in high school, I complained that she needed to spend less time on the computer and in front of the TV and more time doing homework and practicing her trombone. Her mother reprimanded me for not knowing what I was talking about. She didn't call me "beloved," but she probably said something sarcastic like, "Well, dear." She pointed out to me that Lauren had received her report card for the first semester of high school and had a 4.0 and that she was doing very well playing her trombone in band. I made a judgment about her development based on appearances rather than making an informed assessment.

We can't make judgments about growth and development simply based on some assumptions about what people must be doing in order to achieve it. We can warn people about what can cause a decline in growth and development, but we also need to look for the signs of health and provide encouragement in those areas. When we examine ourselves individually and when the church assesses its growth, we need to be able to focus on the ways in which good things are happening, things that are having a positive effect on the life of the church.

CERTAINTY OF SERVICE FOR GOD (6:10)

In verse 10, the author of Hebrews continues to express his confidence in his audience, in this case a certainty of their service for God. He reasons with them. When God evaluates your spiritual condition, he is going to be fair. Since God is characterized by justice, God is not going to be unjust in judgment. God is also not forgetful. Deuteronomy says that God is merciful and will not "forget the covenant with your ancestors that he swore to them" (Deut 4:31). The prophet Amos assures his readers Yahweh "will never forget any of their deeds" (Amos 8:7).

Section Three: Jesus Compared to the High Priesthood of Aaron

What is it that God will remember about Christians? Is it their testimony of a born-again experience? Is it how many times they've read the Bible through cover-to-cover? Or how many times they've presented the gospel to someone? Hebrews says that what God will not overlook is their work and love exemplified by their continuing service and ministry to others.

The word here translated "serving" is the verb form of the Greek word for "deacon." The noun and verb forms are most often found in contexts of serving food at a meal. There's no mistaking the implication of these terms: ministry has more to do with the work and love shown in serving a potluck dinner or helping in a soup kitchen than it does in joining a Bible study or a prayer circle. Yet we, who say we love Jesus and live by the Bible, continually reject service as an attempt to work one's way into heaven. We have so emphasized the Reformation value of salvation by faith through grace that we have ignored the Biblical principles of work and service as indicators of spiritual and moral development.

One of the valuable forms of assessment in the Religious Society of Friends is the practice of the yearly State of the Society. As a part-time pastor, it has been difficult for me to write these things. In my first pastorate I was asked to write the State of the Meeting report. I remember thinking about it and wondering how I was going to write something positive. I certainly couldn't imagine writing about all the things I thought needed improvement. One of the problems was that we had very infrequent activities outside of the hour or two on Sunday morning. Once or twice our church served together at a local soup kitchen. Besides that, we didn't really have much work we did together. As I thought more about the meeting and the people who made up the meeting, I began to change my way of thinking. The woman who was the clerk of our meeting had been going to school to be a nurse and another woman was a nurse working at an extended care facility a few miles away. Another woman had been the middle school librarian and technology resource person for many years. A number of people had grown up in that church and had gone to Earlham College and were involved in service industries, one in particular who regularly gave large donations to help the church. One family had two daughters who were both intelligent, socially sensitive, and very active in the yearly meeting. When you looked at what the people were doing with their lives outside of the local church context, it was an impressive work being done for the good of others.

Signs of Life (6:9-12)

When we measure the health and vitality of our meeting, we are not just listing the programs we have or the small groups that meet, though those can be ways people support each other and grow. We also need to take into account the manner of life people are living. The principle is that the more love one has for God, the more love one will show to others. The deeper the spiritual practice, the greater the capacity for selflessness, sacrifice, and service. The more highly developed the character and the more advanced the faith and moral formation, the more one will recognize one's place as a citizen of the world and one's duties to others and to society.

COMPLETION OF THE SUPREME GOAL (6:11-12)

The author of Hebrews sets before his audience his intense desire that this Christian community work toward the completion of the supreme goal. He wants each person to reach for the same level of diligence. Everyone needs to work hard, pull together, really apply themselves. Don't slow down, don't start taking it easy, but give it all you've got to the very end.

Here's that word "sluggish" again. Remember that we found that the term referred to a sloppy way of thinking about choosing what's right and what will help us to make improvement in our spiritual and moral formation. Instead of being sluggish or sloppy, we need to fix our attention on good moral examples. We need to find models to imitate.

Here we come to that word "faith" again. The question we always need to ask about this word is, is it the kind of faith that is a belief—a passive, mental assent to some sort of teaching or doctrine—or does the context imply constancy, a faithfulness to God in our actions and character. Notice that faith is here coupled with the word "patience." A literal translation of the Greek word is "long-suffering." The implication of the context is endurance and constancy, rather than the content of one's belief system.

The author wants them to remember the saints from biblical history who remained constant in their devotion to God in spite of the difficult circumstances of life. In the next verses the author will give the example of Abraham. In chapter 11 he will give a long list of people in the Bible who remained faithful to God and God blessed them.

Each religious group, denomination or faith community has its success stories. A children's book was published in 1917 called, *A Book of Quaker Saints*. Quakers often talk about the struggles that early Friends endured in England. They tell stories of those who traveled to far off countries. Quakers can list those of their number who were instrumental in social activism like prison reform, establishment of modern mental hospitals, women's suffrage, abolition of slavery, workers' rights, education reform, temperance societies, peace movements, medical and material care, Alternatives to Violence—just to name a few.

Frequently a Friend will say, we shouldn't just talk about the Quaker saints of years gone by. "What have we done lately?" is often the question. Rather than using these people as a way of legitimizing ourselves or to rest on our laurels, we should use them as models for imitation.

There's no such thing as an average Christian. Every Christian has the capability and the duty to reach the goal of our human existence, to have a godly character and behavior. By the end of our lifetime, we should have made progress and developed into a Christ-like person. That's the teaching of the New Testament.

We've settled for much less in contemporary Christianity. We're just satisfied with living a secular life with occasional religious pick-me-ups on the weekend. No, what Hebrews is telling us is that we need to demonstrate diligence and vigilance. The goal of developing our souls toward godlike maturity is set before us. We can do it, and we can do it together.

The author of Hebrews is confident in the signs of good things, there's a certainty of service for God, and hope of their completion of the supreme goal. If a spiritual doctor came and took our vital signs, what would she find? Would she pronounce the patient dead or would she find signs of health and vitality?

You've probably heard about the recent incident in which a van-load of students from Taylor University was struck by an oncoming semi-tractor trailer. One of those people who died was a young woman. A friend of the family identified her, she was given a huge funeral, and the family buried her. Another girl was in critical condition in the hospital in a coma. Family members watched over her, sat with her, waiting for her to revive. She finally did come out of her coma, but the first words they heard was, "Not my parents." The awful realization was, they had misidentified the girls. The father of this girl, I discovered, is the youth pastor of the church where our relatives go to church in Michigan. He had been on a youth trip when he

Signs of Life (6:9–12)

had heard his daughter was dead. He was on another youth trip when he received the news, his daughter is alive.

Many pundits have written off the church. This period of time is labeled "post Christian." They have pronounced the church dead. It is possible, however, that we could prove them wrong. They've given a wrong diagnosis. We've been misidentified. We're not the church that has died, but we are the church who has been revived, is gaining strength, and is on the verge of full recovery. But future survival and growth depends on church life becoming a greater part of people's lives. Each one has to take seriously our own personal growth and maturity in the faith. Together we need to identify how to help people move forward and to discover what the vision is for our work in the community and the world. There are signs of good things in God's church, and we can be confident that life can once again flourish in our communities.

Seize the Day (6:13–20)

Don't you feel sorry for millionaires who get upset about estate taxes? Bill Gates, for instance, has three children. Wouldn't you like to have just the taxes that will be due on the assets he wills to his children?

We use the expression "old money" to talk about family wealth that has been passed down generation after generation. The name "old money" sounds disgusting doesn't it? Wrinkled up bills that have been passed from person to person, stuck in sweaty wallets kept in men's back pockets. We have no idea who had the old money last or through whose hands it has passed. I can guarantee you that any money I'm able to pass on to my children will be new money. As far as I know, no inheritance has been passed down in our family nor do I expect it to be.

My parents are in their eighties and celebrating their sixtieth wedding anniversary. We sometimes talk about their plans for the next—and, in some ways, the last—stage of their lives. They really don't want to devote the rest of their life's savings and investments in assisted living and palliative care. My sister and I tell them, however, to take care of themselves. They deserve it. We don't expect to receive money as an inheritance from them. There are more important things that our parents have passed down to us than wealth or property. Those things are our inheritance.

My father, for instance, has handed down to me some very important guidelines and principles for living that are priceless. I learned from my father the discipline of self-motivation. He had very little formal education and graduated from a Bible institute as preparation for the pastorate. But he has worked long and hard to educate himself and to form himself into a scholar. I can't imagine life different than the one he modeled for me: a Bible on the desk and shelves of books at hand.

My father has also influenced me in the concept of prayer as a way of life. Prayer times are enriching experiences, but a relationship with God is a 24/7 experience. Just as in relationships with other people, that sort of con-

Seize the Day (6:13–20)

nection with God occurs through good times and bad times. It is a dynamic relationship that grows over time. God is a friend I've known intimately for over forty-five years due to the example of my father, as well as my mother.

Believe it or not, I get my sense of humor from my father as well. Some of the most hilarious moments of my life have been with him and his friends and relatives. I'm sure I developed my smirk from my Dad, the only evidence sometimes that I think I have said something humorous. (I said I got my sense of humor from my father, I didn't say it was a good one.)

The most important value is the commitment to God. I'm not talking about puritanical practices, even though my parents tried to teach me that too. I value the idea of a lifetime commitment to God, the idea that service to God is the overarching principle that shapes everything else I do and gives everything meaning.

At the end of chapter six of Hebrews, the author is stressing the importance of valuing what has been passed down from one generation to the next. The generation of Moses was a time of mixed blessing. God rescued them from bondage in Egypt, but because of their disobedience, God vowed not to let them enter the Promised Land. However, God had made a vow before the time of Moses.

Abraham, our grandfather in the faith, had followed God's leading to another part of the world. God promised to give Abraham many descendants and to bless them, in spite of the fact that Abraham and his wife were advanced in age. As John Calvin described it in the early sixteenth century, Abraham and Sarah were "nearer the grave than to a conjugal bed." Abraham remained faithful to God, and God blessed him with Isaac. God tested Abraham by requiring him to take Isaac to be a sacrifice. Abraham followed God's instructions, and at the last moment God stopped him and provided a ram as a sacrifice. The story of that act of complete faithfulness on the part of Abraham was a defining moment in the history of Judaism, Christianity, and Islam.

The author of Hebrews interprets this is in the context of his experience of the recent life and death of Jesus, whom he understands to be God's Son, a fulfillment of the long-awaited priest-king messiah. Hebrews looks back to the event 2000 years ago in which God made a promise, a promise which God confirmed with an oath, according to the book of Genesis. Abraham's descendants have had that promise as an inheritance. Those who are Abraham's spiritual descendants by faith, even us who are living 2000 years after Hebrews, must claim that inheritance which Jesus has validated.

Section Three: Jesus Compared to the High Priesthood of Aaron

The message from this text about hope in the time of testing, put simply, is this: Grandfather Abraham stuck it out (6:13–15), our forefathers substantiated it (6:16), and our generation needs to seize it (6:17–20).

GRANDFATHER ABRAHAM STUCK IT OUT (6:13–15)

Hebrews introduces Abraham as an example: The previous verse says people should be "imitators of those who through faith and patience inherit the promises." Tradition has called him, Father Abraham. But isn't Abraham a little old just to be called Father?

Genesis 22 tells the story of God testing Abraham. The first major test had been the promise that Abraham would have a child in the first place. The second major test, which we read about in Genesis 22, was seeing whether Abraham was willing to give that only child back to God, and whether he would believe that God would still have provided another child even later.

Hebrews describes this as Abraham "patiently enduring" God's testing. As a result, God makes the ultimate gesture of making an oath. A person swears an oath by some powerful force, a parent, a king, or even God. God had to swear an oath by God's own person. In spite of the fact that God by nature cannot lie, God still goes the next step to swear an oath that God will bless Abraham's descendants so that there is no mistake, confusion or debate. Abraham has certainly obtained the promise. Abraham has all kinds of descendants, ethnically, religiously, and spiritually.

The story is told of the Quaker minister Stephen Grellet. While traveling in the ministry he purposed to go into the deep forest of Pennsylvania. The men of the town had cautioned him about traveling alone into the forest. It was dangerous and difficult; the lumber camp was three days journey. When asked who he was, he explained, "Stephen Grellet, of New York, and I go to carry the message of God to those who will listen. I have received my instructions from Above and go without fear, for the Spirit upholds me."[4] As he rode on into the forest, a man remarked, "A Quaker, I know by his speech, and a godly man. But he cannot melt the hearts of those men with his soft tongue."[5]

---

4. Anna Pettit Broomell, *The Children's Story Garden*, Lippincott, 1920; Accessed March 18, 2008. Online: http://www.strecorsoc.org/storygarden/63210_tsitw.html.

5. Ibid.

Seize the Day (6:13–20)

He followed the path through the forest until finally on the third day arrived at the lumber camp. To his surprise, he found a deserted camp, empty sheds, and boarded up cabins.

> Stephen Grellet reined in his mare in great perplexity. The message that had come to him had been very clear, and as was the habit of his life, he had followed the leading of the Spirit in perfect faith. He knew that he was to come to this spot in the heart of the wilderness where a gang of woodcutters, far-famed for their lawlessness, had been operating, and here he was to preach the simple and holy truth of God's presence in the forest. It had not once occurred to him that, as evidently was the case, the lumbermen might have moved on deeper into the forest. He knew without question, however, that this was the place where he must preach. Alighting, he tied his mare to a sapling, leaving her to browse the long wood grass, and made his way to the central cabin where rough tables stood on a slightly raised floor. Mounting this platform, he faced the forest, a strange inner light making his face glow. During his long life he had travelled to the far corners of the earth, defying dangers and discomforts in order to carry the simple assurance of God's love to all people; yet never had he felt more completely the Divine Presence flooding through and around his whole being than when now he stood alone in the deserted camp, surrounded by the mystery of the forest.[6]

In spite of the circumstances, Grellet began to preach out loud to no one but God and the forest animals. When he had finished, he remounted his horse and traveled back, out of the forest back to his home.

Six years later Stephen Grellet was in London, once again following a leading, this time to preach to God's creatures in the streets of London. Nearing the end of the day, Grellet was walking along the Thames, when someone grabbed him by the elbow.

> He turned quickly to face a broad, muscular man, with rugged face and eyes of piercing eagerness, who cried, in great excitement, as he peered into Stephen Grellet's face, "I have got you at last! I have got you at last!"
>
> Stephen returned the gaze calmly, but could see nothing familiar about the man except that he was certainly an American.
>
> "Friend," he replied, "I think thou art mistaken."

---

6. Ibid.

Section Three: Jesus Compared to the High Priesthood of Aaron

"But I am not—I cannot be! I have carried every line of your face in my memory for six years. How I have longed to see it again!"

"Who, then, art thou, and where dost thou think we have met?" inquired Stephen.

"Did you not preach in the great forest of Pennsylvania, three days' trip from the village of Rockville, six years ago last midsummer?"

"I did, but I saw no one there to listen."

The man held out his hands to Stephen Grellet—strong hands that had known hard toil. "I was there," he replied, his voice full of awe as the memory rose again before him. "I was the head of the woodmen who had deserted those shanties. We had moved on into the forest and were putting up more cabins to live in, when I discovered that I had left my lever at the old settlement. So, leaving my men at work, I went back alone for my tool. As I approached the old place I heard a voice. Trembling and agitated, I drew near, and saw you through the chinks in the timber walls of our dining shanty. I listened to you, and something in your face or in your words, or both, stirred me as I had never been stirred before. I went back to my men. I was miserable for weeks; I had no Bible, no book of any kind, no one to speak to about divine things. "At last I found the strength I needed. I obtained a Bible; I told my men the blessed news that God was near us, and we learned together to ask forgiveness and to lead better lives. Three of us became missionaries and went forth to tell thousands of others of the joy and faith you brought into the forest."[7]

Stephen Grellet had been faithful to God's leading in spite of the circumstances. His faithfulness resulted in a blessing that was passed on to generations of those who came to faith as a result of that lumberman and his companions.

Our grandparents in the faith heard the call of God in their lives and they trusted that God would be faithful to fulfill God's promise in their lives. In spite of great obstacles and times of testing, they stuck with it, just like Abraham did.

OUR FOREFATHERS SUBSTANTIATED IT (6:16)

The author of Hebrews probably knew of the wide-spread tradition among Jews in this time period regarding the story of Abraham's test. Most every

---

7. Ibid.

Seize the Day (6:13–20)

type of Judaism that existed around the first century had some explanation and interpretation about this incident in the Bible. Philo, for instance, impresses on his readers the meaning of God swearing an oath by God, "For you see that God does not swear by any other being than himself, for there is nothing more powerful than he is; but he swears by himself, because he is the greatest of all things" (*Allegorical Interpretation*, 3:203). Josephus, the first-century Jewish historian, tells the story in another way. As soon as the altar was prepared, and Abraham had laid on the wood, and all things were entirely ready, he said to his son,

> "O son! I poured out a vast number of prayers that I might have you for my son; when you came into the world, there was nothing that could contribute to your support for which I was not greatly solicitous, nor anything wherein I thought myself happier than to see you grown up to a man's estate, and that I might leave you at my death the successor to my dominion; but since it was by God's will that I became your father, and it is now his will that I relinquish you, bear this consecration to God with a generous mind; for I resign you up to God, who has thought fit now to require this testimony of honour to himself, on account of the favours he has conferred on me, in being to me a supporter and defender. Accordingly you, my son, will now die, not in any common way of going out of the world, but sent to God, the Father of all men, beforehand, by your own father, in the nature of a sacrifice. I suppose he thinks you worthy to get clear of this world neither by disease, neither by war, nor by any other severe way, by which death usually comes upon men, but so that he will receive your soul with prayers and holy offices of religion, and will place you near to himself, and you will be there to me a help and supporter in my old age; on which account I principally brought you up, and you will thereby procure me God for my Comforter instead of yourself." (Josephus, *Antiquities of the Jews*, 1.228–32)

What Josephus says Abraham claimed for Isaac is exactly what Hebrews is claiming for Jesus. Rather than Isaac to be placed near to God, Jesus accomplished through his faithful act in giving himself up to death as a sacrifice and now exalted to the right hand of God.

We are impressed by numbers. If we weren't, politicians and political pundits wouldn't keep throwing numbers around. A poll that says millions of people believe a certain thing only tells us that millions of people believe a certain thing. It doesn't say that they are right or the thing they believe is true. It's the logical fallacy called the *Argumentum ad Populum* or an Appeal to Numbers.

We can't say that because millions of people have been impressed enough by the story in Genesis about Abraham to give their religious commitment to Judaism, Christianity or Islam, it proves that God continues to hold out the promise of blessing on those who, like Abraham, remain faithful to God. We do have anecdotal evidence that, since the time of Abraham, God has blessed Abraham's descendants. Our foreparents can attest to the blessing of God on a life lived faithful to God. Generation after generation substantiate that God blesses those who love God and stay true to God.

OUR GENERATION NEEDS TO SEIZE IT (6:17-20)

The language of Hebrews is so evocative. The author moves from one metaphor to the next. We are pictured as people who are fleeing for refuge, seeking sanctuary in the temple. His words are emphatic; we have a "strong encouragement." Imagine the author of Hebrews preaching this message, reaching out his right arm as a gesture of "strong encouragement" and then tightening his fist in the air and nearly shouting out, "Seize the hope set before us."

Next we are to imagine a ship whose anchor is dropped. We won't drift away from the shore where we've set anchor. Again the scene shifts, now imagining the Holy of Holies in the tabernacle, the inner curtain that separates the first section of the Holy Place from that most sacred place behind the curtain where the high priest alone enters once a year. Jesus enters that inner sanctuary, but the image is of the first person who leads the way, the front-runner in a race or the first rank of an army. Now coming full circle the author of Hebrews arrives back where he started this digression, the mysterious figure of Melchizedek, whose high priestly order prefigures that of Jesus.

One of the most common Latin expressions is *carpe diem*, most commonly translated as "seize the day." In an ode of Horace, we first read the expression, "As we speak, jealous Time flees, Seize the day, believing as little as possible in the next" (*Odes* I, 11.8–9).

The author of Hebrews is saying, "believe as much as possible in the past, believe as much as possible in the future, seize the day. Grab and hold

Seize the Day (6:13–20)

on to the hope that has Jesus as the anchor." Remember the moving speech Robin Williams makes in this scene from the 1989 *Dead Poets Society*?

> "But if you listen real close, you can hear them whisper their legacy to you. Go on, lean in. Listen, you hear it?—Carpe—hear it?—Carpe, carpe diem, seize the day boys, make your lives extraordinary!"[8]

That's what it comes down to. Let's not just think of this as pie-in-the-sky-by-and-by. Hebrews is saying, "Seize the hope, make your lives extraordinary!"

The message from this text about hope in the time of testing, put simply, is this: Grandfather Abraham stuck it out, our forefathers substantiated it, and our generation needs to seize it.

Maybe you have an inheritance and you just don't know it. States are required to report what money and property goes unclaimed. I heard about it on the news, so I went down the list of every state in which I've lived to see if there was any money that was supposed to be mine. I still owe money from living in other states, but apparently none owe me.

In the State of Mississippi, according to an article in the *Clarion Ledger*, June 14, 2006, 450,000 people have unclaimed money amounting to $34 million. We might think, what idiots! People who might have thousands of dollars and it's sitting around unclaimed.

What fools we are if we do not claim the promise given to Abraham and validated in the life and death of Jesus. We are missing something worth so much more than money if we lose sight of God's blessing. Seize the day! God's best is what we receive: an extraordinary life, an extraordinary eternity.

---

8. *Dead Poets Society*, Directed by Peter Weir, screenplay by Tom Schulman, Touchstone, 1989. Accessed March 26, 2008. Online: http://en.wikiquote.org/wiki/Dead_Poets_Society.

Section Four

The Melchizedek Priesthood of Jesus Compared to the Levites
(7:1—8:13)

An Oldie but a Goodie (7:1-10)

"**W**HYYYYY?" THAT'S NOT JUST a way our children respond to everything we tell them to do, it's a question we ask ourselves every time we resist doing what we feel we should do. We can imagine a child who tells her younger sibling to do something—pick up her clothes, put away her dishes, stop playing with the matches—any of those sorts of things that are part of our routine obligations. Her little brother or sister says, "Why? Why should I do what you tell me to do?"

Maybe the older sibling says, "Because Joshua"—he's the oldest of the kids—"told me to tell you to do it."

Then comes the reply, "Who died and made him boss?"

Big brother happens to overhear the conversation, and he adds to the discussion, "Mom told me to tell you to do it."

Now you think that would be the ultimate authority. Wouldn't you expect sissy to say, "Oh, I'm sorry. I didn't understand. Why didn't you just tell me that Mother had left instructions. I will get on that right away."

Mother comes home and sees that the work isn't done and yells at the oldest. The oldest refers her to the next in line, and finally it gets down to little sissy. Mom says, "I left instructions for you to do your chores, now get to it."

And then comes the whining, "Why? Why do I have to do it?" A list of objections then follow: I did it last time, it's someone else's turn; I don't feel well; I'm too tired; I hurt my leg and can no longer walk; it's not fair that I have to do things."

Maybe the mother would do one of those typical—or not so typical anymore these days—"Just wait until your father gets home."

Little sissy doesn't say, but she thinks to herself, "Big deal." She's a smart girl. She may not know the expression "corporal punishment," but she knows that Mom and Dad don't spank. "What are they going to do?" she thinks to herself, "I never go anywhere, so they can't ground me. They

Section Four: The Melchizedek Priesthood of Jesus Compared to the Levites

don't give me an allowance, so they can't take that away. Eventually they will tire out and forget about it."

I heard someone tell a story about his brother who was a zealous Christian. Apparently he had been trying to get his son to eat his vegetables. Perhaps out of a sense of desperation he said, "Eat your vegetables, Jimmy. Jesus likes little boys who eat their vegetables."

Just like little sissy, we go up the chain of command looking for the ultimate moral authority: Why should I do what's right? Just because Mom & Dad taught me it's right? Just because the pastor says so or it's the teaching of the church? Because the Bible says so? Just because the Bible says so, does that necessarily mean that God says so?

The whole purpose of Hebrews is to persuade people to continue to do what's right—in other words, to live faithfully in obedience to God. The author of Hebrews anticipates the question, "Why?" His answer is to point out to his audience what the biblical story says happens when people aren't faithful. The wandering of the children of Israel in the wilderness without being allowed to enter the Promised Land is a case in point.

"That's ancient history," they might say. The author of Hebrews shows in Jesus, God has recently made another attempt to help people become complete and moral people. By comparison, Jesus holds out a better hope for their future than anything that has preceded. Yet, if people failed and received a punishment the first time around, it follows that failure to be faithful regarding something greater means that a greater punishment will be meted out the second time.

Chapter seven of Hebrews is another comparison the author of Hebrews has crafted to demonstrate the way in which what God offers in Jesus excels what God did in the past. The topic for comparison is the priesthood. What can be said about Jesus? Jesus was not from a priestly family. He was from the tribe of Judah, not the tribe of Levi. What can be said about Jesus in connection with the priesthood? It just so happens that Jewish tradition had something of a fascination with a character from the book of Genesis by the name of Melchizedek.

Genesis 14 tells the story of a battle between an alliance of Mesopotamian nations against a weaker alliance of Canaanite cities in the vicinity of the Dead Sea (Gen 14:1–9). The stronger armies from the east get the upper-hand and take captives with them as hostages and spoils of war (Gen 14:10–12). Meanwhile, Abram hears about the defeat and that some of his relatives, including Lot, have been captured. Abram takes

An Oldie but a Goodie (7:1-10)

his own men and leads them in an expedition to catch up to the retreating army (Gen 14:13-14). Abram is successful and heroically brings back their own people plus his own spoils of war (Gen 14:15-16). The king of Sodom is one of those who greets Abram on his return (Gen 14:17). Then Genesis tells about another king by the name of Melchizedek (Gen 14:18). He is king over the city of Salem. Salem is thought actually to have been an earlier name for the city of Jerusalem—we can see it clearly in the end of the English word. In what appears to be a Canaanite religious ceremony, Melchizedek brings to Abram bread and wine. Genesis says Melchizedek is "a priest of the God Most High." This most likely is a term that refers to a Canaanite God known as *Elyon*. The name of the Canaanite deity was *El*; the Hebrews called their God *Elohim*. Melchizedek then gives Abram a blessing (Gen 14:19-20). In return for the blessing, Abram gives Melchizedek an offering, the traditional one-tenth that goes to the priesthood of the deity.

There are a few remarkable things about this person. His name seems significant to later tradition. He's the first person to be called a priest in the Bible, well before the institution of the priesthood and the tabernacle sacrificial system described later in Exodus, Leviticus, Numbers and Deuteronomy. This "priest of the God Most High" gives a blessing to Abram. Nothing else is said about this individual except for one text. In Psalm 110 David is described as a priest-king, "The LORD has sworn and will not change his mind, 'You are a priest forever according to the order of Melchizedek.'" Since the first part of Psalm 110 addresses the messiah and is applied to Jesus, the author of Hebrews takes this stanza of the poem also to apply to Jesus.

Priests in the central sanctuary in Jerusalem took turns officiating. David is the ultimate sort of a king, a king who is also a priest. He's a priest not just for a little while, but he belongs to this special, ancient order of priests, a successor to Melchizedek from the old city.

For the author of Hebrews, Jesus is in this royal order of priests just like David. What can be said of them can be said of Jesus. That makes him better than what people had been used to. Because of the antiquity and perpetuity of the priesthood of Melchizedek, Jesus' priesthood is more authoritative. These verses in Hebrews seven first tell who Melchizedek is (7:1-4), then compares his priesthood to that of the Levites (7:5-6), and finally explains why his priesthood is better (7:7-10).

Section Four: The Melchizedek Priesthood of Jesus Compared to the Levites

GREATNESS BASED ON ETYMOLOGY, GENEALOGY, AND THEOLOGY (7:1–4)

The meaning of his name is significant (7:2). It means "king of righteousness." In actuality, his name probably was "My king is Zedek," but the Hebrew word *tsedek* means "rightness or righteousness," a common description for the deity. Since Salem means "peace" in Hebrew, that makes this king a peaceful king, another common attribute of the Hebrew God, in spite of the tradition of war in the Israelite nation.

The typical pattern of praising an individual in Greek literature is to discuss their lineage, birth, parentage, and the noted features of the person's life and career. In this case, nothing is known of Melchizedek's lineage. In fact, some Jewish tradition, such as what is represented in the Dead Sea Scrolls, considered Melchizedek to be a messianic and even a divine figure.

When it comes to parentage, no information is available from Genesis about Melchizedek (7:3). It's as if he just appears mysteriously in the narrative. Hebrews uses the terms "fatherless" and "motherless" found in classical Greek literature that describe the gods: They are often described as not having parentage. The Psalm text says the Melchizedek priesthood is forever. Therefore, Melchizedek resembles a "son of God," an angelic type figure who is not born nor dies.

Hebrews exclaims, "See how terrific he is!" (7:4). Abraham, the father of the Gentile and Jewish nations, the one who should receive the tithe and the one through whom all nations have been blessed, gave Melchizedek the tithe and received from him a blessing.

Can you imagine some elderly priest who happens to meet the Pope. Since the priest's eyesight isn't so good, he thinks the Pope is a lay person. He greets the Pope with "Bless you my son." The pope realizes the mistaken identity and the switched roles. With humility, the Pope responds with a bow to the old priest. See how great he is! This old priest has been conferred the greatest praise. Think of the honor accorded to him to have the head of the Roman Catholic Church bow to him.

Keep in mind what is being said of Melchizedek applies to Jesus. The predecessor of David was Melchizedek, according to Psalm 110. Jesus, then, is the successor to David in this priesthood. By comparison, the Melchizedekian priesthood surpasses that of the Levitical priesthood.

An Oldie but a Goodie (7:1–10)

PROMINENCE BASED ON PRIVILEGE OF ANTECEDENCE (7:5–6)

In verses five and six, the author of Hebrews draws a formal comparison, a synkrisis, using the Greek *men/de* construction. A literal translation of the beginning of the comparative exchanges looks like this: "(v. 5) On the one hand, the ones from the sons of Levi . . . (v. 6) On the other hand, the one not descended from them . . . ."

On the one hand, Hebrews describes the Levitical priesthood. The descendants of Levi, according to the Old Testament law, are to receive a 10 percent tithe from the people in return for which the people receive the Levitical blessing (Num 18:21–24; 6:22–27). The priests are descendants of Levi, who in turn was a descendant of Abraham: Abraham begets Isaac, Isaac begets Jacob, Jacob begets a lot of children by a lot of women, Levi being the son of Leah. The ones giving the tithe are also descendants of Abraham—it's all in the family.

There's nothing wrong with this. Hebrews isn't criticizing it or saying it's bad. God instituted the law through Moses, it's there in black and white—rather, chiseled in stone, we should say, by the finger of God (Exod 31:18; Deut 9:10).

On the other hand—and here comes the kicker—Melchizedek is outside the family line and even precedes it. Instead of being an Abrahamic descendant who gives or receives the tithes and gives or receives a blessing, Melchizedek is outside the tradition, and it's the whole Abrahamic family before whom the whole Abrahamic line humbles themselves with a tithe and receives the Melchizedekian blessing. How can you beat that?

In writing a eulogy for our make-believe elderly priest, someone could write this.

> See how great he was! On the one hand, his fellow-priests had the great honor of bowing to the Pope and receiving a blessing from him. On the other hand, this priest actually gave a blessing to the Pope and the Pope bowed to him.

SUPERIORITY BASED ON PRIORITY (7:7–10)

Why then is the Melchizedekian priesthood better? Hebrews explains it. Everyone knows that the superior person blesses the inferior. No argument there. In the case of the Levites, they are a group of men who are

Section Four: The Melchizedek Priesthood of Jesus Compared to the Levites

continually dying off and being replaced by others in their tribe. They are the ones who are receiving the tithes from their other relatives from the other tribes. In the case of Melchizedek, he is this divine figure who belongs to a group of priests who live forever. That's how Hebrews is interpreting the text from Psalm 110.

In fact, if you think about it, it's kind of like Levi was not even a glimmer in Abram's eye when he met Melchizedek. If we are somehow generatively in the body of our forefathers, then Levi was in Abraham and it was like Levi himself was giving obeisance to Melchizedek.

Have you known people who play the ancestor game? Suann's mother's side of the family can trace their genealogy to Abraham Lincoln. She's something like an eighth cousin. If she met a descendant of John Wilkes Booth, he could say, "I shot you." It's a bit of a playful argument in Hebrews but one that his audience would have understood.

These verses answer the questions about Melchizedek: who is he, how does he compare with the priesthood of Levi, and why it matters. The comparisons show that the priesthood of Melchizedek—the priesthood claimed for Jesus—is greater, with more prominence, and superior by its priority. This mysterious figure of Melchizedek serves as the prototype of an eternal priesthood.

During graduate school, I took a leave of absence before beginning to write my dissertation on Hebrews chapter seven. I took a job as a typesetter in Massachusetts. There I met a guy who claimed to be a Gnostic. Gnosticism was an early Christian group that considered the material world to be evil, and salvation was to be found in special knowledge through which the individual ascended to higher and higher spiritual planes. Ancient Gnostic texts developed the figure of Melchizedek as divine person. My coworker shared with me a little booklet in which the leader of their Gnostic group described a visitation he had. The hooded figure that appeared to him was none other than Melchizedek. Imagine my honor, to get to see a drawing of what Melchizedek actually looks like. He's held up well over the years.

As we'll see further in Hebrews, it's not Melchizedek who is the Messiah, Son of God, Savior, it's Jesus. The effects of what he has done are like those attributes of Melchizedek. The point is, Jesus is the best God

An Oldie but a Goodie (7:1–10)

has to offer. If we ask the question, "Why should we do what's right?" the answer is clear. God is doing all God can to provide the means for us to live in a right relationship to God, to live life to the fullest, to be the best kind of humans we can be. The rest is up to us.

More Powerful, Longer-Lasting (7:11–17)

Persuasion used to be a good thing. Now persuasion is commercialization. I'll never forget the time I received a phone call and was asked to watch a new television show. I agreed to watch the whole show and then to respond to a survey. I sat down at the appointed time, ready to watch this new sitcom pilot and to share my insight from years of TV viewing. The time came for the phone survey. I had not been impressed by the actors or the script and was prepared to share my opinions about the show. By the second question of the survey I was being asked questions not about the acting or the script but about the first commercial that they aired. I had to tell them, I didn't watch it; I got up to get a snack. The whole thing turned out to be about the commercials, not the show. I felt so used.

We've all experienced the way persuasion is used to get us to buy things. In ancient Greece and Rome, the art of persuasion was about how to urge people toward the best ways to live life. That's not the way it is now. Instead of encouraging determination and endurance, a rabbit wants to sell us batteries that "keep going and going." Instead of urging us to live healthy lives that are conducive to longevity, we should just chew gum that is "longer lasting." Rather than promoting virtuous living, a bread and snack company wants us to "Remember what's good" and eat what they call "indulgent treats." Persuasion is the modern tool to sell things. How do they do it? Mainly by catchy jingles, memorable trademarks, and pleasing images. The old-fashioned way was by reason and logic.

The main concern of Hebrews is the faithful living of followers of Jesus. The author is convinced, not only that we are obligated to be faithful and that negative consequences will happen to the unfaithful but that followers of Jesus have been given what they need to be able to live faithful lives and to become mature Christian people. The main tool in Hebrews' rhetorical arsenal is comparison, a way of praising the excellent qualities

More Powerful, Longer-Lasting (7:11-17)

of something by drawing a parallel to something else that is accepted as having good qualities.

- God gave the law through angels, but Jesus surpasses the angels as the Son of God.
- Moses was faithful to God as a servant, but Jesus is faithful as a Son.
- The high priest serves God through the offerings, but Jesus matches everything about the high priesthood and surpasses it.
- God ordained the Levitical priesthood, but the priesthood of Melchizedek is more powerful and longer lasting. Jesus is that kind of high priest.

In this next section, the author of Hebrews reasons that, if the priesthood of the tribe of Levi had worked, it wouldn't have been changed (7:11-12). But the priesthood has changed to Jesus as High Priest, but not to the tribe of Judah (7:13-14). Jesus' priesthood is not by natural lineage but by divine life (7:15-17).

IF THE PRIESTHOOD OF THE TRIBE OF LEVI HAD WORKED, IT WOULDN'T HAVE BEEN CHANGED. (7:11-12)

Here again is this word "perfection" (7:11). We have a lot of problems with that word. We want to say nobody's perfect. When we say that, we are talking about a different concept than what Hebrews is talking about. The Oxford English Dictionary lists the current usual sense as "The condition, state, or quality of being free from defect; flawlessness, faultlessness; purity." But the first meaning it gives for "perfection" is labeled obsolete. This is the sense in which the word is used in antiquity: "The fact, state, or condition of being completed or perfected; consummation, completion, end. The most complete or perfect stage of growth or development of a person or thing; maturity; ripeness." This is what our English translation of the Greek word in the New Testament means. A change in English usage has brought about confusion in how we understand the New Testament's teaching concerning perfection.

Hebrews has shown that the people of Israel did not come to the end of God's purpose for them. Disobedience caused them to fall in the wilderness before reaching the Promised Land. Consummation, completion, maturity did not come to fruition for the people of God through the Levitical priesthood. If it had, then there wouldn't have been the need for a different priesthood. But, Hebrews argues, there has been a change in the priesthood. Therefore, it follows that the previous priesthood didn't fulfill its intended function for the people of God. God has done a new thing through Jesus.

When I was a teenager, it was still the practice for parents to lay down the law. Somewhere there was a law book that was intended to make good adults out of any kid. The law book must have had a section about clothing and grooming. Boys had to have short hair and no facial hair. Girls had to keep certain portions of their bodies well-covered at all times. Another section must have had something about when and under what circumstances boys and girls could be together. There was a certain age when dating could begin. There was a time by which those dates are concluded and beyond which time trouble was sure to happen. There was a certain progression of intimacy that was permissible: apparently kissing on the first date was a problem and there was some connection between teenage relationships and purchasing milk from cows rather than getting it for free. There must have been a large section on punishment: spanking was good, paddling even better; lashes with a belt gave nice welts for a kid to remember what he did bad; twisting a kid's ear, pinching, pulling hair, wrapping the knuckles, boxing the ears—all apparently good deterrents to childish behavior.

The compendium of rules for enforcing proper behavior and punishing bad behavior was massive and pervasive. Somewhere along the way we have learned a better way. We have realized that strict laws and harsh punishments did not work. Many parents were found to be hypocrites when they had to say, "Do what I say, not as I do." We've also learned that positive reinforcement is a better way to persuade someone to right conduct. And we know that the best way to teach someone proper behavior is to model it for them. Finally, we've discovered that many of the things that we expect from people are superficial things anyway, and what is most important is the kind of person someone is. The goal is essentially the same, however. Parents want their kids to grow up to be virtuous and responsible adults.

The goal for a person in the Old Testament is not essentially different than in the New Testament. Hebrews is saying that what is different is that what God has given to us in Jesus is a more effective way for us to become complete, mature people of God. If we can be convinced of that, perhaps

More Powerful, Longer-Lasting (7:11–17)

we will be more committed and faithful people. And if that's the case, then we have a sure hope that we will enter God's rest when this life is over.

THE PRIESTHOOD HAS CHANGED TO JESUS AS HIGH PRIEST, BUT NOT TO THE TRIBE OF JUDAH (7:13–14)

There was an expectation that God's messiah would be a priest and a king. Some Jewish groups anticipated two messiahs. That makes sense because you couldn't have a priest unless he is from the tribe of Levi, and you couldn't have a king unless he is from the tribe of Judah, like David. In an early Jewish document, possibly from as early as the second century BCE, called the *Testaments of the Twelve Patriarchs*, the testament of Simeon to the children of Israel is this:

> And now, my children, be obedient to Levi and to Judah. Do not exalt yourselves above these two tribes, {because from them will arise the Savior come from God}. For the Lord will raise up from Levi someone as high priest and from Judah someone as king. He will save all the gentiles and the tribe of Israel. For this reason I command these things to you and you command them to your children, so that they may observe them in their successive generations. (*Test 12 Patr*, 2.7)[1]

There's a problem here then. Jesus has the role of a priest. But Jesus is from the tribe of Judah. There's nothing in the Bible about the tribe of Judah serving as priests. How then could Jesus be this messianic figure of the priest-king without being descended from the tribe of Levi?

For many countries who are ruled by dynasty's it means a great deal to be in the right genealogical line. In the United Kingdom, for example, there are nearly 500 people in the line of succession behind the heir apparent, Prince Charles. Hebrews attempts to persuade the audience that he has solved the mystery of the lineage of the priesthood. Jesus is the heir apparent, since he descends from the messianic line and from the Melchizedekean priestly line.

---

1. James H. Charlesworth, *The Old Testament Pseudepigrapha*, 1st ed. (Garden City, N.Y.: Doubleday, 1983), 787.

Section Four: The Melchizedek Priesthood of Jesus Compared to the Levites

JESUS' PRIESTHOOD IS NOT BY NATURAL LINEAGE BUT BY DIVINE LIFE. (7:15–17)

Because Jesus was considered to have been resurrected from the dead and exalted to heaven, he resembles Melchizedek who was said to have a never-ending priesthood. A Levite has a priesthood by physical descent, something that also means he won't be priest for long but will die. Jesus' priesthood is not based on physical descent but because of a spiritual ascent. Not by natural lineage but by divine life.

There's always a stigma applied to someone who moves up in the company when that person is a relative of the owner: Someone claims she got a promotion to vice president because her father owns the company. Or someone passed over for partner consoles himself: He got partner because his mother was a founding partner of the law firm. But we admire the person who goes against all odds, pays his dues, moves up the ladder, and earns the promotion.

Whatever Hebrews might be said to claim for the divinity of Jesus, no one can deny that Hebrews portrays Jesus as ascending to God because he earned it. He's not the great high priest of the heavenly tabernacle because the law says so or just because he has the right parentage. Through his endurance and faithfulness God exalted him having gained an indestructible life. By virtue of that life, he received his appointment to the priesthood in the order of Melchizedek.

~

The author of Hebrews has argued that, if the priesthood of the tribe of Levi had worked, it wouldn't have been changed. But the Priesthood has changed making Jesus the High Priest, but not as from the tribe of Judah. Jesus' Priesthood is not by natural lineage but by divine life.

Imagine if in antiquity they had billboards along the road. You're traveling along the Appian Way and you see a billboard. You say to yourself, "Here's another billboard. Someone trying to persuade me to change my life or urge me to maintain my virtue." There's a big picture of a Jewish man and he's wearing the attire of a Jewish high priest. Big Greek letters (with Latin subtitles, of course) read, "Follow Jesus." Then over the image of the priest it says, "High Priest of Melchizedek." Across the bottom is the motto with a trademark sign, "More Powerful, Longer-lasting."

More Powerful, Longer-Lasting (7:11–17)

The audience of Hebrews would have been impressed by the argument. They would have been persuaded by the comparison. It's up to you to decide, am I convinced that Jesus is what Hebrews says he is? Am I persuaded that by following Jesus I will become a complete, mature person of God because of what Jesus has done and because of who Jesus continues to be, my high priest in heaven?

God's Better Half (7:18–25)

THE SAYING GOES, VOTERS get the politicians they deserve. In a 2005 election in Britain, people were particularly frustrated with the electioneering. One person commented to the BBC News,

> In a democracy the people get exactly what they ask for—the majority of the people in this country get bored by involved policy description. They instead choose to buy papers that focus on gossip and mud-slinging. The politicians then resort to this to try and reach these people. All they do is respond to public demand—this is our fault. If you don't like it change it, stand yourself, just stop whining![1]

Another person related a story from the 1700s.

> The young reporter asked a very wealthy land owner why he wished to go into politics. "Well young man," he replied, "I'm going in to serve the greatest number." "What's that?" asked the reporter. Pointing to his chest he said, "Number one." Nothing has changed in over 200 years.[2]

The people we elect to government are our representatives. We know that if we fail to choose wisely—or we don't choose at all—we get the politicians we deserve. In spite of our failures to understand the issues, to be involved in what our representatives are doing, and to be responsible citizens, we deserve to have the best representation possible. We should be confident that when our elected official has been sworn to duty he or she is the voice of our concerns, an effective legislator, someone who will be a constant presence for us on matters that affect us all.

In the ancient world of the Bible, people didn't have much say about their representatives. Usually the king was a successor to a dynasty or, in

---

1. BBC News | UK | UK Election 2005 | Have Your Say. "Has Politics Become Too Dirty?" Accessed March 18, 2008. Online: http://news.bbc.co.uk/2/low/uk_news/politics/vote_2005/have_your_say/4242765.stm.

2. Ibid.

God's Better Half (7:18–25)

the case of the Roman period, someone appointed by the emperor. People didn't vote to appoint rulers of lesser rank either. Of course, the leadership of the religious institution wasn't decide by a democratic vote. Much of the priestly leadership was dependent on ancestry. If you belonged to the tribe of Levi, you knew that your job would be to take a turn serving at the temple, singing in the choir, butchering the sacrifices, being the grill-master of the altar, or have the clean-up duty. In other words, people didn't choose the priests who would represent them before God and had no say about who they were or how long they served.

The author of Hebrews and his audience knew the stories of the Bible. They knew that after God gave the Israelites the law with all of the instructions for worship and being in fellowship with God, they had gone on to murmur against God and disobey God. Even Moses ended up not making it into the Promised Land.

There were indications in the Bible that God would restore to Israel its kingdom, its royal line of kings, a consecrated priesthood, and a new covenant. For the author of Hebrews and his audience, this all was being fulfilled in Jesus. God was giving people a second chance through the faithful life of Jesus. Even though God had instituted the law and its civil, social, and ceremonial ordinances, by comparison what God was doing in Jesus *would* be effective in bringing people to the goal of life, entering the heavenly rest. It's as though what God has done in Jesus is the second half of God's overall plan. The author of Hebrews perceives it to be God's better half.

In 7:18–25 Hebrews wants us to draw three comparisons: (1) compare the ineffectiveness of the Levitical priesthood to the introduction of a better priesthood (7:18–19); (2) compare the uninaugurated priests to Jesus, whom God appointed as priest (7:20–22); and (3) compare the frequent turnover of Levitical priests to the constancy and efficacy of Jesus' priesthood (7:23–25).

COMPARE THE INEFFECTIVENESS OF THE LEVITICAL PRIESTHOOD TO THE INTRODUCTION OF A BETTER PRIESTHOOD (7:18–19)

You can see the language of comparison in the NRSV translation: on the one hand, on the other hand. Each of the three comparisons in this passage have the same linguistic feature characteristic of formal comparisons,

Section Four: The Melchizedek Priesthood of Jesus Compared to the Levites

but the significant Greek construction goes untranslated in the other two comparisons.

Besides this linguistic problem, there is also the crucial matter of how to interpret Hebrews' language about the Jewish law, the Torah. In the history of the interpretation of Hebrews, Christian scholars have taught that Hebrews was written to argue by Jewish rabbinical methods that Judaism and its law have been superceded by the Church and its salvation by grace through faith without legalism. It was thought that the audience of Hebrews consisted of Jewish Christians who were in danger of lapsing back into their old ways in Judaism. What we understand now is this way of interpreting Hebrews was often done in the last century or so by people who were anti-Semitic. Over the last fifty to seventy-five years, scholars have had to reassess how we interpret the Bible to be careful that opinions aren't shaped by prejudice.

We must try to understand Hebrews within its historical and literary context. I'm convinced that the purpose of Hebrews is to call people to greater faithfulness in time of persecution, an encouragement to progress to a mature stage of human existence, both in the way they relate to God and in the way they relate to others in the community of faith. The assumption has been that a book with so much detail from the Old Testament and whose title came to be "To the Hebrews" was certainly written to Jewish Christians. The reality is the author of Hebrews was not concerned about the ethnic background of his audience. I think it's even possible that the author of Hebrews addressed this document to Gentiles, non-Jews, people who had become adherents to a Hellenized form of Judaism and were now followers of Jesus, a Christian form of Hellenized Judaism.

Having said that, notice that our text refers to the "abrogation of an earlier commandment." Interpreters assume that the linguistic context of Hebrews is law. The term here translated as "abrogation" (*athetēsis*) was used in contexts of annulling or voiding an agreement. The noun form used here is rare in biblical usage. But scholars have been impressed by its usage in Greek papyri. In those instances it is used in the legal sense of annulling and voiding a contract. However, its frequent appearance in those texts doesn't mean it's the normal usage. The Greek papyri are largely legal documents in the first place.

What may help us understand this term is to recognize that the verb form of this word (*atheteō*) does occur in Hebrews: "Anyone who has *violated* the law of Moses dies without mercy 'on the testimony of two or

God's Better Half (7:18-25)

three witnesses'" (10:28). Rather than saying that the earlier commandment has been voided, 7:18 is saying that the earlier commandment, in a broad sense, was violated, rejected by the people through their disobedience. Contrary to what recent commentators have said on this, I think the issue about the law is not that the law was bad, but that it was ineffective in bringing people to perfection, to maturity, to the intended goal. People disobeyed God's commandments, set them aside, and were willful and wandering.

Hebrews says that the law made nothing perfect. It doesn't say that the law wasn't perfect, it says that the law didn't do what God intended it to do because people failed to keep it. In fact, the Bible claims the opposite about the law: "The law of the LORD is perfect, reviving the soul; the decrees of the LORD are sure, making wise the simple" (Ps 19:7). Elsewhere, Hebrews says the law wasn't able to make people perfect. The sacrifices of the tabernacle system were not able to "perfect the conscience of the worshiper" (9:9). Because the law only provided for yearly sacrifices to be made, it did not provide a final way to "make perfect those who approach" (10:1). In two other places, Hebrews refers to the idea that the followers of Jesus will be made perfect (10:14; 12:23).

Notice the other side of the comparative exchange in the middle of verse 19: "there is, on the other hand, the introduction of a better hope, through which we approach God." Into the picture comes a better hope, meaning a different kind of priesthood, the priesthood of Melchizedek, the kind that is more powerful and longer-lasting. Through the priesthood of Jesus we have a better hope of approaching God in worship.

My favorite response when asked for directions is, you can't get there from here. Of course, if you can get to the place from which you can get somewhere, then you can get there from here. It's just that it is a whole lot easier sometimes to get somewhere when you begin at a different starting point.

A man wanted to cross a busy street and couldn't seem to get a lull in the traffic. He noticed another man standing on the other side. He called out to him, "How did you get over there?" The man replied, "I was born over here."

Imagine the complex highways of large cities, the multiple lanes, entrances and exits, cloverleaves that look like you could spend eternity going in a figure eight if you miss your exit.

Hebrews talks about our final destination as being the spiritual equivalent of what the Israelites were heading for and failed to accomplish in the wilderness. From that place in the story, God was telling them, you can't get there from here. Moses looked from the height of a mountain and could see the Promised Land, but he was not allowed to cross over (Deut 34:1–4). There was something stopping the Israelites from being able to live up to God's expectations. Hebrews is saying that God created a bypass. Follow that bypass and you go around the Levitical priesthood. Then look for the entrance that leads to a better road, a way by which we can approach our final destination.

COMPARE THE UNINAUGURATED PRIESTS TO JESUS WHOM GOD APPOINTED AS PRIEST (7:20–22)

We can read in the Old Testament what God set down as the proper installation and ordination procedure for the priests (Exod 29; Lev 8). There's nothing there about requiring the priests to take, what we think of as, an oath of office. However, Psalm 110 says that Yahweh swore an oath that the priesthood of Melchizedek is forever. Hebrews then draws this comparison as a way of saying that the latter type of priesthood is better. How much better can you get than God swearing an oath? Therefore, if God swears that the priesthood is forever, then the presence of Jesus as that sort of priest means that it is certain to last forever.

In the metaphor of a covenant or testament, our inheritance is safe because Jesus is the guarantee and Jesus has obtained an eternal priesthood. One of the ways people went into debt in the first century Mediterranean world was being the guarantor of someone's loan. With the kind of life expectancy people had in the ancient world, it was a very risky business to be a co-signor.

As someone who has had several daughters take out student loans for which I had to be the co-signor, I can tell you I have an additional reason for wanting my daughters to live long and prosper. I've never really thought about it before, but I imagine that bankers have to be concerned about what happens when a co-signor for a loan dies.

None of this is of any concern for us as Christians because of the kind of deal God has given his people. Because Jesus lives forever and God has sworn an oath, there's no chance that we who are the heirs of God will lose our inheritance. We always have Jesus through whom God will make good on his end of the deal.

God's Better Half (7:18–25)

COMPARE THE FREQUENT TURNOVER OF LEVITICAL PRIESTS TO THE CONSTANCY AND EFFICACY OF JESUS' PRIESTHOOD (7:23-25)

Verse 23 is the beginning of the third comparative exchange. The translation should begin with something like "on the one hand." Verse 23 then sets up the topic for comparison. We wouldn't really call this a powerful comparison, but it may have worked for people in antiquity. The Levitical priests, being mortal, only served as priests for ten or twenty years—whatever their lifespan was. This makes obvious sense and is not really a weakness in the system. You can't really blame people for dying.

The translation of verse 24 should begin something like, "on the other hand." According to the psalm text, the Melchizedek priesthood is forever. By virtue of his immortality, Jesus belongs to this order of priesthood, and therefore it is better.

I want to suggest that we may have misunderstood some things about verses twenty-four and twenty-five. The word "permanently" has been taken to refer temporally to the length of Jesus' priesthood. Grammatically, it can modify the word priesthood, but it could also refer to the way in which he remains forever. A more obvious way to understand this word is, not in a temporal sense, but with a word like "inviolable." It is a state of perfection that does not transgress. Jesus holds his priesthood because he remains inviolable forever. This not only fits with the context of Hebrews, it also fits the context of the next verse.

Again, instead of taking this in the temporal sense "for all time," there is much more evidence for translating the Greek expression with words like "completely, entirely." The reason people haven't done that is it doesn't fit with their theology. How can you say that Jesus saves people completely? Isn't someone who is saved either saved or not saved? What I want to argue for is salvation is not just used to refer to being put on the list of people who are to be delivered from damnation and go to heaven. The basic meaning of the word is one of being made well, of making improvement, coming to be made whole. The law didn't make anyone perfect, but Jesus qualitatively saves people completely when they approach to worship God through him.

When people figuratively approach the heavenly tabernacle, Jesus the high priest is there; he will always be there, no one will ever have to replace him. Jesus doesn't even take a break, but Jesus is constantly

Section Four: The Melchizedek Priesthood of Jesus Compared to the Levites

pleading our case before God, making our appeal, keeping before God our prayers.

Have you ever noticed what's on the walls of board rooms? All around the room are pictures of past presidents of the company. There's a larger portrait of the founder, then the next one, and the next. Most likely many of them have the same last name. All around the room are the pictures of people who served their term and then they retired and died—or just died while still on the job.

You can imagine what the priests' room might have looked like in the Jerusalem temple, if they had kept portraits. Maybe a thousand years' worth of sketches of high priests—if they had done that sort of thing. What about the heavenly temple where Jesus serves as high priest? There's just one picture. Maybe it's like our worship room in the church where I am pastor: We have multiple pictures of Jesus. In heaven there's only one high priest, and no room reserved for any others' portraits in the future. Jesus is for eternity employee-of-the-month, and he deserves it for the work he has done: first, for when he lived on earth as a human like you and me, and now for the thorough work he continues to do on our behalf.

⁌

In 7:18–25 Hebrews has drawn three comparisons: We compared the ineffectiveness of the Levitical priesthood to the introduction of a better priesthood; we compared the uninaugurated priests to Jesus, whom God appointed as priest; thirdly, we compared the frequent turnover of Levitical priests to the constancy and efficacy of Jesus' priesthood.

There's another saying I like: If any good, intelligent, young person can grow up to be the president, why doesn't one? It's the nature of politics isn't it? People who are the best qualified to represent and serve people are too good and intelligent to want to run for office. No matter whom we get as leaders, nearly half of us won't have wanted that person and the other half will soon become dissatisfied and eager to "throw the bum out."

It was no different during the time of the writing of Hebrews, when many people considered the temple priesthood to be corrupt. They would have appreciated the idea of Jesus serving in an eternal priesthood, thoroughly capable of being our intercessor, a guarantee that we will make it, we will be perfected, we will reach our final destination. Voters may get the politicians they deserve, but devotees of the living God surely get the high priest they deserve.

He's Just What We Need (7:26–28)

Anyone who has applied for a job or has been responsible for hiring people knows that interviews can be a torturous procedure. The first step is the resume and the procedure known as "padding the resume." An article in the *Kansas City Business Journal*, is titled "Euphemistic engineer titles ease the ego's suffering, but what about the smell?" In that article Michele McInerney pokes some fun at the way we create titles. She lists these three euphemisms:

- Pumps Gas—retail petroleum distribution engineer
- Painter—liquid recoating specialists
- Lifeguards—aquatic oversight engineers[1]

The article goes on to describe the type of job description one finds when job hunting. One example lists a very impressive job.

> Conduct a technical and sociological study of the projects for well rehabilitation/reconstruction and spring catchments, follow and evaluate the creation and capacity-building water committees, and manage water and sanitation programs, budgets and about 50 staff members.[2]

This was for a water and sanitation engineer in Afghanistan.

Since so many people pad their resumes, employers have come to expect it. If you don't put much in your resume, you look worse than you really are. If you have a great deal of experience, the employer only believes half of what he or she reads anyway.

When you finally get to an interview, you then face the standard questions.

---

1. Michele McInerney, "Euphemistic Engineer Titles Ease the Ego's Suffering, but What About the Smell?" *Kansas City Business Journal*. Page 1. Accessed March 18, 2008, 2003. Online: http://kansascity.bizjournals.com/kansascity/stories/2003/06/23/focus5.html.

2. Ibid.

Section Four: The Melchizedek Priesthood of Jesus Compared to the Levites

- Where do you see yourself in five years?
- If you were a tree, what kind of tree would you be?
- What are your strongest qualities? What are your weakest?

An article in *BusinessWeek Online*, "Stupid Interview Questions," lists similar questions. To the question, "What kind of animal would you be," Liz Ryan suggests you might answer, "Oh, any crepuscular animal would do well for me—a rabbit or a bat, perhaps."[3]

On the other end, interviewing people for a job presents its own difficulties. Some of us throw hardballs in interviews and some of the rest of us just play softball. It's after hiring a few people who turn out to be bad in their job that we learn we must be tougher in our expectations. When you think about it, we all deserve to have someone who is fit for the job, someone with exemplary qualifications and an impeccable character—as well as someone who can form proper relationships with people.

The author of Hebrews is winding up a difficult section on comparing the priesthood of Melchizedek with that of the Levitical priests. The rhetorical device of comparison is a tool for praising a subject, and these verses show that clearly. For the author of Hebrews, Christ fulfills all the hopes and dreams of the people of God. Although people failed in the past, when God gave an opportunity to follow Him, this work of God through Christ will surely be the means for people to find their way home, to achieve all that God has for them. When it comes to the character of our high priest, Jesus is all anyone could ask (7:26); if you consider the work of Christ in the continuity of his sacrifice, his is for all and for all time (7:27); a look at the quality of his person as our high priest tells us Jesus is God's Son. Jesus is the one made perfect (7:28).

CHARACTER OF OUR HIGH PRIEST: ALL ANYONE COULD ASK (7:26)

The author of Hebrews says it's only right that we should have the best sort of high priest. If we looked at Jesus' resume, we would find the list with bullet points—every resume has to have bullet points.

---

3. Liz Ryan, "Stupid Interview Questions," *Business Week,* Sept. 21, 2005. Accessed March 18, 2008. Online: http://www.businessweek.com/careers/content/sep2005/ca20050921_1099_ca009.htm.

He's Just What We Need (7:26-28)

- Holy: This word is used in the quotation in Acts 13:35 of Psalm 16:10, "You will not let your Holy One experience corruption."
- Blameless: Here we have an unusual word in Greek meaning "innocent, guileless," not the word typically translated as "blameless." One instance of this term is in the Greek Bible in Jer 11:19. In the NRSV it reads: But I was like a *gentle* lamb led to the slaughter. And I did not know it was against me that they devised schemes, saying, "Let us destroy the tree with its fruit, let us cut him off from the land of the living, so that his name will no longer be remembered!"
- Undefiled: Another unusual term. As a negation of a term meaning "defiled," it invokes the idea of those things that can ritually and morally defile. In the Jewish experience, zones of impurity are all over the place and one must be careful where one goes, what one touches, what one eats. Jesus is undefiled.
- Separated from sinners: Rather than mixed in among those who are defiled, Jesus is apart from them. We often hear people talk about the stories in the Gospels about Jesus and suggest that Jesus had no scruples about those with whom he associated. According to the author of Hebrews, Jesus' life fits the high priestly requirement for having been "separate from sinners."
- Exalted above the heavens: How higher can you get? You can't. Jesus is the ultimate, he is the utmost, he is the transcendent high priest.

When I worked at Kinko's, I would see all kinds of resumes and could often detect the overly padded resume. One resume, for example, had a long list of all the software programs the woman knew. Yet, I had to format her resume for her, since she didn't know how to do it herself!

I'll never forget the letter I had to type up one day. It wasn't for a resume, as I remember. I'm not even sure the gentleman knew where to send his letter. This man believed that he was descended from a royal line and was the rightful ruler of Great Britain. As so often happens with people suffering from this sort of dementia or megalomania, his sentences often made little or no sense and would go off on the strangest tangents. At the end of his letter, he had his name followed by his title. I can't remember exactly what it was, but it was something like Emperor of the Seven Seas.

No doubt some people thought the followers of Jesus were out of their minds for the things they claimed about him. But to those who had lived through the earliest years of Christianity, Jesus fit all the requirements for one who was the Son of God, a heavenly high priest. There was nothing more anyone could ask for.

CONTINUITY OF HIS SACRIFICE: FOR ALL, FOR ALL TIME (7:27)

If the previous verse was a description of Jesus' personal qualifications, this next verse is a list of his work experience. The high priests of Jesus' day might list the numerous times they had served as a priest in the temple. A position of high priest would have been evidence of a promotion. Built into the system of sacrifice was the expectation that the priests would sin. They would need to offer a sacrifice for sins to purify themselves first before they could offer a sacrifice for the sins of the people.

That's not the case with Jesus. Imagine seeing someone's resume. Only one job is listed. You look at the dates for the job and only find that the person worked one day. It could happen. You could be an inventor, and, if you're lucky and really smart, you could invent something in one day that would mean you never had to work another day in your life. What if you did your job so well that you worked one day and your job was done. One way of looking at Jesus' work history is to imagine there is only one item, representing the one time he offered himself. He didn't have to offer sacrifice for himself first. He didn't have to die every day on the cross for the sins of the people. That's the problem with being a martyr, you can only do it once. Jesus only needed to do it once. Once for all people, once for all time.

QUALITY OF THE HIGH PRIEST: HE IS THE PERFECT SON (7:28)

The problem with the law was not that it was bad in itself. The problem was that those who served in the temple and those who were to follow the law were only human. They were subject to weakness.

In our culture we work hard to avoid nepotism. Just because someone is in the family doesn't make that person particularly suitable for the job. But the priesthood was based on family. It was the ultimate in family business.

Remember that the word of the oath is found in Psalm 110:4: The LORD has sworn and will not change his mind, "You are a priest forever according to the order of Melchizedek."

He's Just What We Need (7:26-28)

We shouldn't move too quickly over the language of Hebrews, even though it may make some people theologically uncomfortable. Hebrews portrays the human Jesus as having achieved his status as Son and as the Son he is appointed high priest. The language of verse 26 is Jesus "became higher than the heavens." In verse 28, Jesus has "been made perfect unto the ages." Elsewhere in Hebrews we read similar expressions. God made Jesus, "perfect through sufferings" (2:10). After Jesus was "made perfect, he became the source of eternal salvation for all who obey him" (5:9). This section of Hebrews ends on a superlative note. You can't get better than someone who has become perfect.

When someone is asked in a job interview, "What is your greatest weakness," the interviewee will commonly say something like, "My greatest weakness is that I work too hard." Might we say, "My greatest strength is my perfection." We would be apt not to get the job, either because we would be considered to be a liar, or like the Emperor of the Seven Seas, to be a megalomaniac or at least egotistical and conceited.

Jesus was not subject to the same weakness as the high priests of Israelite experience. It was not the law which appointed him like the others, but a form of high priesthood existed that went above and beyond that earthly type of priesthood. It is as an eternal high priest that Jesus has become perfect.

⸺

When it comes to the character of our High Priest, Jesus is all anyone could ask; if you consider the work of Christ in the continuity of his sacrifice, his is for all and for all time; a look at the quality of his person as our high priest tells us Jesus is God's Son. Jesus is the one made perfect.

You can read this joke numerous places on the Internet. The classified ad said, "Wanted: a very experienced lumberjack." A man answered the ad and was asked to describe his experience.

"I've worked at the Sahara Forest."

"You mean the Sahara Desert," said the interviewer.

The man laughed and answered, "Oh sure, that's what they call it now!"

Before Jesus, the people of God made do with the human frailties of priests, kings, and prophets. Fundamental to Christian belief is that by his resurrection Jesus was exalted to heaven. Through the death that he died,

Section Four: The Melchizedek Priesthood of Jesus Compared to the Levites

he made a purification for sins and was himself seated at the right hand of God. This one is above the heavens, he has been made perfect, complete in every way. There's nothing more we could ask, there is no greater qualification. In every way possible, Jesus has become the ultimate solution to our fundamental need.

Here a Tent, There a Tent (8:1–6)

WHEN WE ARE CHILDREN, we learn to make the best of what we have. It may be that children growing up today will look back in fifty years and say, "We did the best we could with the little we had back in the days of video games and computers."

Like many other kids, I spent much of my adolescent years playing with models, acting out roles, pretending, imagining, creating a world that only dimly reflected the real world. *National Geographic* and *Popular Science* magazines laid out in a grid served as roads for our model cars. Our beds would be transformed into Corvettes or GTOs—never something with an automatic transmission.

Then there were the forts and tents. We knew a family in Aurora, IL who drank so much bottled pop that they built a fort in the backyard out of the wooden cases. For us, blankets or sheets held in place by clothespins would serve as tents, a place to feel like you're hidden from the eyes of parents and siblings.

For many of us, the real thing has never been quite as exciting as the things we made up. I don't think I've been in a tent since I was a child. I did own a Honda Accord with 5-speed transmission, but for the past six years I've been driving a Plymouth Grand Voyager—not something I would have dreamed of driving as a kid. If I had pretended to be driving a van, the girls in the back wouldn't have been five daughters. Even though the things we made up to represent the way real people live in the world served their purpose, most of us would choose to experience life in its real forms.

It wouldn't be fair to say that the descendants of Israel, who found themselves living in the mountainous wilderness of the Sinai peninsula, were just pretending when they would erect a large tent within a fenced enclosure in order to worship the living God that spoke from the mountain-top. They passed along the story of how God had told Moses on Mount Sinai to build this tent of worship, to place within it sacred objects,

Section Four: The Melchizedek Priesthood of Jesus Compared to the Levites

to organize a group of people to serve as priests through the offering of various sacrifices and oblations, to recognize an annual cycle of festivals meant to remind the people of their dependence on God and how God has helped them. As real as it would have been to the Israelite worshippers, they knew that it was not the real thing but symbolized a divine pattern revealed on Mount Sinai. The temple in Jerusalem was a firmer reality, but even it was a foreshadowing of a divine reality that Jews imagined would come down from heaven and fulfill all their hopes and dreams of the presence of God in the world.

For the author of Hebrews, Jesus resided in a heavenly tent. Jesus is there as a high priest. The presence of God is enthroned in the holiest place, the place of atonement, the place which embodies the faithfulness and covenant mercy of God. What the people of God constructed in order to worship God in the best way they could served its function, but it was only a model, a human construct, not the reality of divine perfection and blessed existence. This is something that Jesus brings to the world as the God-man, the one who has gone before us to make a way for us all to experience the fullness and completeness of being. The real tent there in heaven (8:1–3) surpasses the replica which existed here on earth (8:4–5). It's Jesus who gives us the better deal (8:6).

REAL TENT (8:1–3)

At the beginning of chapter eight, the author of Hebrews is summing up, recapitulating, what has been said so far. We have a high priest, Jesus. Jesus is said to be seated on the right, the place of power and privilege, next to the heavenly throne where exists the one who is the most high and majestic one. Like the high priest who is appointed to make offerings, Jesus was not only appointed but was sworn into office by God. Jesus has offered himself as the sacrifice in a single act of faithfulness, obedience, and holiness.

What's new in this text is the beginning of the discussion about the tabernacle itself. Looking forward, chapter 9 will take up this topic in the form of a comparison. In chapter eight Hebrews introduces the idea that Jesus is the servant in the Holy Place or sanctuary of the heavenly tent. It is not set up by human hands, but Yahweh put up this "true tent," the genuine article, the real thing.

Here a Tent, There a Tent (8:1-6)

I remember the time as a child when my family lived in a tent. It was a church camp, and my Dad must have had some role in directing the camp that week. The campers stayed in cabins, but for some reason we were staying in a large tent next to the main building. I'm sure it was a great campground. I can remember there was a cave at one end of this forested gorge that served as the campground. I can remember the hillside where the cabins were, because I rolled down it. My brother and his friends were doing somersaults down the hill so I tried. I could start to do the somersault but I couldn't stop rolling head over heels until I got to the bottom. One night we had a terrible, cold rain. Everything in the tent felt wet. My sleeping bag felt wet, and the cold went right through me. I developed a cough and was miserable. I don't remember much about the experience, but I do remember what happened that morning. I was brought into the kitchen. Maybe they had the kitchen oven on or maybe they had a wood-burning stove, I don't recall. All I remember is the glowing warmth of the fire, a warmth that penetrated into my body. Compared to the tent, the building was a bit of heaven.

Humans have been trying for millennia to represent what divine existence is like. Holy places and sacred spaces all over the world are monuments to human imagination about the divine. Religious literature contains the dreams and fantasies of priests, prophets, and even philosophers as they speculate about divine beauty, holiness, and serenity. We close our eyes and stare into the enlightened darkness of our minds, seeking to see a glimpse of God's being—that which grounds all things and transcends all things. We've had our best people working on it: the best artists, the best authors, the best architects. Still we are not able to come close to what the true reality of God's presence is.

REPLICA TENT (8:4-5)

The language of verse four and verse six is again the language of comparison. Verses four and five describe the earthly worship that Moses created. Verse six will argue that Jesus brings a better former of worship, a better covenant, and better promises.

Hebrews here makes the point that, if Jesus were here on earth, he couldn't be a priest. He's not from the priestly lineage; others serve God as priests. The Holy Place in which the priests serve is a faint reflection of the heavenly sanctuary. The tabernacle was only a representation of

Section Four: The Melchizedek Priesthood of Jesus Compared to the Levites

what God's dwelling is. It was a model or example meant to help people imagine the reality of God's presence. Perhaps the language of Hebrews here is an allusion to the ideas and forms of Platonism. The earthly tent is only a shadow, the dim light casting a darkened image representing the form of what the ideal truly is.

Hebrews again refers to the language of Torah, "And see that you make them according to the pattern for them, which is being shown you on the mountain" (Exod 25:40). Remember the experience of Moses?

> The LORD said to Moses, "Come up to me on the mountain, and wait there; and I will give you the tablets of stone, with the law and the commandment, which I have written for their instruction." So Moses set out with his assistant Joshua, and Moses went up into the mountain of God. To the elders he had said, "Wait here for us, until we come to you again; for Aaron and Hur are with you; whoever has a dispute may go to them." Then Moses went up on the mountain, and the cloud covered the mountain. The glory of the LORD settled on Mount Sinai, and the cloud covered it for six days; on the seventh day he called to Moses out of the cloud. Now the appearance of the glory of the LORD was like a devouring fire on the top of the mountain in the sight of the people of Israel. Moses entered the cloud, and went up on the mountain. Moses was on the mountain for forty days and forty nights. (Exod 24:12–19)

During that time Moses was said to have seen God's temple, and what he brought back was the earthly representation of divine presence—a way to bring heaven to earth.

Museums try to help us experience what life was like at another time, to enter buildings, even an entire village or streets of a city. When we lived in New England, we visited the Plymouth Plantation and Old Sturbridge Village. While in Williamsburg, VA, we walked the streets of Old Williamsburg. The Conner Prairie Living Museum in Indianapolis lets you walk back in time to country life in the 1800s. More recently I had the opportunity to explore the Indianapolis Children's Museum. In one area they had a replica of a trading post. Some children had entered the mock building before me, and I heard them talking. Inside the trading post seemed so real that one girl was not quite sure they were supposed to be there. It was as though she expected someone to appear behind the counter and want to know what she wanted to buy.

Here a Tent, There a Tent (8:1-6)

There's no doubt that the tabernacle was a holy place that drew people into an experience of God's presence. To them it was the real thing. But the reality is, it was still only a sketch and shadow of the real thing. As much as we might enjoy churches and cathedrals, they are only works of human hands, a faint representation of what awaits us, of what exists beyond the veil of physical existence, of what pervades our world but evades our perception.

JESUS GIVES THE BETTER DEAL (8:6)

Here we find the other half of the comparative exchange. On the one hand in verses four and five, there is the earthly, the sketchy, the shadowy. On the other hand in verse six, Jesus has obtained something better. Remember that Jesus is different than the earthly high priests. His ministry was a single act of sacrifice for all time. As the Son who holds the priesthood forever, Jesus is the mediator of a better covenant. The promises of God through the one who is God's Son are sworn by God with an eternal oath.

If you go into a store to purchase something and that store carries a family name, whom are you going to want to talk to? If you go into Miller's Bakery to place a special order for a party, whom do you want to talk to? You want to talk to a Miller. If you go into Taylor's Clothing to order a suit or dress, you don't want to be talking to Hank Jones—you want Ms. Taylor or Mr. Taylor to be waiting on you. If you go into a Ford dealership to buy a car—chances are you won't be talking to a Ford, but you get the idea. We know that if we talk to the owner or we talk to the son or daughter of the owner, we are most likely to get the best deal.

To say that Jesus, God's Son, gives us the best deal seems a bit crude. But that's what a covenant is, it's the deal God makes with us through Jesus. We don't want to have a deal where we only experience God through a tent made of animal skins and gold embossed objects. I love a good barbecue, but I don't want to worship God by killing animals and roasting them on a fire. But that's my preference.

The better deal is what God is doing through Jesus and what God promises will be ours some day. The tabernacle served its purpose, the priests fulfilled their function in the way God intended for that time, but the human systems and structures will give place to the celestial, the ethereal, the ineffable presence of Spirit.

Section Four: The Melchizedek Priesthood of Jesus Compared to the Levites

What Hebrews has said is that the real tent there in heaven surpasses the replica which existed here on earth. It's Jesus who gives us the better deal. Try to imagine what it must have been like for the citizens of St. Andrews in Scotland, that tiny hamlet next to the North Sea, to walk past the village shops, through the muddy streets, and then come upon a huge cathedral, as long as a football field, spires soaring into the sky. Entering the cathedral certainly would have been like passing into another world, a world of beautiful stonework, evocative stained glass windows, sculptures and tapestries all telling the gospel story. The music of voice and instrument lifts the soul upward, the smell of incense leads one into the place of worship. What else could one call it but the house of God?

Yet today what remains of that cathedral is called ruins. All of that work and expense to give people a taste of what God's presence is like is now nothing more than a tourist spot, a place to take a little time to rest one's feet. Our buildings and our forms of worship are the best we can do, and we should make the best of them. But forms and facades pale in comparison to the real presence of Jesus.

New Deal (8:7–13)

The ceremony of married couples renewing their vows is an interesting practice. Suann's parents renewed their vows after fifty years of marriage. Maybe after fifty years the marriage certificate had become so old that the ink was fading and the paper was falling apart. I'm sure there are some couples who renew their vows because they know that the vows have been broken at some time or other. Maybe by renewing them, the new vows will have more staying power.

In a sense, the covenant God made with the Israelite nation at Mt. Sinai was a marriage certificate. The marriage vows would be considered sexist by today's standards, but the agreement was that God as the husband would take care of the wife, Israel. Israel, as the virgin bride, was to remain faithful to her husband. As we know from reading the Bible, Israel often cheated on God by following other gods and other ways. The book of Hosea, in fact, represents Israel as a whore who is continually unfaithful. That unfaithfulness would cause God to back away and remove his protection from her. Consequently, foreign nations would dominate her and lead her off to their own country and defile her.

The prophet Jeremiah looked forward to the day when God would make a new covenant with Israel, a renewal of that marriage vow made at Sinai. Jeremiah hoped that this covenant renewal would not only tell Israel what is right but would somehow implant within her a heart and mind to live faithfully.

The author of Hebrews believes that the inauguration of Jesus as high priest in the heavenly tabernacle is a signal that this new covenant will soon be established. In these verses of Hebrews, the first covenant has been pronounced faulty (8:7), a new covenant has been prophesied for the future (8:8–12), and the old covenant is passing away (8:13).

Section Four: The Melchizedek Priesthood of Jesus Compared to the Levites

THE FIRST COVENANT
HAS BEEN PRONOUNCED FAULTY (8:7)

The author of Hebrews has concluded that Jesus is the one who has mediated a better covenant between God and God's people. If there is to be a better covenant, it means that the Sinai covenant will be followed by a second covenant. It is logical that the need for a second covenant implies that there was something wrong with the first one.

What was that first covenant, the one God made with the Israelites at Mt. Sinai after they has escaped from Egypt? Remember how it began? What happened to the Israelites even before Moses returned to them with God's instructions for them on how to be God's people, a holy nation committed to Yahweh? God desired to punish the Israelites, but Moses convinced God to give them another chance. According to their own history, the Jewish experience from the days of the judges to the formation of the kingdom was a cycle of the people going after pagan gods and goddesses, experiencing the discipline of God through the oppression of foreign nations, and then the repentance for sin and God's forgiveness and salvation for the people.

Imagine a young couple, anxious about getting married but able to walk the aisle and say their vows to each other. Somewhere between the church and the honeymoon suite, the man finds himself alone with an old girlfriend. Before the ink is dry on the marriage certificate, he has broken his vows.

That's the story of God's people. The Israelites vow to be God's people, but before the dust has settled from inscribing the tablets of stone, they are making an idol and holding a pagan festival.

For Christians, it's the experience of making a commitment to follow Jesus and then, when trials and temptations come our way, we turn our back and forget what we had promised God we would do. Are we being unfaithful to God? Are we cheating on God by our devotion to the good life: looking out for number one, filling our time and our minds with meaningless pleasure, spending all we have to have the things that show off our status and power. We need that renewal. Not just to say words again but to have a renewal that comes with the power to make it real in our lives, to making a lasting difference in who we are, something that transforms us from the inside.

New Deal (8:7–13)

A NEW COVENANT HAS BEEN PROPHESIED FOR THE FUTURE (8:8-12)

The author of Hebrews lays the blame for the condition of the relationship established in the Sinai Covenant with the people. The extensive quotation from Jeremiah 31:31-34 recalls the time when Israel had been defeated by the Assyrians and Judah had been exiled to Babylon. The Jewish people considered this to be a sign that God was punishing them for their waywardness, their inability to faithfully follow Yahweh as their God. The prophecy of Jeremiah points toward a future restoration of God's people when there will be a new covenant with the Jewish people.

He doesn't say that the entire foundation of the Sinai covenant with the giving of the law is to be done away with but that a revised agreement will be made that will achieve the original intention for Yahweh to be their God and for them to be God's people. This revised covenant will not be like the first one specifically because "they did not continue in my covenant." Consequently, Yahweh's response was "I had no concern for them."

In this future time, according to Jeremiah's prophecy, God will take greater measures to ensure that the people will remain faithful and obedient. Rather than relying on the people to be responsible to teach the law publicly and in their homes, God will inscribe his laws in their very being so that they remember and want to perform their duties to God. This will result in a time when God will no longer punish them for the breaking of the covenant; their iniquities and sins will be wiped clean and not remembered any longer.

I can't help but think about this in computer terms. There are three main parts of a computer's memory. Most of us know the language of storing data on a disk drive or the hard drive. Information there is saved when the computer is turned off. It's a pretty reliable way for the computer to remember its instructions for operating the computer system and the data you've stored in its memory.

You might also be aware of what's called RAM. It's sort of like short-term memory. Programs are loaded to perform their functions and make changes to your data. Many of us know what happens if something goes wrong before the computer has written the data to the hard drive. Whatever we were working on has disappeared; even worse, something

Section Four: The Melchizedek Priesthood of Jesus Compared to the Levites

can get corrupted on the hard drive and we are in danger of losing much of our work—not to mention all the games we've installed.

The other part of the computer is the ROM. These are instructions for the computer that have been installed in the chips. Here lives the computer's BIOS, that which forms the basic life of the computer, no matter what software is installed or what hardware is attached.

We are only human, we say. But that is at the root of our problem. As humans, what we know and the character we have developed which guides our behavior can be corrupted. We can easily forget—or choose to forget—what decisions we have made for how we choose to live life. If there were only some way to write that into our BIOS so that no matter what we encounter in the world, we will always operate in conformity to the new way we've been wired. That's the prophetic hope, that's what has begun to happen with the presence of God's Spirit within us.

THE OLD COVENANT IS PASSING AWAY (8:13)

Hebrews has argued that a new covenant means that there is a second one following the first. If there is a second one, the first one must have had something wrong with it. Now the author of Hebrews argues that for there to be a "new covenant" it must mean that the previous one is an "old" one.

The word translated "obsolete" is the Greek verb meaning "to become old" or "to be said to be old." It is used often to talk about the effect of becoming old, that something is "wearing out." The implication is that what is wearing out will eventually be of no use: a garment that wears out will have to be replaced. The other term is also a word that has to do with aging, a word from which we get our English word "geriatric." The last word in the sentence, "to disappear," is a term used frequently in the Old Testament for the desolation of a city that has been abandoned, like we might think of an old ghost town. According to the author of Hebrews, the first covenant made at Sinai is beginning to show its age. It has lived out its purpose, it is showing signs of fading and will soon disappear altogether.

Think of a marriage certificate as being the only proof of your marriage contract. Maybe it wouldn't survive the first argument before one or the other tears it up and throws the confetti. Imagine, though, that you carry it around with you. Maybe it's stuck in a man's wallet. Every time you need to prove your marriage, you have to take it out of the wallet and unfold it. Back it goes into the wallet. Then comes the inevitable time when the wallet goes through the washer and dryer. After many years, the certificate begins to show its age. The fold lines are visible and some creases have holes where it has worn out. Maybe a few places have tape holding it together. Corners are missing. The ink is faded and the paper is thin.

That's the image Hebrews evokes. The old covenant is deteriorating and will soon disappear. That may seem sad, but the good news is that God is renewing God's covenant. The second one will be much better. Why? Because Jesus, who lived faithfully to God in human existence, is the one who is our high priest in heaven. What Jesus has accomplished and what Jesus does on our behalf each moment of our existence has brought about transformation. In the coming age, that new covenant will be fully realized, all will know God, all will love God, and God's blessing and grace will be poured out on God's creation.

We have seen in these verses of Hebrews that the first covenant has been pronounced faulty, a new covenant has been prophesied for the future, and the old covenant is passing away.

Let me use another joke from the Internet. A woman was going through her husband's desk drawer and discovered three soybeans in an envelope containing thirty dollars in cash. So she asked him about it.

And the husband said, "Well, I have to confess. Over the years I haven't been completely faithful to you. But every time I cheated, I put a soybean in the drawer to remind myself."

"So where did the thirty dollars come from?" she asked.

"Well, when soybeans hit ten dollars a bushel, I decided to sell."

About marriage, the joke is an exaggeration. But it's no exaggeration that God's people are often unfaithful to God—and it's no joke. Perhaps it's time to renew our commitment to God and to the new covenant that Jesus brings.

Section Five

The Heavenly Sanctuary Compared to the Earthly
(9:1—10:39)

The Ineffectiveness of Worship under the First Covenant (9:1–10)

THE OLD RHYME GOES, "Man may work from sun to sun, But woman's work is never done." I'm old enough to have grown up during the time when the work of men and women was clearly divided. Women's work was largely what was done inside the house. And, yes, it was a never-ending job. Men's work mostly involved keeping the house functioning and caring for the outside of the house. When it comes to the outside of the house, a man's work is never done. Women might exclaim, "Yeah, a man's work is never done because he never does it."

Like many tasks inside the house, tasks outside the house also have to be repeated. Here's a case in point. I can't imagine what it must have been like when people owned houses that needed to be painted every few years. I remember a job my father gave me to do when I was a teenager. The north side of our house had a lot of shade, so the moisture had caused the paint to peel. That summer I scraped and I scraped. When I think about that summer, the only picture I can form in my mind is the tedious task of preparing the side of the house. Up the ladder, down the ladder, scraping, scraping, scraping. I hardly remember getting to do the fun part, actually getting to paint and then stand back and admire the finished product.

It's a nice feeling to finish the job. A fresh coat of paint covers over whatever imperfections may have occurred since the last time the house was painted. There is some sense of satisfaction and of relief that the job is done. Nevertheless, there is always the knowledge that it isn't permanent. Eventually it will have to be done all over again.

Thank God it's not every year the house needs to be painted. But as soon as you finish, you know you'll need to do it again. It doesn't last forever. You are the house's servant, and it will need your attention. Think of the time you sacrifice for your house, the blood that's shed from scraping not only the siding but also your knuckles; the fear you face as your life is at risk 10 or 20 feet up from the ground. You did it last time for your house, and you'll have to do it again.

The house of God was once a tent, a special tent filled with mysterious objects, objects intended to bring God's power and God's mercy into one special place. No one needed to paint it, but they did need to care for this place day after day, year after year, interminably. The author of Hebrews contends that the work done at the house of God in the wilderness did not suffice because the work had to be continuously repeated.

Chapter nine of Hebrews begins a major section about the tabernacle, the tent which contained the Holy Place. The language of this chapter is one in which the author employs comparison. As we've learned previously, this means that 9:1 contains an untranslated Greek word *men* that begins the first half of the comparative exchange and is followed in 9:11 with the other half introduced by the Greek word *de*. A better translation of these terms is,

> *On the one hand*, then, the first covenant had regulations for worship . . . during which gifts and sacrifices are offered that cannot perfect the conscience of the worshiper . . . . *On the other hand*, Christ . . . entered once for all . . . obtaining eternal redemption.

Here in verses 1–10—the first part of the comparative exchange—the author of Hebrews describes the place of worship as well as the practice of worship and then states that this place and practice is not able to perfect the worshiper.

THE PLACE OF WORSHIP (9:1–5)

The first covenant, the one made at Sinai, contained regulations for how those who were to be God's people should worship God (9:1). The Israelites were a nomadic people, so it makes sense that they were to carry with them a portable place of worship (9:2). Obviously, they didn't travel each day and then stop and set up camp for the evening. Instead, they set up camp in a good area that provided water and a place for animals to graze (Exod 15:27). After a time, they would break camp and move the group to a new site (Exod 17:1). Slowly, they made their way north, depending on the local terrain and the tribes of people already living near an area (Exod 23:20–33).

At Mt. Sinai God inaugurated the covenant with Israel and gave them instructions for how to be the people of God and to worship God

The Ineffectveness of Worship under the First Covenant (9:1-10)

through ceremonies and sacrifices (Exod 19:1—23:19). The instructions included directions for constructing the tabernacle and all its furnishings. This Holy Place was the house of God where God would meet the people and the people would worship God (Exod 25ff).

The Holy Place was a tent inside an enclosure, the court of the tabernacle (Exod 27:9-18). Outside of that inner tent was the altar where sacrifices were made (Exod 27:1-8) and where some animal sacrifices were burned over the fire.

Inside the tent were the special objects that symbolized the way in which God was to be worshipped (9:2). Light from the seven oil lamps of the menorah joined to brighten the inside of the first space within the Holy Place (Exod 25:37; 37:23; Num 8:2-3). A golden table functioned like a place setting for Yahweh (Exod 25:28-30). Twelve cakes, similar to pita bread or tortillas, were lined up on the table along with dinner service for one. Each Sabbath day the priests ate the bread and new loaves were laid out (Lev 24:5-9).

Behind the curtain was the Holy of Holies or in other words the Holiest Place (9:3). In that space were the holiest relics of worship (9:4-5). The golden altar of incense would have added to the sights and smells of worship (Exod 39:38; 40:5). The ark of the covenant was a wooden box overlaid with gold (Exod 25:16-22). According to Hebrews, it contained the special objects from Israel's experience of the exodus: the golden urn that held some of the divinely provided manna (Exod 16:32-34); the wooden staff or rod of Aaron which had miraculously come to life and budded (Num 17:8-11); and the stone tablets—second edition—were also placed in the box (Exod 25:16, 21; 40:3, 20-21; Deut 10:2-5; 1 Kgs 8:9, 21; 2 Chr 5:10). Although the Old Testament doesn't describe in any one place all of these as being present in the ark the way Hebrews does, later Jewish tradition also claims that the ark contained these ancient relics (*b. Yoma* 52b).

The cover of the box was designed with two angelic cherubs, the cherubim, whose outstretched wings formed the focal point of the divine presence—the throne of God, the mercy seat, the place of atonement and expiation of sin (Exod 25:18-22). This was the house of God and the furniture it contained.

Most people have some style of furniture in their homes. Some people have Early American or Mission style, for example. The special style in our home is what I call Eclectic. The end tables in the living room were passed down from my grandmother. The dining room table is an antique from

Section Five: The Heavenly Sanctuary Compared to the Earthly

Suann's parents passed down from her great uncle Jake. In the corner of our bedroom is a black recliner. It belonged to Suann's grandmother. Even though the chair is worn out and now serves as a place to hang clothes, it stays in its place. It brings back memories for her. She can look at the chair and remember her grandmother. As a young girl, Suann can remember her grandmother sitting in that chair while Suann played the piano for her. Some of our furnishings don't have great sentimental value, but most everything has a story and represents some phase of our life together.

The tabernacle of the Israelites was a tent not too dissimilar from the kind of tents they lived in. What made it special was the furnishings. Some reminded them of their past, some represented their beliefs about God, but all were well-cared for and greatly valued. It would be wrong for us to diminish the beauty and sacredness of the worship of God in the tabernacle. Psalm 84 expresses the feelings of those who worshipped there.

> How lovely is your dwelling place, O LORD of hosts! My soul longs, indeed it faints for the courts of the LORD; my heart and my flesh sing for joy to the living God. Even the sparrow finds a home, and the swallow a nest for herself, where she may lay her young, at your altars, O LORD of hosts, my King and my God. Happy are those who live in your house, ever singing your praise. Selah. (Ps 84:1–4)

Hebrews views this holy tent and all its trappings—as beautiful and meaningful as they were—to be temporary "until the time comes to set things right" (9:10).

THE PRACTICE OF WORSHIP (9:6–7)

The day-to-day practice of worship in this holy tent was carried out by the priests (9:6). This bustle of activity signified the continuous effort made by the priests to present worship to the deity on behalf of the people. As long as sin continued, sacrifices continued.

The high priest alone was allowed to enter the Holiest Place, and he only entered once a year on the Day of Atonement (9:7; Exod 30:10; Lev 16:1–34). On this day the high priest sacrificed a bull for his own sins (Lev 16:6, 11) and a goat for the sins of Israel (Lev 16:15). The blood was brought into the innermost part of the sanctuary, and the blood was sprinkled on the top and the front of the ark of the covenant (Lev 16:14–15). Only the

The Ineffectveness of Worship under the First Covenant (9:1–10)

high priest was allowed to do this. No one else was permitted to be in the tent of meeting (Lev 16:17).

I'm always curious about places I can't go, places whose doors say "Authorized Personnel Only." You see people going through the doors. They must be authorized personnel. You wonder what's in there that people have to be authorized before they can enter. Is it a secret? Is it dangerous in there? Do you have to be specially trained to be able to be inside? Is it bright or dark inside? Are there valuable things there: diamonds, gold, stacks of money?

Can you think of places that you wondered about and then got to visit? Perhaps you've had a tour in a factory? Maybe you've been allowed backstage at a theater. As a custodian in my college days, I got to go behind-the-scenes in places like a telephone company. I was fascinated to be in the room with all the telephone switching and could actually hear multiple phone conversations at once. Another time I was working on a college campus. I knew that the science building had a closet in which they kept a cadaver. One night I used my keys to look in the closet, pull back the wet towels soaked with formaldehyde, and see the hand of what was an elderly woman. I remember I had a cold then and was using a throat spray. I can no longer use throat spray, since the smell reminds me of dead bodies soaked in formaldehyde.

There's a special feeling we get when we enter a place that few people get to see. But there's also a feeling of exclusion when we are prohibited from entering where only authorized people are able to go. The practice of worship in the tabernacle was exclusive. You had to belong to the special tribe of Levites and descendants of Aaron to work in the outer court of the tabernacle. If you didn't belong to the group, you didn't belong inside. Out of all the people that made up the tribes of the sons of Israel, only one person entered the holiest place, and he only entered once a year. No one else really knew what he saw. The Holiest Place was a place for authorized personnel only, and only one person was authorized.

THE PERFECTION OF THE WORSHIPER (9:8–10)

From all indications in the book of Hebrews, the Jerusalem temple was still in existence. At least Hebrews says nothing about the destruction of the temple in 70 CE. It is an assumption, since Hebrews doesn't actually talk about the temple, only about the house of God in terms of the tabernacle described in the Bible. For Hebrews, the presence of the temple system means that its regulations still function as the way to God (9:8). But the temple system was not so much a way to God as it was a way to restrict people from coming to God. That sounds harsh, but this is the argument that Hebrews makes.

Look at it this way. The people were kept at the foot of Mt. Sinai while Moses met with God. The series of enclosures kept people at a distance from the Holy Place where only priests were able to enter. Every day was another day that the priests had to perform sacrifices for the benefit of the people. Each year the high priest made the sacrifices to cover—to atone—for the sins of the people. What took place in the Holy Place was hidden. Whatever happened inside was hidden from the worshiper. As long as the tabernacle or the temple still stands, it means that the way into the Holiest Place has not been made possible (9:8).

It's a symbol or illustration (literally a "parable") of the current situation for those to whom Hebrews is addressed (9:9). The place of worship is there and the practice of worship is conducted, but the perfection of the worshiper does not take place. There is not a consciousness of forgiveness, the mind is not relieved, the spirit still feels guilt. People are not given what they need to be free. They are only given regulations that guide the proper kosher diet and the ways to maintain the purity of the body (9:10). These practices were established until the time when God would straighten everything out. That's the literal sense of the term at the end of 9:10. Hebrews looks forward to the time when God will amend what has been set forth and bring about reformation. It will be something that will bring about the intended effect of the wholeness of the worshipper of God and not something that will just deal with external practices.

We're all aware of the ways in which medicine can treat symptoms without effecting a cure. We get headaches and so we take pain reliever. As my doctor would say, the problem is not that our body lacks pain reliever. Taking pain reliever doesn't necessarily cure what's wrong, it treats the symptoms. We take all sorts of remedies when we have a cold, but if we stopped and thought about it we would remember that a cold is a virus. We're not treating the cold; we're just trying to be able to lessen the symptoms.

There are ways to not just treat symptoms but to get to the root of the problem. Rather than making an itch stop itching, we can cure the rash that causes the itch. Instead of wearing glasses all the time to correct poor vision, doctors can now correct the vision with laser surgery. Where

The Ineffectveness of Worship under the First Covenant (9:1–10)

someone might have used braces or crutches to help them walk, now doctors can repair misalignments and other types of skeletal abnormalities. One step further than the cure is the prevention of the disease or illness in the first place. Both are better than a continual effort to cover over or undo the damages of the past.

The existence of the tabernacle system meant that no other way had been found. There was no way to take care of the problem of sin once and for all. No way to prevent the sin from occurring in the first place because the person might not know all the laws intended to guard against eating the wrong thing, going to the wrong place, coming too close to the wrong person. There was only the hope that some day in some way God would straighten everything out.

༄

The author of Hebrews has described the place of worship, as well as the practice of worship. He then has argued that this place and practice that necessitates a constantly repeated sacrifice is not able to perfect the worshiper.

I can imagine what it must have been like for people of a previous generation who lived in the same house year after year, decade after decade. The number of times they had to go through the whole process of getting their house painted, knowing that it was going to have to be done again within a few short years. Then along came aluminum siding. No more need to paint the side of the house! "The younger generation doesn't know how good they have it," they might say. With aluminum siding the whole house is covered, and it's pretty much taken care of once for all. A crew of workers is no longer needed to cover over the impurities and imperfections.

Human sin continues, there's no denying that. But we no longer need to carry our guilt, to be in fear of God's wrath. That's the message of Hebrews. How many men served in the tabernacle and temple? How many sacrifices were offered? But how many men did it take to straighten it all out? It only took the One and the work is done.

The Effectiveness of Worship under the New Covenant (9:11–17)

Most of us city folk don't know what it means to butcher an animal. We even get squeamish when the meat we buy at the grocery store has too much red liquid in the package. I was disillusioned to discover that some farmers don't do their own butchering anymore. Our unfamiliarity with the process of raising livestock and preparing it for consumption makes it difficult for us to comprehend sacrifice in the Bible.

If we think about it, we can begin to understand how important animals were to the people of the Middle East in ancient times. Livestock for nomadic hunter-gatherers in a desert culture was often a lifeline. Animals not only provided food in the form of dairy products and its flesh as meat, but also the hair, skin, bones, and tendons provided material with which to clothe themselves and make implements. Animals also produced more animals. The more animals you had the wealthier you were. Livestock was so valuable that it was used like currency, even to the extent that marriage dowries consisted of herds of animals.

Think what it meant to kill one of the animals or offer it for sacrifice. Slitting an animal's throat and draining its blood is an act of it pouring out its very life. You have taken its life for your benefit. The ritual animal sacrifice, however, means that the animal dies because of your own faults, your transgressions against the laws of God. And when you make a sacrifice to God, you don't take the runt of the litter, so to speak—a poor expression here, since it refers to animals like dogs and pigs. You don't bring your gimp cow or a diseased goat to be sacrificed. You bring the best of your animals to be a sacrifice to God. Because you sin—and even if you are an upright person, you may sin unknowingly—you continue to have to give up your best livestock to atone for your sins. Does it make you feel better? No, not really. It's a constant reminder of your own failing and of the awful judgment due to that failing.

The Effectveness of Worship under the New Covenant (9:11–17)

The book of Hebrews relates that concept to the effect of Jesus' execution. Because Jesus was a righteous, innocent person, his death was considered a noble sacrifice for the benefit of others. His death was similar to the animal sacrifices practiced in the tabernacle. But, in comparison, his death went beyond that of animals, and his sacrifice transcends that offered by priests on an altar.

The Sinai covenant involved a system of regular sacrifices intended to atone for the sins of the people and maintain their relationship to God and God's blessing on them as God's people. Although the instructions for building the tabernacle was given by God to Moses on Mt. Sinai, the tabernacle was a human structure in an earthly sphere. The tent itself was made with human hands, no different than the idols they had worshipped before had been made with their own hands. This tent and its pattern of sacrifice and worship was given by God, but it was only an earthly model of a heavenly tabernacle Moses had seen when he was in the presence of God.

Even though they had this tent and all that went with it, and they traveled everywhere with it, the Israelites still ended up sinning against God. Their failure was so extreme God cursed them to wander in the desert until the first generation died off. The Sinai covenant didn't have the power to remove sin and free people from being bound to repeated sacrifice and repeated times of blessing and cursing.

The prophecy of Jeremiah spoke of a time when a new covenant would be made and that covenant would give people the power to be right with God without written law, without the need for continuing sacrifices (Jer 31:31–34). The followers of Jesus believed that the death of Jesus brought about this new covenant with God and a way finally to receive all the promised blessings of God for eternity. Through Christ the people of God are released forever from sacrificial obligation (9:11–12), their minds are reprogrammed to worship the living God (9:13–14), and they will ultimately receive their eternal inheritance (9:15–17).

RELEASED FOREVER
FROM SACRIFICIAL OBLIGATION (9:11–12)

Verse 11 begins the other half of a comparative exchange which started in 9:1: "On the other hand, Christ . . ." As is typical in synkrisis, the comparison in the second part shows how this subject is better or greater than the preceding. Christ has now come, and he is like a high priest in what he did. He is a high priest of "good things" (9:11).

By enduring a death for the benefit of others, Jesus' death is like a blood sacrifice, but in this case he is both priest and sacrifice (9:12). Rather than repeatedly entering into the Holy Place year after year, Christ enters once. He doesn't go into a tent that humans have made, not something existing in this world of perception. Rather, the metaphor is he went into a celestial tabernacle. He doesn't bring with him bowls filled with blood drained from a goat or a calf, but it is as though he carries his own blood into the Holy of Holies. This was a sacrifice to end all sacrifices. What the others couldn't do, Jesus did. A single act had an eternal consequence. The redemption or release was secured; humans are free from the need to offer daily or annual sacrifices to atone for sins.

I want you to imagine that you have agreed to a binding contract. It seemed simple, but you didn't realize what you had gotten yourself into. You are to live in a large pit in the ground. You are to keep digging until the you hit bedrock. You are told that bedrock is only some twenty to thirty feet down, but you are in a pit already twenty to thirty feet in the ground. You begin digging, but the dirt you dig piles up on the other side of the pit. Days come when a rainstorm washes the piles of dirt back into the place where you've been digging. No matter how hard you try, you can't dig yourself out of the hole. Every day you dig, but you never get any closer to the goal. Everyday you are reminded of your inability to remove all the dirt and be done with it once and for all. Your boss is happy that you are fulfilling your part of your contract, but you're still not any closer than you were twenty or thirty years ago.

How do you get out of this? We'll have to imagine that someone comes to help you who happens to be thirty-feet tall and has a really big shovel. With one scoop the job is done and your contract is fulfilled. You are free!

Okay, a thirty-foot Jesus with a big shovel is a corny illustration. At least I didn't give him a big, blue ox as a companion! But I want you to understand the point Hebrews makes. The issue is not that the tabernacle system was legalistic and onerous, something that humans invented to try to please God with their human effort. According to Hebrews, the weakness of the system was, by these animal sacrifices people couldn't be released from their cycle of sin and were not given the power to prevent themselves from sinning against God.

The Effectveness of Worship under the New Covenant (9:11–17)

It was only through the death of Jesus that the followers of Jesus could understand the implication of his resurrection and ascension to heaven. It meant that Jesus could bring about in the heavenly tabernacle what they couldn't accomplish in the earthly one.

REPROGRAMMED TO WORSHIP THE LIVING GOD (9:13–14)

The ordinances contained in the Mosaic law provided a way for people to be consecrated or made holy. By certain actions, such as contact with dead animals (Lev 11:24; 17:15), bodily fluids (Lev 15:2, 16–19, 25) or unclean people or animals (Lev 5:3; 13:14; 22:5–6), they could become defiled and impure. By offering certain sacrifices the priest could pronounce the person pure. In our culture we think of blood as something that stains. We don't associate blood and ashes as things which make something pure and clean, but that's how they thought. Rather than one's own body and blood receiving the punishment for sins committed, it was, in a sense, transferred to the animal.

The author of Hebrews makes the point that, if this worked with animal blood and the ashes from a burned cow, it stands to reason that a greater case can be made for the effect of Christ's sacrificial death. Christ was considered to have been sinless, a perfect human. He was obedient to death and endured execution. Animals given for sacrifice had to be spotless, without blemish. That's what Jesus was like.

The purifying effect of his sacrifice, however, was at a deeper level. It was not the flesh that was no longer impure, like with animal sacrifices. It was the very consciousness of the human mind that was wiped clean from the effects of wrong-doing. It was a transformation from the earthly sphere of bondage to sin and death to the heavenly sphere of being free to worship the living God.

I've chosen to describe this process of purifying the conscience as reprogramming in a psychological sense. I'm thinking about the person who spends years and years as a prisoner. Everyday they go through the same motions, not only the body but also the mind is captive to the world of imprisonment.

I remember a TV show that had a family take in a prisoner after he had been released. He wasn't happy in his new bedroom because it wasn't what he was used to. Finally, the family learned that to make him feel at home they had to change his surroundings and his way of life to what he had been used to in prison. But he wasn't truly free because he was living as a prisoner within the confines of the world. What he needed was to be reprogrammed to think like a free person.

The transformation that Christians talk about in the New Testament is based on the ideal of Jeremiah's prophecy about the new covenant. Paul describes it this way in Romans 12.

> I appeal to you therefore, brothers and sisters, by the mercies of God, to present your bodies as a living sacrifice, holy and acceptable to God, which is your spiritual worship. Do not be conformed to this world, but be transformed by the renewing of your minds, so that you may discern what is the will of God—what is good and acceptable and perfect. (Rom 12:1, 2)

In the words of Hebrews, "the blood of Christ ... purifies our conscience." Our minds, our consciousness, is wiped clean from the effects of sin and transgression. We no longer devote ourselves to buildings and boxes we've built with our hands, but we are reprogrammed to worship what is alive, the living God.

RECEPTION OF OUR INHERITANCE THROUGH A NEW COVENANT (9:15–17)

In verses 15–17 the author of Hebrews makes a play on the word for covenant. The same word for covenant is used to talk of what we call a person's "last will and testament." The expression "new covenant" from Jeremiah 31:31 is where we get the name New Testament.

Not only is Jesus the sacrifice and the high priest offering the sacrifice, Jesus is also the mediator of the new covenant, the new testament (not in the sense of writings). He mediates his own "last will and testament." His death means that this "new testament" is now in effect.

Those who are named in his will, so to speak, now receive their inheritance. What has been promised is a heavenly rest, an eternal inheritance. They are no longer bound by the effects of their transgressions under the first covenant. The effect then was that they would not enter into their rest, but God has provided a new covenant which redeems them from their curse.

All of these ways of talking about the meaning of the death of Jesus are metaphors for the deeper meaning. Preachers are notorious for over-

The Effectveness of Worship under the New Covenant (9:11–17)

dramatizing the metaphors. There's a film that a so-called archaeologist has made that claims to prove the literal meaning of the figurative language. He claims that he explored a cave that goes into the hill thought to have been Golgotha, where Jesus was crucified. Deep inside this network of caves, he claims, was hidden away the actual Ark of the Covenant, thought lost since the days before the Babylonian Captivity. According to his reconstruction, when Jesus' blood dripped from his body, it would have seeped through the crevices finally to sprinkle the mercy seat of the ark of the covenant. It makes for sensational preaching, as one preacher I knew in my childhood would do, to dramatize how Jesus would have scooped up his blood from the earth, entered into heaven, and placed it on the heavenly throne between the cherubim.

Hebrews is the ultimate in mixed metaphor: Jesus is the sacrifice, Jesus is the high priest, Jesus is the mediator of the covenant, but he is also the testator of the will who dies. These are all metaphors to say through Jesus' death we are redeemed, and his death is a fulfillment of what wasn't accomplished in the past.

It is faith in the power of Jesus' death and exaltation which gives us the power to move forward with boldness and claim what is offered to us: to be God's children, God's heirs, God's people and together to reach the heavenly rest God has waiting for us.

∿

Through Christ the people of God are released forever from sacrificial obligation, their minds are reprogrammed to worship the living God, and they will ultimately receive their eternal inheritance.

Not only is history filled with examples of people whose unexpected deaths have had a great impact, but we continue to experience it. Think of the impact of those who died on 9/11, especially those on the airplane whose own lives were sacrificed to save those who were intended to die on the ground. The legacy of people like Ghandi, Mother Theresa, JFK, Martin Luther King Jr., and many others continue to change and mold lives for the betterment of our world. Jesus' death was a monumental event in human history, even when simply viewed as a death like any other. The core belief of Christianity, however, is that Jesus' death was not like any other in that his death was the change of an epoch, the dawn of a new era, the fulfillment of what was promised in the past and the ultimate hope for what the future promises to be.

Jesus' Single Treatment for the Cancer of Sin (9:18–28)

It's an awful part of human experience when our own bodies turn on us. Think of the many ways that our bodies can be our worst enemy. For some of us, our bodies don't control appetite in the way it should. We don't get the signal of being satisfied until our stomachs have had more than they should. Some people don't feel pain the way they should, and they can burn themselves. Some diseases are the result of cells in the body that attack other cells. Multiple Sclerosis, the degenerative nerve disease, is thought to be caused by the body's natural defenses actually attacking its own myelin, the covering of nerve fibers. Cancer is another instance of a disease in which abnormal cells keep dividing and forming new cells without control or order. These and others are ways in which we ourselves, our own bodies, can become our worst enemy.

The human condition is one of imperfection, not just physically but morally. For whatever reason, whether we are born into sin or we learn wrong behavior, we do what is wrong even when we know it is wrong.

The Biblical teaching is God is a holy God and an aspect of God's holiness is justice. Justice deals with sin, either by atonement or by judgment. The book of Hebrews stands in that tradition and places the cross of Jesus at the crux of time. What God intended to do for those people with whom he made a covenant at Sinai to be their God and for them to be God's people was to provide a means for them to maintain their relationship to God by atoning for sins. It was a practice that went on continually, day after day, year after year. It took the sacrifice of animals, one after another.

The gospel message is the death of Jesus was a sacrifice for sins. Everything that the first covenant was intended to do, Christ's death accomplished through a new covenant in his own blood. Sin, that awful cancer of human existence, was dealt with once for all.

This long section of Hebrews summarizes what the author has been saying about the work of Christ as a High Priest in the heavenly sanctu-

Jesus' Single Treatment for the Cancer of Sin (9:18–28)

ary. Hebrews is here saying, if the blood of sacrifice was needed to enact the first covenant and consecrate the tabernacle system (9:18–22), then a better sacrifice was needed for the heavenly sanctuary (9:23–24). This ultimate sacrifice was a culmination of an age and a removal of sin once for all (9:25–28).

THE BLOOD OF SACRIFICE WAS NEEDED TO ENACT THE FIRST COVENANT AND CONSECRATE THE TABERNACLE SYSTEM (9:18–22)

The prophecy in Jeremiah 31:31 of a new covenant said nothing about a sacrifice needing to be made. The author of Hebrews argues that a death is necessary for a covenant to be in effect. In the previous verses Hebrews interprets covenant in terms of a will, which is not in effect until the person dies. Now the author of Hebrews argues that a covenant is enacted only when there is a bloody sacrifice. That's true of the first one, he says. It was inaugurated with blood. He relates the event recorded in Exodus 24 as the main example, but he expands on the story with rituals from other texts in Exodus, some having to do with purification rites for lepers. Although one cannot find a text in the Bible in which all of these features take place, together they represent the function of blood in ratifying a covenant with God. The blood drawn from sacrificial animals is ceremonially sprinkled on those people and objects to be symbolically designated as purified and consecrated to God. The red splashes signify the errors of the people which have now been set right.

There was a time when red ink on paper indicated the errors of a student. In graduate school I wrote a seminar paper in which I challenged my professor's theories on the book of Romans. I went through his work and carefully quoted what he wrote. I thought I had done a decent job of using his own writing to challenge his conclusions. When I received my paper back I was horrified to see the amount of red ink on every page of my paper. In fact, I was so stunned that I didn't even want to defend what I had written. I knew I had done the best I could, but there was all the red.

Once I had to use a red ink pen when I applied for a job at a Christian publishing company. I was to take a test on proof-reading and editing. The only red ink pen I had was something that had been in my drawer for who knows how long. The pen leaked and my fingers were red from me using it to prepare for the test. Pages of my copy of *The Chicago Manual of Style* still have red blots where my pen had been bleeding over the grammatical sins of people.

The book of the covenant at Sinai was not written with red ink, but red splatters would have been visible on everything connected with the covenant God made with the children of Israel. The splatters were reminders that transgressions of the covenant were atoned for by the blood of animal sacrifices. A covenant with God is a matter of life and death: death for the sacrifice to atone and life passed on to those whose sin brings death.

A BETTER SACRIFICE WAS NEEDED FOR THE HEAVENLY SANCTUARY (9:23–24)

In the ancient world, the blood from animals was a necessary aspect of ritual sacrifice. There was no release from the consequences of sin without blood being drained from the animal to bring about its death. Remember that Hebrews has described the tabernacle system as revealed on Mt. Sinai as only an earthly model of a heavenly reality. The heavenly Holy Place was much better than the earthly example. It follows that, while the earthly, "hand-made" model had these bloody purification rites, the heavenly sanctuary required a better type of sacrifice. Christ entered into heaven itself, the high priest who is himself a sacrifice for our benefit.

We've probably all experienced entering the make-believe world of a child. What little girl's room hasn't had a pretend kitchen set with tables and chairs? It's really quite a sexist thing for us to do, but that's been the tradition, and it was true in our house. There might be a place to pretend to bake in an oven or cook on the stove with little plastic pots and pans. The old-fashioned tea party could now be a seven-course meal for daughter, parent, and guests, usually dolls and stuffed animals.

In another part of the house was the real thing, the kitchen itself. Real oven, stove, refrigerator, table and chairs, sink, and counters. In the kids' room we went through the motions of preparing the meal, serving it up, sharing it together, and then putting everything away. We would look rather funny if we stood at the stove without the burner on and stirred an empty pot. We wouldn't be satisfied with a full place-setting at the table but with an empty plate and glass filled with nothing but air.

The earthly tabernacle was designed to imitate the heavenly reality of worshipping God, of doing what's needed to be in right-relationship

Jesus' Single Treatment for the Cancer of Sin (9:18-28)

with God. The high priest in full costume with a hyssop branch dipped in blood would have been as out-of-place in heaven as we would be pretending to have dinner with Pooh, Teddy, and Paddington Bear.

In the case of a tabernacle, we aren't able to conceive of what that heavenly reality is. We can only express our faith in the work of Christ, who died for us, in terms that we have experienced, knowing that our physical enactment and our theological reenactment in words are only crude expressions of the inexpressible reality of what Christ has done for us.

THE ULTIMATE SACRIFICE WAS A CULMINATION OF AN AGE AND A REMOVAL OF SIN ONCE FOR ALL (9:25-28)

The author of Hebrews repeats the idea that Christ's sacrifice was not repeated. He has already described how the High Priest would enter the Holy Place once a year, year after year. That's not how it is with Jesus. If it had been the case, then Jesus would have had to go through the suffering of crucifixion year after year. Not just every year for the last two millennia but every year since the beginning of time. Instead, the death of Christ was a single event that not only had implications for what followed but for what preceded—it was once for all time.

Our time is described as being the culmination of an eon when Christ's sacrifice removes sin. The first time Christ was present on earth was for him to be presented as an offering and be offered up "for the sins of many." The second time Christ appears will not be for judgment but will be for those who are anticipating his coming, eager for the one who died for them to come in cosmic salvation to bring all things to completion. The idea that Christ comes a second time does not go against the teaching that Christ's acting in the world was once for all, not to be repeated.

We've all read the instructions on the shampoo bottle that, when taken literally, leads to something absurd. The joke is told this way: Why did the blonde run out of shampoo? She kept following the instructions: lather, rinse, repeat! We want to have clean hair, but if you follow the directions you might not have any shampoo left—or hair!

Under the law, the High Priest would have to kill an animal, offer its blood—and repeat. The cleansing effect of Christ's blood symbolically offered in the heavenly temple did not need to be repeated. All that's left is to wait for Christ's return for salvation to be fully realized in the world.

Section Five: The Heavenly Sanctuary Compared to the Earthly

The argument Hebrews has constructed followed this logic: If the blood of sacrifice was needed to enact the first covenant and consecrate the tabernacle system, then a better sacrifice was required for the heavenly sanctuary. The ultimate sacrifice, which Jesus endured on the cross, was a culmination of an age and a removal of sin once for all. The cancer of sin had been treated daily along with an annual procedure carried out by a specialist.

A woman named Charlotte tells her story of how she dealt with cancer. One morning in December, 2005 she realized something was wrong. She felt so tired she was unable to get out of bed to go to work. A few weeks later she determined that she was going to get out of bed and try to go to work. She crawled out of bed to get to the shower and within minutes collapsed. Her husband came home from work and took her to the hospital. The results came back from the blood test and she was told she had Acute Myelogenous Leukemia (AML). She was in shock, unable to believe the diagnosis. Right away she began chemotherapy. The treatment made her even worse.

> The doctors showed me a list of some things I might get from the chemo. Well, I got them all, like vomiting, blood gushing from my nose and mouth, sores on my privates and very painful hemorrhoids that needed morphine to take away the pain.[1]

After two months in the hospital, Charlotte learned she needed a bone marrow transplant. There was about a month and a half of remission before she learned the cancer was back. She was taken to the Dana Farber Cancer Institute in Boston. They began to prepare her for treatment and the cells donated from another person.

> It was a very emotional day for me, knowing that someone out there cared enough to do this for me, all I know is she's from California and a female. I think about her every day and would love to talk or even meet her some day, after all, she's saved my life!![2]

---

1. Accessed July 16, 2006. Online: http://www.cancersurvivors.org/Support/emotional/stories2.htm. Accessed March 18, 2008. Online: http://www.dianawalkerbreastcancerfoundation.com/survivorstories.htm.

2. Ibid.

Jesus' Single Treatment for the Cancer of Sin (9:18–28)

At the time of her writing Charlotte had only been recovering for thirty-six days. Listen to the joy she is experiencing because someone made a sacrifice that took care of her predicament.

> I see life in a very different way now, I cherish all the little things in life and every morning when I awake, I know it's going to be a beautiful day.[3]

Cancer is a terrible corruption within the human body. But sin is corruption within the soul. What this woman did for Charlotte was great, but it pales in comparison to what Christ has done for humanity. Charlotte says she would love to talk to this woman whom she credits with saving her life. In the words of Hebrews, Jesus' return is expected, "to save those who are eagerly waiting for him" (Hebrews 9:28). The result of Christ's sacrifice and the once-for-all cleansing of the cancer of sin should engender the same sort of response from us that Charlotte experienced. We're not quite there yet; we still have many more days left. But we see life in a different way; we cherish all that life has to offer us. We know what we have to look forward to and we can say with Charlotte, "It's going to be a beautiful day."

---

3. Ibid.

Jesus Is the Key to Lasting Fulfillment (10:1–18)

If you need help in life, you probably shouldn't go to the bookstore and look in the self-help section. There are a ton of books there to help people become healthier, happier, more successful, and generally find a better way of life. But out of the hundreds of books, which one has the answer? Do you have to read all of them to achieve a well-balanced life? Many self-help books tell you they have the key to unlock the mystery of human existence. Here's a list of books whose titles contain the word "key."

- Keys to the Deeper Life
- The Master-Key to Inner Peace and Relationship Harmony
- Lunar Nodes: Keys To Emotions and Life Experience
- Twelve Keys for Living: Possibilities for a Whole, Healthy Life
- Thin for Life: 10 Keys to Success from People Who Have Lost Weight and Kept It Off
- The Abundance Principle: Five Keys to Extraordinary Living
- Transformational Healing: Five Surprisingly Simple Keys Designed to Redirect Your Life Toward Wellness, Purpose, and Prosperity
- The Myth of Tomorrow: Seven Essential Keys for Living the Life You Want Today
- Starting Over: Five Keys To A New Direction In Life
- Six Keys to Creating the Life You Desire: Stop Pursuing the Unattainable and Find the Fulfillment You Truly Need
- Get the Prize: Nine Keys for a Life of Victory
- Balance 20/20: Six Keys to a Harmonious Life
- What the Angel Taught You: Seven Keys to Life Fulfillment

So how many keys and how many books do we need? If you spend some time browsing the shelves of the self-help section, you'll walk away think-

Jesus Is the Key to Lasting Fulfillment (10:1–18)

ing, "I don't know any of these keys. I'm so messed up and there's no way I can fix it all."

Humans in all cultures have asked themselves, "What's my situation in the world and how do I make it the best it can be?" The ancient Israelites viewed themselves as having a covenant relationship with their God, Yahweh. The law of the land for them described how they were to remain faithful to God and serve God. They would be God's people, and God would be their God. It's clear from their own history that at various times Israelites worshipped other gods and Yahweh withheld blessing from them and punished them. The Assyrian captivity and Babylonian exile were devastating reminders that merely conducting sacrifices to Yahweh in a temple were not enough to please God. The prophets called the people to live lives of greater faithfulness to God.

For the author of Hebrews, the coming of Jesus was the final and ultimate answer. Although the law couldn't make anyone perfect (10:1–4), we have now been sanctified through the offering of Christ's body (10:5–10) and made perfect for all time (10:11–18).

LAW CAN'T MAKE PERFECT THOSE WHO APPROACH (10:1–4)

The author of Hebrews sets forth an argument in these verses seeking to prove his thesis that the sacrificial system contained in the law was not capable of bringing people to the state of perfection, a condition of completeness and finality. The tent with its priestly system of sacrifice was only a copy of the heavenly reality. Anything that's done continually year after year is not something that reaches a culmination—it just keeps going. Therefore, it can't bring people to completion, in other words, to perfection.

Put another way, if people were able to reach completion, then those worshipping in the tabernacle would have been freed from their pervasive awareness of sin and would have discontinued making sacrificial offerings. But that wouldn't happen because it is not possible for animal slaughter to remove the consciousness of sin.

I think of it this way. Think of the person who wants to be physically fit and healthy. So the person goes to the gym to exercise once a week, maybe even every day. Each time the person goes through his routine. There's the warm-up time. Then a series of various machines for building strength in the various muscle groups of the arms, shoulders, back, chest, abdomen, thighs, and calves. Then comes the cardio-vascular work on the stationary cycle or stair machine.

At some point, he goes to the scale and weighs himself. There's a problem. Even with all this exercise, he stills weighs the same. He looks at himself in the mirror—the typical wall-size mirror that gyms have. He looks the same as when he came in the first time, only sweatier. He goes home and has a bowl of cereal while he waits for his pizza to come out of the oven. He sits down in front of the TV with his pizza and six-pack of beer and wonders why he can't look like the people on TV. Just because he worships at the altar of the human body in the gym, doesn't mean it will change who he is. The most noticeable effect is that he is reminded every day of how he doesn't match up to the standard. He's not able to reach his goal.

The daily sacrifices in the temple had that effect. They were a constant reminder of the failure of the people of God. There was no end to their sin, no end to their failure to live up to God's standard. There was no way to bring the cycle of sin and redemption to a completion, to be forgiven for sin and to have the power no longer to be sinful people of God. Bull's blood and goat's blood had no power to remove sin.

WE HAVE BEEN MADE HOLY THROUGH THE BODY OF JESUS CHRIST (10:5–10)

Hebrews quotes from the Psalms to support his argument.

> Sacrifice and offering you do not desire, but you have given me an open ear. Burnt offering and sin offering you have not required. Then I said, "Here I am; in the scroll of the book it is written of me. I delight to do your will, O my God; your law is within my heart." (Ps 40:6–8)

You may notice that the wording is a bit different. The author of Hebrews writes "a body you have prepared for me" rather than "you have given me an open ear" as we read in Ps 40:6. As different as these two phrases seem, it is really only the difference of one word in the ancient texts. Hebrews follows the reading that is found in the ancient Greek translation of the Hebrew Bible. Rather than simply opening the ears for obedient action, as the Hebrew text reads, the Greek translation interprets the text as saying that the whole body is prepared to do God's will. The author of Hebrews goes the next step to put this in the context of the incarnation, the embodiment, of the one to whom this prophetic psalm refers.

Jesus Is the Key to Lasting Fulfillment (10:1–18)

The sense of the argument contains first the negative statement: God does not desire for the people to make sacrifices without changing their character and conduct. That's a common theme of the Hebrew prophets. The positive statement is applied to Jesus, who is the one who "had a body prepared." It is Jesus who said, in effect, "I have come to do your will."

The offering of sacrifices is set aside, but doing God's will is established as the appropriate mode of action. Jesus does God's will and endures the suffering of death and offers his own body as the ultimate and completing sacrifice.

There are many times that we try to do something for someone to show them our love. One of the things I hate the most is cleaning up the kitchen and doing dishes. The time seems to drag and it feels like I'll never get the job done. When my wife, Suann, was having difficulty with her eyesight, I decided I would surprise her by cleaning up the kitchen and doing the dishes. It's funny the way families think that cleaning up their own messes is supposed to make Mom happy. I emptied the dishwasher and then began rinsing the sink-load—and counter-load—pile of dishes. When I finished loading the dishwasher, I began clearing the stove of leftover pots and pans. I finally completed the work, which actually took me less than an hour but seemed like an eternity. I then waited for Suann to arrive home. I proudly followed her into the kitchen, waiting for her to exclaim, "Who's the wonderful person who did all this work? Who is it who deserves my lavish affections?" Instead, there was no recognition that the kitchen was any different than it had been that morning. As you can imagine, I asked, "Do you notice anything different?"

Still no response. Frustrated, I said, "Can't you tell I cleaned up the kitchen?"

"Oh, I was wondering about that," she answered. "I just thought I had cleaned this morning and had forgot."

That's the way it is when people perform obligations for the purpose of pleasing God. "God, have you counted how many animals I've sacrificed to you? Doesn't it make you want to lavish your blessings on me?" God's response is, "I am so tired of your sacrifices and offerings. Don't you know that what I want is for you to do my will and not commit the sins and transgressions in the first place?" We keep trying to clean up our messes to make God happy, when God wants us not to make messes in the first place.

Section Five: The Heavenly Sanctuary Compared to the Earthly

THE SANCTIFIED ARE PERFECTED FOR ALL TIME (10:11–18)

The author of Hebrews here includes another brief comparison. The first part begins in verse 11 where the Greek text has the untranslated particle *men*. Verse 12 then switches to compare what has been said of Christ. On the one hand, every priest stands offering sacrifices. On the other hand, Christ offered one sacrifice and sat down.

One more time, the author of Hebrews repeats the theme of the never-ending sacrifices of the priests with the once-for-all-time sacrifice of Christ. Notice he says the priest stands, and Christ sat down.

Within the language of the text is another point of comparison. There were numerous priests who carried out the function of offering sacrifices. Verse 12 reads in the Greek, "This one," in other words, "this single guy" made a single sacrifice, and he was done.

Again Hebrews quotes from Psalm 110, "Yahweh says to my lord, 'Sit at my right hand until I make your enemies your footstool.'" Jesus sat down at God's right hand and is ... doing what? He's waiting. Who would have thought the throne room of God is a waiting room?

What are we to make of this reference to a "footstool for his feet"? First Chronicles 28:2 says that David wanted to build a temple to house the ark of the covenant "for the footstool of our God." The Psalms call people to worship at the temple, to "worship at his footstool" (Pss 99:5; 132:7). Isaiah says the entire earth is Yahweh's footstool.

> Thus says the LORD: Heaven is my throne and the earth is my footstool; what is the house that you would build for me, and what is my resting place? All these things my hand has made, and so all these things are mine, says the LORD. But this is the one to whom I will look, to the humble and contrite in spirit, who trembles at my word. Whoever slaughters an ox is like one who kills a human being; whoever sacrifices a lamb, like one who breaks a dog's neck; whoever presents a grain offering, like one who offers swine's blood; whoever makes a memorial offering of frankincense, like one who blesses an idol. These have chosen their own ways, and in their abominations they take delight. (Isa 66:1–3)

In this sense, the whole earth is to be made the place of worship, no longer limited to sacrifices performed in a tent or building, a tabernacle or a temple.

Jesus Is the Key to Lasting Fulfillment (10:1–18)

The key sentence is in verse 14, that the single offering of Jesus has brought about the condition of completeness for all time. In verse 16 the author of Hebrews brings his discussion back around to the key text of Jeremiah regarding the new covenant and quotes the text again. He concludes in verse 18 by saying, with the inauguration of the new covenant in which the Lord forgives sins and lawless deeds, there is no longer any need to have any sacrificial offerings for sin.

What Jesus did sounds like a hero's tale. You know the Grimm's fairy tale of "Seven at One Blow." The little tailor had work to do and was waiting until he was finished to eat his bread and jam. Noticing that flies had gathered on his snack, he swatted them and killed seven flies with one blow. He made himself a belt that announced to the world, "Seven in One Blow." As he struck out to seek his fortune, his reputation gave him an advantage. Whether it was slaying giants or capturing unicorns and wild boars, there was nothing the little tailor couldn't do, even feats that could not be accomplished by a hundred men. In the end, he was rewarded with a place in the kingdom and eventually ascended to the throne himself. An old, English version of the story concludes with these words.

> So the brave little tailor became ruler over the whole kingdom; and his motto throughout his whole life was, "Seven at one blow."[1]

It's a Herculean effort, one person able to accomplish with one act what no one could do before. Like the tailor, Jesus ascended to the throne, his motto, "Forgiveness attained with one sacrifice."

The sacrificial system wasn't able to bring people to the condition of completeness, but Jesus' offering of his own body has removed sin and made us to be a holy people of God. That act of Jesus brings us to the state of completeness and wholeness before God.

There aren't hundreds of books with thousands of keys to solving the problem of the human condition. The book of Hebrews identifies the one key that unlocks our freedom and forgiveness, the one key that opens the door to our future rest. That key is Jesus.

---

1. Grimm, "The Brave Little Tailor," Accessed: March 18, 2008. Online: http://www.ongoing-tales.com/SERIALS/oldtime/FAIRYTALES/tailor1.html.

Time Is of the Essence (10:19–25)

WHAT IS YOUR VISION for ministry in the twenty-first century? The world keeps changing around us in many different ways. The way in which people prepare for careers has made a dramatic change in recent years. Rather than leaving home after high school and attending various schools until relocating for a job, many are finding alternative ways to prepare for vocations while continuing their current lifestyle. For families, the school system provides a great deal of the socialization for children, the social network for adults in parent/teacher organizations and booster clubs, and sometimes the primary focus of scheduling family activities to attend sporting events and concerts. People are able to be connected with others in many more ways and at all times of the day. Computers, personal information managers, and cell phones enable people to widen their community to include people from around the world.

The twentieth century pace of life no longer exists for the vast majority of people in the developed world. The seasons of the year are no longer set off by harvest, but are delineated more by sports and entertainment. The work-week continues to blend through the week-end as people are more able to do their work wherever they are. No longer do people need to wake up with the roosters, since the global market never sleeps and technology enables millions of people to do their work any time of the day. In the ever-transforming information age, people are able to keep up with what's going on in the world, have greater access to a diversity of viewpoints, and consume and construct knowledge about any topic or interest imaginable without having to go anywhere.

Meanwhile the country church or the church on the corner for the most part continues to function the way it did for the last century or so. One response has been the mega-church movement. The one-stop shopping approach provides everything the modern Christian family could want, including shopping. The multiplex church campus is an attempt to respond to the changing needs of people and restore the church as the center of Christian life. In the midst of cultural change and social crisis, the church needs to maintain its core identity and primary function.

The Jewish people in the first century were experiencing this sort of cultural and social upheaval. The influence of Greek culture from previous centuries had brought a different language along with various cultural institutions and customs. The Roman occupation not only controlled political and civic life, it had a way of transforming private life in ways that affected people's ways of doing business, where they traveled, and how they planned for the future. For a particular group of Jews, their lives were being changed by the life and teachings of their fellow-Jew, a Galilean, named Jesus. His exemplary life, his endurance of suffering in death as a martyr, and the supernatural events related to his appearance after death and ascension into the sky, convinced many that this Jesus was indeed God's Son and was a fulfillment of what was described in the Hebrew Bible, which many of them knew through reading it or hearing it read in its Greek translation.

The author of Hebrews has completed a final section in which he has compared Jesus and the new covenant with its heavenly tabernacle to what had been described in the law and the prophets. In what follows, the author will once again raise encouragement and warning regarding the necessary faithfulness to be shown by the people of God lest they experience God's judgment as did the Israelites who failed to complete their journey and enter God's rest provided for them. In a time of crisis and change, it's vital that God's people continue to worship God genuinely and faithfully (10:19–22), withstand pressures to conform (10:23), and work hard to encourage each other to lovingly care for others (10:24–25).

WORSHIP GOD GENUINELY AND FAITHFULLY (10:19–22)

The author of Hebrews begins this section with "therefore." It's a good indication that a transition is taking place. From this point on, the type of language the author uses is sometimes called paraenetic or hortatory. It's language that uses exhortation ("let us do this or that"), encouragement ("keep doing the great things you're doing"), advice ("this is a good way to go"), imperatives ("act in this way"), admonishment ("stop doing that"), warning ("if you don't, this will happen"), and giving examples, both negative and positive ("be like this person, not like that").

Section Five: The Heavenly Sanctuary Compared to the Earthly

After each section of comparison in Hebrews, the author has followed it with this kind of language. This final section of comparison is followed by a longer and more intense appeal to the audience. He first refers to what has been concluded in the comparative section just prior. Jesus, as our great priest, has, in effect, rededicated the worship center of God enabling us to enter the holiest place. His death as a sacrifice was a blood atonement with his own flesh serving as the curtain pulled aside to allow passage. It is a new and living way since it is the resurrected life of Jesus that provides entrance rather than dried blood that symbolizes the death of the animal. On this basis, the author exhorts the audience to approach as worshippers into God's heavenly temple.

Whereas worshippers in the tabernacle might have experienced the sprinkling of animal's blood or a ritual of washing with clean water, those who approach God now are to be aware of their forgiveness of sin and the cleansing of their soul, not just ritually, metaphorically, or symbolically, but in reality. We come to God with genuineness, a true heart. We are fully who we are as people, not people who are represented by someone else, a priest, not someone for whom an animal has had to be slaughtered, but people who appear before God just as we are, body, soul and spirit. Because of the death Jesus died, the example his life gives, and the empowering presence of God's Spirit within us, we are able to approach God with a full assurance of faith.

Most of us have had the experience, at one time or another, of having to meet with a boss when we know that something has not been right. We dread the day when we have our meeting with the boss. We imagine what it's going to be like. The big boss will be sitting behind a huge desk towering over us as we sit in our little chair cowering behind a plant. When asked why something wasn't done right or wasn't done on time, we have to make our apologies and promise that it will never happen again. We feel so rotten that our stomach aches and our eyes are burning. We just want to get away and have it be done with.

There are other times when we know we've done well and, while we may still be apprehensive about meeting with the boss, we are confident that we are going to be praised for what we've done and be encouraged to keep up the good work. Rather than skulking into the boss's office, we strut in with our head held high, a smile on our face, and greet the boss with a firm handshake. Instead of sitting on the edge of the chair with our hands in our lap, we sit back relaxed. Instead of looking at the floor,

Time Is of the Essence (10:19–25)

we make good eye contact and smile confidently. Rather than "yes, sir" and "no, sir," we are able to be ourselves, talk about the work we are doing together, and be more personable.

When worshippers came to the tabernacle, they wouldn't have known to what degree they may have displeased God. The only thing you could do is throw another cow on the fire, so to speak. The point is, when we come to worship God together, we should be cognizant of where we stand before God based on what Jesus has done for us. Rather than entering into worship fearfully, we come confidently. We have a backstage pass to visit God in worship. Our boss has an open door policy to come to God at any time in worship and prayer. We have been cleansed and purified; our sins have been taken care of. There's no reason to be demur when we come together to worship God. We don't have to fake piousness. God knows who you are and what you have done. Your sins are forgiven and you are beckoned to approach God as the person you are.

WITHSTAND THE PRESSURES OF CONFORMITY WITHOUT WAVERING (10:23)

Next the author of Hebrews urges them to stay committed to the message they have shared. The story of the Bible contains a basic message about what God is doing in the world, and this is the message we share in common. We tell it to each other, we remind each other of it, and it's what we pass on to the next generation.

Throughout Hebrews the author warns the readers about what has happened in the past when God's people have wavered in their allegiance to God. If people disobeyed God in the past and received judgment, we should expect that disobedience to a greater work in this age will deserve a greater punishment. The previous people failed to receive the promise God had given them, but this time the hope is God's people will remain true and receive the promise God still holds out, the promise of entering God's rest.

We know that politicians often have a message they want us to receive. Each day the president of the United States has certain talking points that he wants to get across to people. Those who are loyal to the president stick to the message. No matter how difficult the situation gets, you must stick to the message. Sometimes it seems like it doesn't matter what question is asked during press briefings, the answer comes back with the same message.

Holding to our confession doesn't necessarily mean following the party line. The traditions we were taught as a child or the formulations of denominational groups don't necessarily amount to our common confession. Our allegiance is to God and to the message about God's work in the world from creation to redemption. There's a core message there that should be something that we will not waver on. Together we will stand firm for the message no matter the consequences.

WORK HARD TO HELP OTHERS TO WORK HARD FOR OTHERS (10:24–25)

The author of Hebrews has talked about how the church of his day is to come together to worship God boldly and how to withstand the pressure of conformity. Here he is talking about how the community functions together to do God's work in the world. The verb he uses implies great concentration: we are to contemplate, to challenge our minds. He then uses a word that has come into English as the word paroxysm. A paroxysm is a sudden outburst of emotion or action; it's like having a seizure or an attack. We're supposed to apply our minds to coming up with ways to make each other experience a paroxysm. The result of this sudden outburst of action is to be two things. We're supposed to break out in attacks of love for others and of doing good things for others.

Along with this are two things we should be doing. The first is actually what we shouldn't be doing. We shouldn't abandon or forsake getting together as the church. Apparently, some people in his day had gotten in the practice of skipping church meetings. It's rather stronger than that since it refers not just to missing church once in awhile, but rather leaving the church community completely.

The positive action is that we should be encouraging one another. The author of Hebrews adds that this should be our practice all the more when we consider that the day of Christ's return is closer now than it was before.

There are people who have the gift of bringing out the best in other people. Some teachers have a way of being a good encourager and of getting students to do their best work. Some people become the captain of their sports team because they help others to do their best; they provide opportunities for others to perform to their best ability. A good boss is one who knows how to set an example and be someone others want to follow. People do good work because they are in an environment where excellence is expected and rewarded.

How can we figure out how to cause people to have an outburst of loving care for others? We certainly need to set good examples by what we do in our own lives. We also need to nurture others and give them the opportunities to be involved in work that impacts the lives of others. In that work, we need to support and encourage each other, holding each other to the high standard of selfless work to benefit other people. It takes the commitment of everyone to work together to accomplish this highest of ideals, to love others and to do good work for others.

⸻

Our world continues to change in the twenty-first century, but ministry needs to continue to be shaped around these three ideals: to worship God together in genuineness and faithfulness, to withstand the pressures to change our core values, and to work hard to promote love and good deeds in our community and around the world.

I hear the language all the time about how the church needs to change in the postmodern world. Our pluralistic world is now a post-Christian society. We know what's behind us, but we don't know what's ahead. A pessimist sees the church as post-something, but the optimist sees the church as pre-something—pre-revival, pre-revolution, pre-transformation. What the church will become is largely in our hands. The responsibility has been given to us. We have the knowledge of what has taken place in the past and the knowledge of what God's promises are. It is left to us to respond faithfully to the needs of a new world with a new church firmly based in an ageless message of God's redemption.

A Pep Talk for the Last Quarter (10:26–39)

Sermons are supposed to be a sort of pep talk for Christians. One of the classic scenes in American cinema is the pep talk Knute Rockne, played by Pat O'Brien, gives to his Notre Dame team at half-time when they're losing:

> Well, boys, I haven't a thing to say. Played a great game—all of you. Great game. I guess we just can't expect to win 'em all. I'm going to tell you something I've kept to myself for years. None of you ever knew George Gipp. He was long before your time, but you all know what a tradition he is at Notre Dame. And the last thing he said to me, "Rock," he said, "sometime when the team is up against it and the breaks are beating the boys, tell them to go out there with all they got and win just one for the Gipper. I don't know where I'll be then, Rock," he said, "but I'll know about it, and I'll be happy."[1]

The long speech we call the book of Hebrews is coming to the pep talk section. He's coaching and coaxing them to draw together everything he's been saying and go out and play the second half to win.

In Christian terms, before the turn of the millennia was the first half. The people of God were losing, in spite of all the great things God had done on their behalf. In the second half there was going to be a new player on the field, number seven, a guy named Jesus. Coach Hebrews is sure that the team can win, if they work together and don't give up, even when the going gets tough.

The author of Hebrews tells his audience to be warned about the consequences of future failure (10:26–31), to be reminded of the condition of past accomplishments (10:32–34), and to be admonished about the conclusion to give up in the present (10:35–39).

---

1. *Knute Rockne All American Hero.* Directed by Lloyd Bacon. Warner Bros., 1940. Accessed March 26, 2008. Online: http://www.filmsite.org/knut.html.

A Pep Talk for the Last Quarter (10:26–39)

BE WARNED ABOUT THE CONSEQUENCES OF FUTURE FAILURE (10:26–31)

In the midst of Hebrews' language of exhortation comes another warning. It's a warning that's been repeated throughout Hebrews. The logic goes like this: A is good, but B is greater than A. If going against A results in X, then going against B results in Y, which is greater than X.

Hebrews explains that the people of God are in a more dire position than the Israelites were who were judged for their disobedience by not being allowed to enter the Promised Land. The argument Hebrews makes goes like this: If the followers of Jesus make a deliberate decision to break with their religious tradition under the duress of persecution, they need to understand that what Jesus did was a one time thing. For the people to commit such a sin means that they can't go back to sacrificing in the temple, and what God did through the death of Jesus can't be repeated. There's nothing left but judgment.

The law of Moses teaches in Deuteronomy that judgment is made on the basis of two or three witnesses. Here's three witnesses against this people who would reject the work God has done in Jesus: (1) They will be literally trampling under foot the Son of God; (2) They will have treated as profane the blood of Jesus that inaugurated the new covenant; and (3) they will have insulted the grace of God poured out by God's spirit. That's the three-strikes-and-you-are-out of blasphemy and utter disregard for the work of God in the world!

If there's one thing you learn from reading the Old Testament, you learn that God doesn't take infidelity lightly. According to the Hebrew of Deut 32:35, "Vengeance is mine, and recompense." The ancient Greek translation (LXX) reads, "In the day of vengeance, I will repay." Hebrews cites the text with words closer to the Greek Bible. Interestingly enough, Paul in Rom 12:19 quotes Deut 32:35 with exactly the same words as Hebrews does here. In any case, the message is the same. God responds to infidelity with vengeance.

Next Hebrews quotes from a section of the next verse in Deuteronomy, "For the Lord shall judge his people" (Deut 32:36). In a terrifying climax, Hebrews issues the warning, "It is a fearful thing to fall into the hands of the living God" (10:31).

We've talked about the concept of a greater judgment in a number of ways as we have encountered it in the book of Hebrews. Here's another way of thinking about it. The average clock on the wall does the job for which it is intended. You can tell what time it is and be reasonably assured that it is accurate, as long as you make sure to set it once in awhile and keep electricity going to it. We rely on our clocks to tell us the time so we can keep to a schedule. We depend on clocks having approximately the same time so we can do things together at the scheduled time. There are devices that tell time that are much better than the average clock on the wall.

According to the web site of the National Institute of Standards and Technology (http://tf.nist.gov/cesium/fountain.htm) NIST-F1, the nation's primary time and frequency standard, is a cesium fountain atomic clock developed at the NIST laboratories in Boulder, Colorado. NIST-F1 contributes to the international group of atomic clocks that define Coordinated Universal Time (UTC), the official world time. Because NIST-F1 is among the most accurate clocks in the world, it makes UTC more accurate than ever before. This clock is expected not to gain or lose a second in 60 million years.

If someone tinkered with your clock on the wall, the consequences would probably not be very severe. I did once change the time of a clock. It was the last class before graduation at the Bible institute my wife and I attended. I was sitting by the wall and the clock was just above me. We were waiting for the instructor to arrive and we were all feeling a bit playful. So I reached up and pushed the clock about twenty minutes forward. In a few minutes, the instructor arrived, and he began his last class of the semester giving his concluding thoughts on Bible study methods. By that time I had forgotten all about the clock, until he glanced over at the wall and saw that time was up. He quickly wrapped up the class period and dismissed us. No one in the class said anything, and I became the hero for the day.

If someone were to go to Boulder, CO and somehow managed to sabotage the NIST-F1, not only would we all suffer, but that person would receive a greater punishment than I would had I been caught. But come to think of it, it was a very conservative Bible institute, so maybe my punishment would have been equal to the saboteur of time.

What this illustration doesn't demonstrate is the way in which the disobedience and punishment are not focused on individual action but of corporate responsibility. We are in the same boat with the people of the first century. The warning they received in the first century is the warning we need to hear as Christians of the twenty-first century. Together we are

A Pep Talk for the Last Quarter (10:26-39)

obligated to remain true to the knowledge we have received lest we also are guilty of "spurning the Son of God" or "profaning the blood of the covenant" or "outraging the Spirit of grace."

How would we be guilty? We would be guilty if we continue to let the tenets of Christian faith have less and less influence in contemporary society. We would be guilty if we continue to let ourselves be secularized so that science and philosophy become our only moral guides. We would be guilty if we continue to ignore the action that faith requires and did not respond to the needs of our world. The standard by which we will be judged will not only be different than in biblical times but the consequences will also be greater.

BE REMINDED OF THE CONDITION OF PAST ACCOMPLISHMENTS (10:32-34)

Hebrews now uses the language common in exhortation which reminds the audience of their past accomplishment as a way to encourage continued good behavior. From what Hebrews says, we get a picture of the recent history of this group of people. At some earlier point, they were enlightened. It reminds us of the stories in Acts when the apostolic missionaries would come to a city and teach. Acts 8:5-8 describes Philip visiting the city of Samaria. They listened to what Philip said and saw the miraculous signs he performed. Acts says, "there was great joy in that city" (Acts 8:11). The people believed the message proclaimed to them and experienced the presence of the Holy Spirit.

Acts 9:32-35 tells the story of Peter coming to the city of Lydda. After Peter heals Aeneas, a man who had been paralyzed for eight years, "all the residents of Lydda and Sharon saw him and turned to the Lord" (Acts 9:35).

Acts 11:19-21 relates the circumstances after the martyrdom of Stephen. The disciples of Jesus were scattered because of the persecution taking place. Some men came to Antioch and preached about Jesus to the Greek-speaking Jews there. Acts records that, "The hand of the Lord was with them, and a great number became believers and turned to the Lord" (Acts 11:21).

Whatever group it is to whom Hebrews is addressed, they experienced this sort of conversion to being followers of Jesus. Some time afterward there came a time of persecution. Hebrews characterizes the conflict as an athletic struggle (10:32). The abuse and persecution was theatrical in the way people were publicly treated (10:33). Groups were sometimes treated maliciously. In the midst of that period of persecution, this group demonstrated their sympathy for people who had been imprisoned as part of their punishment (10:34). In spite of having their property taken from them, they were able to respond with an attitude of joy because of their experience of a risen Christ with a promise of a better possession and one that lasts forever.

The history of the early church has its stories of persecution and imprisonment. The book of Acts records those periods, and the letters of Paul refer to his own experience of imprisonment as well as the persecution others experienced. We can imagine what was possible in these situations by reading an account of a time of persecution suffered by Jews in Alexandria in the year 38 CE, around the same time as the early church was beginning. Philo, in his work on the prefect of Egypt named Flaccus, writes the following about the persecution of the Jews in Alexandria:

> They drove the Jews entirely out of four quarters, and crammed them all into a very small portion of one; while the populace, overrunning their desolate houses, turned to plunder, and divided the booty among themselves as if they had obtained it in war. And then, being immediately seized by those who had excited the seditious multitude against them, they were treacherously put to death, and then were dragged along and trampled under foot by the whole city, and completely destroyed, without the least portion of them being left which could possibly receive burial; and in this way their enemies, who in their savage madness had become transformed into the nature of wild beasts, slew them and thousands of others with all kinds of agony and tortures, and newly invented cruelties, for wherever they met with or caught sight of a Jew, they stoned him, or beat him with sticks, not at once delivering their blows upon mortal parts, lest they should die speedily, and so speedily escape from the sufferings which it was their design to inflict upon them. And those who did these things, mimicked the sufferers, like people employed in the representation of theatrical farces; but the relations and friends of those who were the real victims, merely because they sympathized with the misery of their relations, were led away to prison, were scourged, were tortured, and after all the ill treatment which their living bodies could endure, found the cross the end of all, and the punishment from which they could not escape. (Philo, *Flaccus*, 1:55–77)

A Pep Talk for the Last Quarter (10:26–39)

There have been times of persecution in more recent years. Samuel Janney writes of a Quaker who experienced the kind of treatment Hebrews describes.

> Among those convinced of the principles of Friends about this time, the name of Robert Widders must not be omitted. He was born in the year 1618, at Upper Kellet, in Lancashire, and before his acquaintance with Friends was a seeker of heavenly truth. In the year 1652, George Fox held a great meeting at his house, at which many were convinced, and it is supposed he was one of that number. He frequently travelled with George Fox, who speaks of him "as a thundering man against hypocrisy, deceit, and the rottenness of the priests." Being zealous in his religious efforts, and a severe reprover of "spiritual wickedness in high places," he suffered much, and his life was often in peril from the rude assaults of his adversaries. On account of his faithful testimony against tithes he suffered great loss of property, but was not the least dejected or disheartened by it, knowing well that the cause for which he suffered was the promotion of Christian truth.[2]

We need to be reminded of what others have experienced, times of much greater struggle than we in North America know now. What we remember is how they handled the persecution, how they endured the loss of property, how they persevered even though they or their loved ones were imprisoned. We need to be guided by that kind of fortitude to stay true during the times of our own testing.

BE ADMONISHED ABOUT THE CONCLUSION TO GIVE UP IN THE PRESENT (10:35–39)

In this section the author of Hebrews admonishes his audience not to give up. "Don't throw it all away," he says. "Don't lose your nerve." "Don't abandon your confidence; it has great consequence." Hebrews said earlier in 3:6, "we are his house if we hold firm the confidence." What the people need is endurance, perseverance. At the end of it all, if they have done God's will, they will receive what God promised.

Again, Hebrews quotes from several places to substantiate his claims. He first uses a phrase from Isa 26:20 to set the time frame for God's ac-

---

2. Samuel Macpherson Janney, *History of the Religious Society of Friends from Its Rise to the Year 1828*, vol. 1, (2nd) Hayes AND Zell, 1860, 142–43. Accessed: March 18, 2008. Online: http://dqc.esr.earlham.edu/toc/E11340417A.

tion. It will be "in a very little while." The next phrase comes from the end of Hab 2:3, "the one who is coming will come and will not delay." Then Hebrews reverses the two clauses in the next verse quoted from Hab 2:4 and makes a slight change to the order of one word. With this quotation, "my righteous one will live by faith," Hebrews introduces the topic of faith, which will be the central theme of Heb 11. The one who is God's righteous person will live a life of faith. God takes pleasure in one who does not shrink back from the time of persecution and by doing so lose faith. Hebrews emphasizes this point: In the contest of faith, we are not among the losers but among the winners.

But people get disappointed, including pastors. Take the example of Pastor Larry. He had been a good pastor to his congregation.

> But the community has deteriorated as markets shifted. Many left for better jobs and were replaced by transient families with lesser skills. Schools and stores changed overnight. Larry, an African-American, felt alienated in a community that once embraced his encouragement. He was ready to throw in the towel.[3]

We can understand his discouragement. Often pastors feel like they work alone and are undervalued by their congregations. Just when Pastor Larry was feeling defeated, an elderly member of his congregation stopped by his office. She said to him, "I've watched you for nearly 10 years, consoling, shepherding, and ministering to this community. You've been an encouragement to everyone."[4] Larry appreciated her kind words but wanted to know, "Then why are so many leaving and being replaced by individuals hostile to God's Word?"[5] Pearl replied, "God's brought them for you to grow in your ministry. I believe God gifted you with an encouraging heart for a time such as this."[6]

We can't throw in the towel and give up on the plain truth of the gospel message. We have to endure the difficult times and stay true to God's will. We mustn't shrink back from our duties but move forward in faith.

---

3. David Farr, *God's Man*, ed. Don M. Aycock appearing as an excerpt in "Men of Integrity," Nov/Dec 2001. Accessed: March 18, 2008. Online: http://www.christianitytoday.com/moi/2001/006/nov/7.7.html.

4. Ibid.

5. Ibid.

6. Ibid.

A Pep Talk for the Last Quarter (10:26-39)

In this concluding section of chapter 10, Hebrews has warned us about the consequences of future failure, reminded us of the condition of our past accomplishments, and admonished us about any conclusion we might have to give up in the present.

Do you remember what happened to George Gipp, the character played by Ronald Reagan in *Knute Rockne, All American*? He had been an inspiration to his team and all those who knew him. He died in the prime of life, but his life was an example for others to give the best they have and even in death to think of others. With his dying breath he had told his coach, "Some day, when things are tough, maybe you can ask the boys to go in there and win just one for the Gipper."

We're well into the second half now. Maybe we're in the fourth quarter. Maybe there are only seconds to play. I don't know if we know whether we're winning or not. But we can't give up. We must finish and finish well. We must win this one for Jesus.

Section Six

Examples and Exhortations to Faithful Living
(11:1—13:25)

Faith Is Made Evident in Faithful Lives (11:1–7)

BIOGRAPHIES ARE CATALOGUED IN the library as non-fiction, but there is something fictional about the way an author portrays someone by looking back on the entire scope of a person's life. Real lives are messy sorts of things. Where we end up in life may have nothing to do with what we set out to do in the beginning. Successes and failures are often as much a result of "dumb luck" as they are of careful planning and discipline. However, all things being equal, someone who sets out to accomplish something in his or her life and achieves those goals can be a valuable example to encourage us to work hard and dream big.

I've read a number of biographies and autobiographies in my life. They have helped to guide my vision of what I want to accomplish in life. It shouldn't surprise anyone to learn that I read biographies of biblical scholars, theologians, missionaries, and pastors. In my early years, I read biographies of Charles Spurgeon, the prolific author and preacher from London, and Dwight L. Moody, the evangelist who formed the Moody Bible Institute in Chicago. Reading a biography of Albert Schweitzer gave me the desire to do more than one thing in life: Schweitzer is impressive as a medical doctor and missionary to Africa, but along with his skills in playing and repairing pipe organs is his great contribution as a New Testament scholar. The biography of Adoniram Judson also tells the story of someone who is a scholar of the Bible and who applies that knowledge to missionary work; in his case to Burma, what is now Myanmar. Imagine how Judson, while captive in the hold of a ship, translates his Hebrew Bible into Latin just to keep himself sane. Most of us would think doing that would lead to insanity. Biographies of F.F. Bruce and William Barclay emphasize their roles as ministers in the church while also being New Testament scholars. A biography of Edgar J. Goodspeed portrays a man who achieved great things as a scholar and collector of ancient manuscripts at the University of Chicago. The biography *J. B. Phillips: The Wounded Healer*, written by Vera Phillips, narrates her husband's accomplishments

Section Six: Examples and Exhortations to Faithful Living

but also gives insights into his battle with dark moods and depression. Along with the success that marked his career, there were difficult times, great controversies, and dark moments. When we read biographies, we learn by example. Imitating the examples of others can be a powerful way to guide us as we continue to write the stories of our own lives.

Ancient Greco-Roman rhetoric is concerned with the power of persuasion. While sophists tried to teach aristocrats, such as lawyers and politicians, to use persuasion to gain power, prestige, or wealth, philosophers sought to use that power to help people make their lives better. One effective technique in rhetoric is to provide examples. Often these examples would praise the illustrious individuals from the past or present who most ably characterize virtuous living.

One such author was the second-century philosopher Plutarch. Besides his massive work on moral philosophy called the *Moralia*, he also wrote an immense work on the *Lives of the Noble Greeks and Romans*. Plutarch, as we've already learned, also wrote comparisons in which he would juxtapose the essential qualities of great people and demonstrate which one, the Greek or Roman, was the better person.

Hebrews has followed a pattern of comparing Jesus and his work with individuals and institutions of the Old Testament. Each comparative section has been followed by a section devoted to exhortation to the audience. Near the end of Hebrews comes a series of examples of people known from biblical literature. Their lives and experiences are held out as examples of faithful living. Chapter 10 had concluded in verse 38 with an allusion to Hab 2:4, "My righteous one will live by faith." Chapter 11 now begins with that transition. It answers the question, what is faith?

The author of Hebrews gives us two parallel phrases at the beginning of chapter 11, "Now faith is the assurance of things hoped for, the conviction of things not seen." The first clause refers to hope and the second clause to things we can't see. Hope is something we do with regard to the future and in that way is not something we can see. The future doesn't exist yet. There is much about faith that involves things we can't see, like God. It is faith that places hope and invisible things into the realm of reality. We exist and we think; we think of events that have not yet happened and of substances that are not tangible. Our faith makes those things real to us in our world.

This table of heroes of faith proves that living by faith commends us to God. The stories of the Bible substantiate through its testimony that

Faith Is Made Evident in Faithful Lives (11:1-7)

our ancestors in the faith lived lives that God accepted, in spite of the many difficulties they faced. The notable thing about chapter 11 is the way the author repeats a single Greek word at the beginning of sentences that mark the transitions from one paragraph to the next. It is translated in English with the phrase "by faith."

As we begin this litany of leaders we should be aware of where the author of Hebrews is leading us. At the end of this section, he says, "Yet all these, though they were commended for their faith, did not receive what was promised, since God had provided something better so that they would not, apart from us, be made perfect" (Heb 11:39-40). Although Hebrews praises these people for their exemplary lives, he comes around to say that what Jesus has now done for us is something even better, something that will in the end get us to the ultimate goal in this life and in the next.

The first group in chapter 11 covers the time of creation and names three individuals: Abel, Enoch, and Noah. First, the beginning of the world as created by God is to be accepted by faith (11:3). Secondly, from the story of Abel we learn that a better sacrifice is approved by God for righteousness (11:4). Thirdly, from the story of Enoch, we discover that belief in the God who rewards faithfulness meets God's approval (11:5-6). Lastly, from Noah, we find out that being warned and acting faithfully brings about righteousness (11:7).

BEGINNING OF THE WORLD AS CREATED BY GOD IS ACCEPTED BY FAITH (11:3)

Verse three begins the repetition of the phrase "by faith." In this first instance Hebrews does not name an individual but refers to the creation of the universe in the opening pages of the book of Genesis. Much of what is described in the early chapters of Genesis goes beyond human experience and understanding. How are we to have knowledge of God creating the world and forming the universe in space and time? We can't know it in any scientific sense. But Hebrews says we can comprehend it by faith. Our minds can imagine the process of creation, either ages of geologic time and the phenomenon of an expanding universe shrunk into an instance of divine fiat or the explosion of matter guided by a God who has designed the physics and biology of the universe to gradually result in a world—or maybe worlds—in which life blooms and evolves. It is faith that gives us the ability to look at the world around us and begin to understand the way the world works and what might be our place in it. Creativity within humans is a microcosm of the nature of God.

My daughter Lauren has been painting for a few years. I had known she had canvases and paints, and I had seen paintings laying around. I wasn't really aware of what she had been doing. One night she brought her paintings out to the living room, and I got a chance to study them. It wasn't until I looked closely at them and let my imagination be free to experience her creativity that I began to see relationships and meaning in the colors and shapes. I was moved by what I discovered in her artistic expression. I came to know her better through what she created.

With the universe as the canvas, God has expressed God's creative energy, taking what did not exist or existed as thought, and shaping it into a reality of matter, space, and time. God's brush was God's voice. If we could imagine someone standing before a canvas and singing a song, and, rather than hear the music, we would instead see the music take shape and form color. That's the world God created; that's the world we experience; that's the divine creation we accept through faith.

BETTER SACRIFICE IS APPROVED BY GOD FOR RIGHTEOUSNESS (11:4)

We know the story of Abel from Genesis chapter four. After the expulsion from the Garden of Eden (Gen 3:22–24), Adam and Eve become parents (Gen 4:1–2). The first son is Cain. They become parents again with another son and name him Abel. In this very first story of family life we get a glimpse of the age-old feud between farmers and ranchers. Cain is a farmer and works the soil; Abel is a rancher with a herd of sheep (Gen 4:2). They each bring the produce of their work to God (Gen 4:3–4). In some way that the text doesn't explain, God accepts Abel's animal sacrifice but rejects the "vegetarian diet" Cain offered (Gen 4:5–7). Cain plots against his brother and kills him in secret (Gen 4:8). The evidence of the blood-soaked ground calls out Cain's guilt (Gen 4:10).

God's approval of Abel's gift, according to Heb 11:4, demonstrates not only that Abel's sacrifice was better than Cain's but also that Abel is regarded as a righteous person. Although Abel had been murdered and his blood called for justice, Abel's faithfulness in offering the better sacrifice calls out to us as the better example.

Faith Is Made Evident in Faithful Lives (11:1–7)

The classic illustration of this is the difference between what the chicken and pig contribute to one's breakfast. For the chicken an egg is a generous contribution, but for a pig, his is a total sacrifice. It is a greater sacrifice to offer to God the life of an animal than the crops of a field.

Why God chose one and not the other is something of a mystery. One might say that it makes sense for the Israelites as nomadic shepherds to pass down a story that favors the sacrifice of an animal. Another tradition told by an agrarian community could just as well have passed down a story in which the hero is the younger son who brings the best of the crop to honor God. We know from this vantage point that animal sacrifice would come to be part of the instructions given by God for the atonement of sin within the covenant with Israel.

Hebrews interprets the Genesis text to say that Abel acted in faith when he offered an animal sacrifice and because of that action God approved of him, which demonstrated the righteousness of Abel.

BELIEF IN GOD WHO REWARDS MEETS GOD'S APPROVAL (11:5–6)

Enoch has remained one of the most mysterious of people from antiquity. We know nothing about what Enoch did to deserve such notoriety. The Hebrew text of Genesis says twice that Enoch "walked with God" (Gen 5:22, 24). The ancient Greek translation of the Hebrew, which is what Hebrews quotes, says instead that Enoch was "well-pleasing" to God. We find support for the same reading in early Jewish texts. For example, the text called the Wisdom of Solomon reads, "There were some who pleased God and were loved by him, and while living among sinners were taken up" (Wisdom 4:10). Likewise, the book of Sirach says, "Enoch pleased the Lord and was taken up, an example of repentance to all generations" (Sirach 44:16).

What happened to Enoch? Perhaps Enoch died a mysterious death, and they never recovered his body. For some reason it was felt that Enoch was a righteous person and in some mysterious way was transferred from this world to the next. Hebrews argues that Enoch must have been a faithful person. It is impossible to please God without being a faithful person (11:6).

Remember the Habakkuk quotation, "My righteous one will live by faith" (Hab 2:4). The next phrase in the quotation of that text, based on the Greek translation of Hab 2:4, is the opposite of living by faith: "My soul

Section Six: Examples and Exhortations to Faithful Living

takes no pleasure in anyone who shrinks back" (10:38). The unfaithful person shrinks back from walking with God. God has no pleasure in that person. That person is not someone with whom God is pleased, as the Genesis text says as quoted by Hebrews. Hebrews then says that there are two essential components to faith. The first is that a person must believe that God "is." The second is that God is a just God who rewards those who seek God.

Enoch is a wonderful example of faithful living. Can you imagine visiting the Heroes Hall of Fame in heaven. You're walking through the exhibits and talking with the inductees. You come across Enoch. The display is almost non-existent it's so small. Enoch is sitting nearby watching people pass. You approach him and introduce yourself. Not knowing much of the story of his life and not remembering that there was much to know, you begin to question him.

"Tell me, Enoch, what was it that you did? Did you build an ark like Noah or a temple for God like Solomon?"

He replies, "No, I didn't build anything."

"Well, did you engage in battle and sacrifice your life heroically?"

"No," he says, "I didn't fight in any battles."

You continue to think how you can get him to tell you what he did. "How about writing books and sharing your wisdom, poetry or prophecy?"

"I never wrote anything," he confesses.

"Maybe you had children you raised who did something tremendous with their lives, something I would have heard about?"

"Yes," he says excitedly, "I did have a son who gained some notoriety."

"Go on," you prod, "who was he, what did he do?"

You can almost see Enoch's chest puff out. "I had a son named Methusaleh."

"Yes, what did he do?" you ask.

"Do? He didn't really do anything, I suppose. He did live to be 969 years old. That's something."

How many people have you known that also deserve to be with Enoch in his wing of Faith's Hall of Fame, people who have simply lived their lives. They've learned what they needed to know. They've provided for their families. After a mere 365 years—in the case of Enoch—God takes them.

Faith Is Made Evident in Faithful Lives (11:1–7)

Their nobility is in the quality of who they are rather than what they have accomplished. It's as though one moment the person was on the porch in his or her rocking chair, just watching life around them. The next moment the person has vanished. All that's left is the empty chair, slowly rocking back and forth until it stops. God has taken the person. Like a piece of bread toasting to a state of perfection, which pops up and is gone. The person of faith pleases God, and that person belongs to God, whether here or there.

BEING WARNED AND ACTING FAITHFULLY BRINGS ABOUT RIGHTEOUSNESS (11:7)

The story of Noah takes up about four chapters in the book of Genesis. Here in Heb 11 the author summarizes Noah's life in one sentence contained in verse seven. First, Noah is warned by God about something that would happen that had never happened before ("events as yet unseen"). Noah was asked to build a boat in dry dock without any apparent way to put the boat into water. Not just a boat, but he was to build a huge barge. Noah obeys God ("respected the warning"), accepts that God is going to save just his immediate family ("save his household") and no one else ("he condemned the world")—them and a bunch of animals. His faithfulness to God despite all signs to the contrary becomes a great example ("became an heir to the righteousness that is in accordance with faith"). Gen 7:1 records the approval of God, "For I have seen that you alone are righteous before me in this generation."

A person who is called upon to have a faith like Noah's is as rare as the circumstances that called forth such a faith. There are people who have such a prophetic insight into the future of world events or a vision of what God may be doing in a particular place and time. There have been godly men and women who have had such a vision. In simple words, George Fox described his vision for the people of God. He wrote in his journal,

> As we travelled, we came near a very great and high hill, called Pendlehill, and I was moved of the Lord to go up to the top of it; which I did with much ado, it was so very steep and high. When I was come to the top, I saw the sea bordering upon Lancashire. From the top of this hill the Lord let me see in what places he had a great people to be gathered.[1]

---

1. Fox, "Journal," in *Works*, vol. 1, 140. Accessed: March 14, 2008. Online: http://dqc.esr.earlham.edu/toc/E12877488A-000.

Section Six: Examples and Exhortations to Faithful Living

It is by faith that we receive such visions from God, and it is by faith that we act upon them. Those sorts of visions may be rare, but we must be open to what God may call us to do. Maybe it will be a life like Enoch or maybe it will be something like Noah. We can't simply live by what we know and what we see. Living by faith is being open to the unseen events and movements of God in the world.

⸺

From the stories of creation and of the lives of Abel, Enoch and Noah we learn that God approves and is pleased with the person of faith: the one who believes that God exists, that God is the creator of the world, and that God rewards those who seek God.

Who knows what our lives might be, if we live our lives "by faith." The biographical examples from Hebrews look at a very small aspect of these lives of people from antiquity. But they are examples from which we can learn. For us it's not too late to start a new chapter in our lives, a life characterized by faith.

Samuel Goldwyn once said, "I don't think anyone should write their autobiography until after they're dead. Who knows what might yet happen." The Jewish philosopher Abraham J. Heschel put it this way, "The course of life is unpredictable, no one can write his autobiography in advance." May each paragraph of the new chapter we're writing with our lives begin with the words, "by faith."

Abraham: Our Journey of Faith That Leads Home (11:8–16)

As someone who has moved around a lot in life, I'm still not sure where to claim as my home. I haven't yet made the transition to claiming Indiana as home. Here's an example of what I mean. I recently had to go to a podiatrist. My doctor's first choice couldn't give me an appointment until a month later, so I had to go to the second choice. There's something about the name of the medical group that didn't give me much confidence. It is called Hoosier Foot and Ankle. For one thing, the name reminds me of "hoof and mouth" for some reason. The other is that I don't connect the name Hoosier with intellectual and scientific achievement. I realize that's my problem. Just because a file in the receptionist's area was labeled with a misspelling doesn't mean the doctor is not qualified. In fact, I received very good treatment there. I shouldn't judge people on their appearance, I know that. I know there's no reason why a well-educated and experienced doctor shouldn't have a mullet. Just because a woman wears a NASCAR or Indianapolis Colts jacket doesn't mean she isn't trained and qualified as a nurse. I've lived in Indiana for seven years now, and it's about time I accept that I'm a Hoosier. Here I am and here I will probably stay.

I'm not the only one who has a problem settling down. On the campus where I work we have many people who have moved from elsewhere. There are times when we go around the room to introduce ourselves and invariably we are expected to say something about our church affiliation. It seems like ninety percent of the people say that their church is somewhere else in the world, but they attend such and such a church nearby. One of the expressions people use is to say they are "sojourning" at a particular church currently. I wonder if some of them have been sojourning at churches longer than they attended their home church.

About a year ago I was in a Spanish class. We were supposed to say where we were from. That's hard enough for me to explain in English.

Eventually I started to make things up to make it easier: *Yo soy de Michigan.* You see, my formative years were complicated. I'm not really from Michigan, but that's where I lived during adolescence and started my adult life. Before that I lived in Illinois; that's where my earliest memories are. But before that I had been born in Michigan. Our married life began in Indiana. Then we moved to Illinois and then to Rhode Island and Massachusetts. We lived in New England for fifteen years, but, as a Midwesterner, I consider that time to have been a sojourn. I never intended to stay there; I never even intended to be there that long. So here I am back in Indiana but haven't yet settled in to call it home.

This faith chapter of Hebrews is moving through the primary individuals in the history of the Bible. We now come to the story of Abraham (11:8ff). The recurring word at the beginning of sentences that mark transition in this chapter is the word translated in English with the words "by faith." Abraham will get four "by faith" sections, three of which we will deal with here.

The first "by faith" thing Abraham does is leave where his father settled his family and travel to a new place in obedience to God's direct calling (11:8). The second "by faith" thing is Abraham's taking up residence in the new land, though to the author of Hebrews it seems temporary since Abraham lives in a tent (11:9–10). The third "by faith" thing is the beginning of a new family line, even though Abraham and his wife Sarah are pushing their nineties (11:11–16). Hebrews interprets the account of Genesis about Abraham to say that although Abraham and his descendants lived in a land that was promised and given to them by God, there is a heavenly place that is the ultimate destination that fulfills the promises and blessings of God.

We can learn from the example of Abraham. Our spiritual journey mirrors the experience of Abraham as he followed God's call. Put simply, as we go through life we are seeking the place where God would have us be (11:8), we sojourn in that place (11:9–10), and in a sense we settle into that place with our family (11:11–16).

SEEKING GOD'S PLACE (11:8)

Genesis narrates the travel of Abram (remember he is first called Abram) from Mesopotamia to the land along the eastern coast of the Mediterranean, what we refer to as Palestine. Abram's father had brought

Abraham: Our Journey of Faith That Leads Home (11:8–16)

his family from the east following the fertile crescent to the west (Gen 11:31). After Abram's father died (Gen 11:32), Abram received the call from God to take his family to a new land where God would bless Abram and his family.

> Now the LORD said to Abram, "Go from your country and your kindred and your father's house to the land that I will show you. I will make of you a great nation, and I will bless you, and make your name great, so that you will be a blessing. I will bless those who bless you, and the one who curses you I will curse; and in you all the families of the earth shall be blessed." So Abram went, as the LORD had told him; and Lot went with him. Abram was seventy-five years old when he departed from Haran. (Gen 12:1–5)

Heb 11:8 remarks that Abraham obeyed God's call by faith. Abraham didn't know where God was going to bring him, he just knew that God would show him the place and that God was going to bless him.

Moving to a new location is not the only way that people can seek God's place in their life. As a preacher's kid, I always had a sense that wherever I lived was temporary. When Suann and I were married, we moved to Winona Lake, Indiana so I could go to college there. That began our journey, a journey that was to lead back to Indiana about twenty-two years later.

The move that required the most faith was setting out for Providence, Rhode Island from Illinois. I went ahead during the summer to spend a week looking for a place to live. One apartment I found was owned by a Jewish family. They were very nice to me, they served me iced tea out on their back patio. During the interview they realized that we had no source of income established for when we moved. They even called Suann back in Illinois to talk with her about her job prospects in Rhode Island. Of course, she had no idea what she was going to do. I considered myself to be like Abraham, following the leading of God, not knowing how everything was going to work out but going with God by faith. It was ironic that these descendants of Abraham wouldn't help me as I sought to follow God's leading to a new place.

In a way, even if we don't make big moves in our lives, each one of us has to seek the right place for us as we follow God's direction in our lives. As children become adults and begin to discern what their place is in the world, there are many uncertainties. The choice of whether to attend college or which college to attend can have a dramatic impact on the future course of one's life. There are big choices to make: education, marriage, career, where to live. The choices we make should be guided by our sense of calling. We don't just seek God's path at the beginning of the journey but continue to seek our place in the world, that place to which God has called us.

SOJOURNING IN A NEW PLACE (11:9–10)

According to Genesis, Abram takes his wife Sarai (remember that was Sarah's name at first) and his nephew Lot along with their possessions and sets out for the land of Canaan (Gen 12:5). After Abram arrives in the new land, he begins to sojourn there as a nomad. He "pitched his tent" (Gen 12:8) and "journeyed on by stages toward the Negeb" (Gen 12:9). Yahweh appears to Abram at Shechem and says, "To your offspring I will give this land" (Gen 12:7).

Hebrews refers to this sojourn as Abraham's act of faith. The fact that Abraham lived in a tent (11:9) seems to imply to the author of Hebrews that Abraham wasn't putting down permanent roots in the land, even though he continued to live there (with the exception of trips to Egypt during times of famine, you will recall). Hebrews interprets this to mean that Abraham considered his residence on earth to be temporary (11:10). A permanent place would be one with foundations. A heavenly place would be one that God creates and builds.

Anyone who has made a move knows what it's like to box up your life and remove it to a new place. There's that period of time when most of us live for months or years with boxes still unpacked. It may just be that we're lazy, or it may be that we haven't made the new place permanent. For those of us who rent for awhile before buying a home, there still can be a sense that it's not really our house yet. Maybe there's a point at which you consider a house to be your house; maybe after you redecorate, buy new appliances, put some work into it.

For me there was always a sense that we were sojourning when we moved to a new place because I never intended to stay there after I finished going to school in that area. I was always thinking about what the next place would be, always thinking of what the next opportunities and challenges would be.

We know that in the big scheme of things there is no permanency about this world. Even if we find just the right place to live, and we fix up

Abraham: Our Journey of Faith That Leads Home (11:8–16)

everything just the way we want, we won't live there forever—we don't live forever. We are sojourners in this world. What we anticipate is the final place, that place we believe we will inhabit for eternity. God is the one who has come up with the plans for that city and has built it for us. We live by faith in this world, but it is a life that we see and experience. The faith we exercise by living our lives not by sight is the belief that God has that place for us all to share.

SETTLING IN WITH FAMILY (11:11–16)

For the third time Hebrews uses the expression "by faith" to refer to Abraham (11:11). Abram and Sarai were very old by this time in the story in Genesis. They still had not had any children. God had said to Abram that God would bless him. But Abram didn't know how God was going to do that when he and Sarai were still childless. Abram's heir at this point was a slave in his household (Gen 15:2). Yahweh assured Abram that he would be given offspring and from that offspring would come an uncountable number of descendants (Gen 15:5). Abram's response was faith, "and the LORD reckoned it to him as righteousness" (Gen 15:6).

God promised Abram a child. At first Sarai attempted to give Abram a son through her maid (Gen 16:1–2). Abraham didn't complain about that too much, and nine months later he had a son through Hagar. They named him Ishmael (Gen 16:15). Genesis 21 tells the story of what happened with Hagar and Ishmael. His many descendants are named in Gen 25:12–18.

When Abram is ninety-nine years old, Yahweh makes a covenant with Abram, changing his name to Abraham and his wife's to Sarah (Gen 17:1ff). Yahweh makes clear that Sarah is going to give birth, even though she is ninety years old (Gen 17:19). Sarah gives birth to Isaac and from this one has come many branches of a family tree, whose story unfolds in the Hebrew Bible.

Hebrews 11:13–16 once again interprets the Genesis account in terms of a future and heavenly place. Hebrews says these descendants of Abraham lived faithful lives ("all these died in faith"), but they didn't receive the promise God offered. The metaphor that Hebrews uses is of seeing people at a distance and waving to them ("from a distance they saw and greeted them"). It reminds me of that final text about Moses in Deuteronomy when Moses is not allowed to enter the Promised Land following the exodus and the wandering in the wilderness. Moses looks from the heights of Mount Pisgah and Yahweh says,

> This is the land of which I swore to Abraham, to Isaac, and to Jacob, saying, "I will give it to your descendants"; I have let you see it with your eyes, but you shall not cross over there. (Deut 34:4)

It is as though Moses could have viewed the prospects that lay before the Israelites and waved to a next generation who would experience the promises God had given.

Although the descendants of Abraham are innumerable (11:12) and have formed a nation, Hebrews still sees them as seeking another homeland (11:14), a better country, one that Hebrews calls a heavenly one (11:16a). Hebrews says of the descendants of Abraham that God is not ashamed to be called their God and that God has prepared a city for them (11:16b).

Once we have sought our place in the world and have moved out to sojourn through life, many of us choose to marry and have children. Or perhaps we choose not to not have children, if you know what I mean. At some point we begin to settle down and settle into a place. We begin to set down roots and let our family tree flourish. Some of us have more flourishing trees than others. Once in awhile I hear someone say they have six or seven children and my response is, "That's just crazy." As if my having five children these days isn't.

The more we settle down and put down roots the harder it is to ever leave. I suppose that's the way it is when families grow up around Grandma and Grandpa and then one day the grandparents say, "Bye kids, we're going off to live the rest of our retirement in Florida." As hard as that is, it's even harder when we have to see them leave this world for the next.

As important as the Promised Land has been to the Jewish people, Hebrews regards the future city of God to be more important. Even as we settle into our lives in this world, we should live lightly here and hold on to our loved ones lightly. This is not our final destination, this is not our place of rest, we're not home yet.

⸺

God leads us in life to seek the proper place to fulfill our calling, and there we live as sojourners, only settling in for a temporary stay.

Abraham: Our Journey of Faith That Leads Home (11:8–16)

Over the years I've learned quite a number of songs, most of which are hymns or gospel songs. There's one song that I try not to sing when I'm driving. I discovered that one night when I was roaring down the highway singing songs and suddenly realized I was singing, "This world is not my home, I'm just a passing through." I stopped singing and put my hand over my mouth. After all, I didn't want God to get the wrong idea.

It's like the Sunday School teacher who asked the kids how many of them wanted to go to heaven. Everyone raised their hands except one boy. The teacher said, "Johnny, don't you want to go to heaven when you die." Johnny replied, "Oh, you mean when I die. I thought you were getting a group together now."

Remember the words to that gospel song?

> This world is not my home, I'm just a passing through.//My treasure's all laid up, somewhere beyond the blue.//The angels beckon me from heaven's open door//and I can't feel at home in this world anymore.

We really shouldn't feel too much at home in this world. With Abraham we are looking for another place, a place that transcends city, state, country, or even planet. That's the home we're looking for . . . by faith.

Abraham to Joseph: The Blessings of Faithfulness
(11:17–22)

TRACING A FAMILY'S GENEALOGY can be very interesting. It's like unraveling the plot of an intricate story. When I was pastor of a historic Quaker meeting in Massachusetts, I decided to do some genealogical study of the families. Actually, I began to use genealogical software just to try to figure out who belonged to whom in the church. As so often happens in a small, rural church, most everyone seems to be related to each other in some way. When you live in an area where a family's ancestor came over on the Mayflower and the area was settled so early in the history of our country, connecting the dots of family relationships can be quite a task. My genealogical research developed as I traced back the lineage of various families. The Howland family, for instance, was a prominent family in the Dartmouth Monthly Meeting of Friends. Their ancestor was a Mayflower passenger. Another woman traced her ancestry back to Peleg Slocum, who also was a descendant of a Mayflower passenger. He was one who had given the church the property for their meetinghouse back in the 1690s. Peleg's wife, Mary Holder, had relatives with connections to Anne Hutchinson in Boston and Roger Williams in Providence. I was fascinated to see how these family relationships grew over time, became inter-connected, and had so much positive influence for the future.

Hebrews 11 traces the genealogical relationships of a family that had its beginning in Adam and Eve and passed on through many generations. Abel (11:4), Enoch (11:5–6), and Noah (11:7) were the earliest ones to receive treatment in this chapter as people who lived "by faith."

Another starting point was the life of a man named Abraham, whom we started to get to know in the previous chapter. Like a family member who starts a new life in a new world, Abraham had followed the leading of God, traveled to a new land, and set about to begin a new branch of a family tree. In spite of getting a late start creating that tree, Abraham and Sarah had an only child whom they named Isaac.

Abraham to Joseph: The Blessings of Faithfulness (11:17–22)

In Heb 11:17–22, Abraham will face a trial of his faith in God's plan for him when God tells him to offer his only son as a burnt sacrifice. In three brief verses, we read about the faith expressed in the future by Abraham's descendants (11:17–19). In verse 20 Isaac blesses his sons, Jacob and Esau. Then in verse 21 Jacob, the one whose name is changed to Israel, blesses the two sons of Joseph. Finally in verse 22, Joseph, with his dying breath, points forward to the future blessing of the sons of Israel as they re-enter the Promised Land following the exodus. The faith they show in the future is the example for the faith we should have in life. Like them, we should act in faith regardless of the present consequences (11:17–19). Along with them we should also act in faith regarding the future circumstances (11:20–22).

ACTING IN FAITH REGARDLESS OF THE PRESENT CONSEQUENCES (11:17–19)

Genesis 22 gives us the account of Abraham offering his son Isaac as a sacrifice. The account begins:

> After these things God tested Abraham. He said to him, "Abraham!" And he said, "Here I am." He said, "Take your son, your only son Isaac, whom you love, and go to the land of Moriah, and offer him there as a burnt offering on one of the mountains that I shall show you." (Gen 22:1–2)

What an incredible test! Remember that God had promised Abraham a son in spite of his advanced years. Finally, the near-miraculous happens and Abraham and Sarah have a son. Through this son God is going to bless Abraham with future generations who will be a blessing to all people. After this great blessing occurs to Abraham and Sarah, God tells Abraham not only to kill his son but to burn his body as well.

It's not the first time that Abraham has been confronted with some extraordinary news about God intending the death of someone. When God wanted to destroy Sodom and Gomorrah, Abraham talks God into not destroying the cities if Abraham can find 10 righteous people there (Gen 18:19–33). Remember how Abraham negotiates with God? What if there are 50 righteous in Sodom? How about 45? What if there's 40? Do I hear 30? Who will give me 20? Will you take just 10? When I read the story of Abraham and Isaac, I have to ask myself, "So why doesn't Abraham bargain with God for the life of Isaac?" He could have said, "God, does he

Section Six: Examples and Exhortations to Faithful Living

really need to die? What if I just rough him up a little bit? How about if I just take away his favorite camel?" Instead, Abraham takes God at his word, packs up the kindling, and takes Isaac off to the mountain-top for a bonfire.

Why would Abraham act that way? Hebrews explains it as an act of faith (11:17). Abraham believed God (Gen 15:6) when God said Abraham would have descendants through Isaac. If God wanted him to kill Isaac, it must mean that God will raise Isaac from the dead in order for God to fulfill the promise (11:19).

Abraham went as far as a person can in completing the act of sacrifice without actually having killed the sacrifice: The wood was ready to be lit, Isaac was tied up on the altar, the knife was raised and ready to plunge (Gen 22:9–10). The angel of the Lord called a halt in the nick of time (Gen 22:11–12). Abraham recovered his son from the jaws of death because of his willingness to trust God's promises.

How can we learn from the faithfulness of Abraham in this story? When are we called upon to exercise such faith, the kind of faith in which we are asked to do something that seems contrary to what we believe God is doing in our lives?

In the movie, *One True Thing*, based on the novel of the same name by Anna Quindlen, a young woman named Ellen is hot on a career in writing for a magazine. It's been her goal in life to become like her father, a professor of literature at a local college. Just when her career is about to take off, her father expects her to drop everything to return home and take care of her cancer-stricken mother. Ellen is left without any choice but to leave what she thought was her destiny and see her dreams disappear. She resents her mother and becomes a disaffected child desperately seeking her father's blessing. After all she goes through, she ends up getting a job at another magazine, not a mainstream news magazine but a magazine called *The Voice*. It's only by going through these unexpected and difficult experiences that Ellen is able to find her own voice.

Life sometimes takes a detour, and sometimes the detours look like dead-ends. It's difficult to keep trusting God that what you thought was your destiny is still ahead for you, but it might take a little longer to get there. Abraham trusted that God would fulfill the promises of descendants through Isaac. Abraham acted in faith regardless of what the present consequences might seem to be. God then blessed Abraham for his faithfulness (Gen 22:15–18).

Abraham to Joseph: The Blessings of Faithfulness (11:17–22)

ACTING IN FAITH REGARDING THE FUTURE CIRCUMSTANCES (11:20–22)

In three short, stylistically-related verses (11:20–22) the author of Hebrews covers the second half of the book of Genesis. Each of these verses describe the way in which the person acts in faith regarding future circumstances.

The first two describe the practice of saying a blessing over children (11:20–21). It's sort of like stating your last will and testament, but it gives the parent's hopes and dreams for the children. We remember that Jacob, with the help of his mother, had tricked his father Isaac into giving his blessing intended for the firstborn son to him rather than to his older, fraternal twin Esau (Gen 27:1–29). Hebrews simply recalls the blessing (11:20). From Genesis we read the blessing.

> May God give you of the dew of heaven, and of the fatness of the earth, and plenty of grain and wine. Let peoples serve you, and nations bow down to you. Be lord over your brothers, and may your mother's sons bow down to you. Cursed be everyone who curses you, and blessed be everyone who blesses you! (Gen 27:28–29)

Esau is distraught at missing Isaac's blessing and asks if Isaac has anything left with which he might bless him. Isaac has nothing left with which to bless the other son. Hebrews simply acknowledges that Isaac blesses Esau, but it is more of a curse than a blessing.

> See, away from the fatness of the earth shall your home be, and away from the dew of heaven on high. By your sword you shall live, and you shall serve your brother; but when you break loose, you shall break his yoke from your neck. (Gen 27:39–40)

Hebrews moves quickly on to the story of Jacob's blessing of the sons of Joseph. Remember that Joseph's brothers had sold him into slavery in Egypt (Gen 37:28, 36). But Joseph's presence and power there had rescued the family from famine (Gen 47:11). Joseph was a favorite son of Jacob and in his last hours he met with Joseph and Joseph's two sons, Ephraim and Manasseh (Gen 48:1). Joseph tried to get his father to favor the eldest son Manasseh by placing him at Jacob's right hand and the younger Ephraim on his left (Gen 48:13). But Jacob crossed his hands, placing his right hand on Ephraim's head and his left on the head of Manasseh (Gen 48:14). He then states his blessing.

Section Six: Examples and Exhortations to Faithful Living

> The God before whom my ancestors Abraham and Isaac walked, the God who has been my shepherd all my life to this day, the angel who has redeemed me from all harm, bless the boys; and in them let my name be perpetuated, and the name of my ancestors Abraham and Isaac; and let them grow into a multitude on the earth. (Gen 48:15–16)

Hebrews 11:22 refers to the death-bed scene of Joseph. Joseph makes what amounts to a prophecy.

> Then Joseph said to his brothers, "I am about to die; but God will surely come to you, and bring you up out of this land to the land that he swore to Abraham, to Isaac, and to Jacob." So Joseph made the Israelites swear, saying, "When God comes to you, you shall carry up my bones from here." (Gen 50:24–25)

Joseph acted in faith by believing that a future for his family lay back in the Promised Land, that not only would God bring them back but that his own bones would be laid to rest in that place of promise.

Living by faith is an investment in the future. For example, when we get an education as a young person, we are committing ourselves in faith to whatever the future might hold. When we choose a path in life, whether it's a career, home-making, marriage or whatever our choice might be, we are acknowledging that the future is a place in which we can find purpose and fulfillment. When we have children, for instance, we are saying that we are trusting that life was not only meaningful for us but that the future holds blessing and promise for our descendants. At the end of life, we demonstrate our faith when we pass on to next generations our blessings for their future, our hope for good things to come.

We don't know what the future holds; it's not something we can see. Nevertheless, we must go forward by faith, placing our future and our children's future in the hands of God.

☙

If we want to continue to build a future in which the mission of God in the world is carried forth, we must learn to live faithful lives regardless of the present consequences and be willing to be forward-thinking and forward-believing regarding future circumstances.

I've asked a number of times about my family's genealogy. I'm afraid our family tree is more like a family bush, since my ancestor from a few

Abraham to Joseph: The Blessings of Faithfulness (11:17–22)

generations ago decided not to pass along our history. Probably our family comes from somewhere in Germany. Maybe the Seid family was actually Jewish since many Seids from another branch of our family tree are all Jewish. No one seems to know and no one seems to be working at figuring it all out.

For me, I'm more concerned about the future of the tree. You might think without sons I would be concerned about the Seid name in my family. It's ironic that the only male who is carrying on the Seid name from me and my siblings is adopted. In fact, I'm proud that my nephew David carries on the Seid name; the Seid name is in good hands with him. More important than the name, however, is the family tradition. My five daughters may not pass along the family name but they are blossoming—and perhaps one day they will also be fruitful and multiply. I look forward to giving my blessing to marriages and whatever else the future might hold for my family.

My family and your family has connections that go back to earliest times. We honor that tradition by living by faith and adding our own testimonies to God's faithfulness in our journey together.

Moses: Faithful Leadership for the People of God (11:23–28)

PERSONAL CONVICTIONS CAN GIVE a normal person the strength to act heroically. Some examples might illustrate the point. For instance, I once witnessed a man hitting a woman in a car and was compelled to get him to leave her alone. I expected that he might attack me for interfering, but it was more important to help someone being brutalized. At our neighborhood grocery store, an elderly woman who worked there was accosted as she left work one day. The assailant took her purse and knocked her down. Some man ran after the purse snatcher, risking his own life to retrieve the woman's possessions.

Every day, perhaps not in these dramatic ways, we are forced to decide whether we have the strength of our convictions to help someone who is oppressed, abused, and victimized. We don't know how things will work out. But we have to act by faith, believing that we are doing the right thing and that our actions outweigh whatever danger or difficulty we might face.

Moses is another example of someone whose life was characterized by faith according to chapter 11 of Hebrews. Moses gets four occurrences in chapter 11 of the expression "by faith." How Moses was protected as an infant was an act of faith (11:23). He acted in faith when as a young man he chose to side with his Hebrew kinsmen (11:24–26). Moses displayed faith in God when he left Egypt for a time to tend sheep in Midian until God was ready for him to be a shepherd to lead the Israelites out of Egypt (11:27). Finally, Moses faithfully kept Passover with the Israelites and protected them from experiencing the death of the firstborn in the tenth plague on Egypt (11:28).

For us to be people of faith, we should learn these four lessons from Moses' actions: Do what's right in spite of retribution (11:23); choose reproach that brings rewards (11:24–26); withstand the rage of others for

Moses: Faithful Leadership for the People of God (11:23-28)

the sake of what's real (11:27); and do what's "rite" to provide release from bondage (11:28).

DO WHAT'S RIGHT IN SPITE OF RETRIBUTION (11:23)

Hebrews 11:23 transports us to the beginning of the book of Exodus. The Hebrew people have been flourishing in Egypt, though they have become an enslaved group, put to work on the building projects of the pharaoh (Exod 1:7-11). In spite of Pharaoh's attempts to decrease the population of the Israelites living in his land, they continue to multiply at an alarming rate (Exod 1:12). The Egyptians increase the amount of work given to the Hebrew people and become even more ruthless (Exod 1:13-14).

Pharaoh's Plan A is a long-range strategy to decrease the male population of the Hebrews by having them killed as they are born (Exod 1:15-16). But when the Egyptian midwives are instructed to kill any baby boys born to a Hebrew woman, they refuse to do so because they fear God (Exod 1:17). They make up an excuse and tell Pharaoh that the Hebrew women experience a shorter period of labor, which doesn't allow the midwives to arrive in time to take the baby boys and kill them (Exod 1:18-19). God, therefore, rewards the midwives with families of their own (Exod 1:20-21).

Pharaoh falls back on Plan B: He orders his people to engage in the infanticide of Hebrew baby boys. They are commanded to throw every male child into the Nile, presumably to be drowned or eaten by crocodiles (Exod 1:22). We might surmise that the daughters born to Hebrew parents are preserved so that they might function as servants for Egyptian families.

It was at that time that a couple, both from the tribe of Levi, have a baby boy (Exod 2:1). The Hebrew Bible says that the couple saw that the baby was *tov*, "good" (Exod 2:2). The text of Hebrews (11:23) follows the Greek translation of Exodus, "they saw that he was handsome."

They keep their baby under wraps for the next three months (Exod 2:2). Although Hebrews 11:23 seems to imply that it was the parents who were not afraid of the edict of the king, the context of the story in Exodus points more toward the action of the midwives: "But the midwives feared God; they did not do as the king of Egypt commanded them, but they let the boys live" (Exod 1:17). It was a joint effort on the part of the Hebrew midwives and the family of this baby boy to do what was right even though it could mean retribution from Pharaoh.

Section Six: Examples and Exhortations to Faithful Living

People have been faced with this dilemma throughout human history. What are we willing to do to help those who are oppressed even though it might mean we receive punishment? Jews under the Nazi regime were protected by families who feared God more than they feared Hitler's soldiers. Families along the underground railroad hid runaway slaves because they believed all humans deserved life and liberty. People now do such things as take in abused women and their children, risking their own lives in some cases, because they believe that no one should be subject to enslavement and abuse.

We show ourselves faithful to God when we determine to do what's right in spite of the consequences. It may mean that a young person sticks up for someone who's being bullied at school because they are different in some way. It may mean that we join with those at our jobs who are mistreated because of sexism or ageism. Living by faith means valuing the sanctity of life, not just for a fetus, but for human beings of every race, every religion, every region of our own country and the world.

CHOOSE REPROACH THAT BRINGS REWARDS (11:24–26)

We remember the story of how this Hebrew boy is placed in a water-proof basket in the Nile (Exod 2:3). Apparently, his mother chooses the spot where the Egyptian princess will discover the baby. Sure enough, the boy is rescued and taken into the care of Pharaoh's household (Exod 2:4–6). He is given the name Moses to recall his having been drawn from the water (Exod 2:10). The cleverness of the plot is complete when the boy's own mother is asked to be the wet-nurse for the infant (Exod 2:7–9).

The story in Exodus jumps ahead to Moses as a young man (Exod 2:11ff). He witnesses an Egyptian guard whipping a Hebrew, someone of his own race. At that point, he chooses to side with the oppressed of his own kind rather than with the wealth and privilege he enjoyed as an Egyptian-raised man in the king's court (11:25). He looks around to make sure there are no other Egyptians watching and kills the guard, burying his body in the sand to cover up his deed (Exod 2:12). Word gets out, however, and Moses becomes a marked man, fleeing into the desert away from Pharaoh's soldiers (Exod 2:14–15).

The text of Hebrews indicates that Moses chose to share in the afflictions of his own people rather than in the transient indulgence of sinful pleasure (11:25). The author of Hebrews represents his own ethnic preju-

Moses: Faithful Leadership for the People of God (11:23-28)

dice by characterizing the lifestyle of another culture as decadent. Here it is a metaphorical device by which Egyptian life with its monuments and golden, jewel encrusted objects represent the life given to extravagance and pleasure.

In verse 26 Hebrews again interprets the action of a biblical figure to have been done because of foresight. Abraham looked forward to a heavenly city (11:16). Isaac and Jacob anticipated the blessing of God on the Hebrew people (11:20-21). Joseph prophesied the return of the people to the Promised Land (11:22; Gen 50:24). In Heb 11:26 Moses values the future messianic reproach more highly than the present Egyptian treasure. Moses is looking ahead to the future and the heavenly or eschatological reward that is to come to the people of God.

When we side with the oppressed or abused, we take on ourselves the stigma that applies to those people. We take up their cause and sometimes risk our own livelihoods or even our own lives. The Garden of the Righteous Among the Nations at the holocaust memorial Yad Vashem in Jerusalem, as of January 2007, lists 21,758 non-Jews who risked their lives to help Jews during the Holocaust. Many whites in the early nineteenth century helped in the formation of an "underground railroad" to assist runaway slaves to make it to freedom in the North and Canada. In a letter dated 1786, George Washington comments on Quakers in Philadelphia, who were attempting to liberate a slave, saying that they were "acting repugnant to justice." Many more cases could be cited where one group of people helped another and thereby took upon themselves the opprobrium of that group.

People today who fight for the rights of gay and lesbian people to hold jobs, find housing, and live securely in neighborhoods, bear people's scorn. At times they are said to promote homosexuality or that they must be gay themselves. Most recently we are experiencing a time in which people are suspicious and even vengeful toward Arab-looking people, those who look like they might be Muslims. What would we do if a Muslim family moved into our neighborhood?

It is the faithful person who chooses to accept the reproach of the oppressed. We believe that God rewards those in the future who treat people right in the present. It may mean a loss of friendships, a loss of status among our peers, or even the loss of income if we are fired for standing up for marginalized people. We must be willing to accept that loss and reproach, believing that God's reward for doing good is better than what we gain by choosing worldly goods in contradiction to our principles.

Section Six: Examples and Exhortations to Faithful Living

WITHSTAND RAGE FOR WHAT IS REAL (11:27)

Verse 27 resumes the story of Moses. After the incident in which Moses killed an Egyptian, Moses leaves Egypt, having heard that Pharaoh wants to kill him. It might sound to us like Moses flees from Egypt because he is afraid of the anger of the king of Egypt. But that's not how the author of Hebrews sees it: Moses was "unafraid of the king's anger" (11:27). Moses takes up residence in the land of Midian, that area we now call the Sinai Peninsula (Exod 2:15). There he meets a priest of Midian, the father of seven daughters. Moses comes to the defense of the sisters and helps them water their flocks (Exod 2:16–17). Eventually Moses marries one of them, Zipporah, and together they raise a son named Gershom (Exod 2:21–22). After many years Pharaoh dies and the Israelites are said to groan and cry out to God because of the length and severity of their enslavement in Egypt (Exod 2:23–25).

Moses is living as a shepherd in Midian and one day takes his flock to Horeb, the place called "the mountain of God" (Exod 3:1). There Moses sees the burning bush and hears the voice of God (Exod 3:2–5). Yahweh there reaffirms his covenant with the Israelites and chooses Moses to be the one to lead them out of bondage and back to the land God promised them (Exod 3:6–10).

Perhaps this is what Hebrews has in mind when it says that Moses "persevered as though he saw him who is invisible" (11:27). Perhaps what this text means is that Moses survived his encounter with the divine. He sees the invisible God (Rom 1:20; Col 1:15; 1 Tim 1:17) in the flames of the burning bush, hears God's voice calling him, and Moses lives to tell about it. The Hebrew people worshipped a God who was not represented in figures of stone like the Egyptian god Anubis, portrayed in hieroglyphics like the sun god Ra, or painted on papyrus like the falcon-headed god Horus. The Hebrew people worshipped an invisible God. Yet, God had shown himself through the angel of the Lord and now appeared in this theophany of a burning bush. Moses' faith was bolstered, and he agreed to represent God to the new pharaoh and lead his people to freedom.

Although Moses had fled from Egypt to Midian, Hebrews regards Moses' actions to be prompted by faith. Perhaps a fearful person would have just given themselves up to a pharaoh. An adherent of Egyptian religion would have considered it useless to run away from a divine figure

Moses: Faithful Leadership for the People of God (11:23-28)

like a pharaoh. Yet Moses leaves the Egyptian king behind and preserves his life to meet Pharaoh another day.

We can imagine the situation in which people take on an unpopular cause. Think of situations in which the Ku Klux Klan would target families who tried to help their black neighbors by burning crosses on their lawns. People might feel the need to move away to a new home where they might find safety.

In a fictionalized story ("North Fork," *Have Gun, Will Travel*, aired June 21, 1959), a young woman in the frontier days of the old American west, stood up for the Mennonite families who had settled in their town. They were ostracized for the way they dressed and spoke. They were made fun of because they were peaceful people and refused to fight against neighboring Native American Indians. After the local men had burned much of their crops, the Mennonite group decided they would have to move to a new location. The young woman was willing to associate with them and even to leave her home to settle in a new area with the Mennonites.

When we identify ourselves with those who are oppressed, we must be prepared to encounter the rage of those whose hatred is sparked by bigotry. We might discover that we are no longer safe in our own neighborhoods. Like Moses, we might be forced to leave the place we know. Moses acted in faith, and God came to him at last. Leadership like Moses' is born out of the heat of battle, but the fire of God's presence inspires us to do the work God calls us to.

DO THE "RITE THING" TO PROVIDE THE RELEASE FROM BONDAGE (11:28)

The author of Hebrews ignores the Exodus account in which Moses shows a lack of faith. What we hear Moses saying is, "Who am I to talk to Pharaoh? What if the Israelites don't listen to me?" Then Moses says in effect, "I cain't talk too good." In the words of Exod 4:13, "Please send someone else." What Hebrews remembers is that Moses did return to Egypt with his brother Aaron, convinced the Israelites to follow him out of Egypt, and finally wore down the will of Pharaoh after 10 plagues to let God's people go.

The Israelites observe a ritual that Jews continue to practice today called Pesach or Passover. Homes are ceremonially cleaned of all leaven in a seven-day preparation period in which no work is allowed. Families join together to eat roasted lamb with unleavened bread and other garnishment.

When the institution of Passover began in Egypt, the blood of the lamb was splashed upon the sides and tops of the doorways of the Israelites' homes. When the destroyer, the death angel, came to each house, the angel would pass over those homes with the blood upon the door. But when the destroyer came to the Egyptian homes without the sign of the blood, the death angel would put to death the firstborn male offspring, human and animal. The book of Exodus reports that every Egyptian house experienced death that night. But no Israelite house that observed the ritual lost a firstborn.

How are we to understand the action of God against the Egyptians? Pharaoh was evil to conduct the infanticide that wiped out the Hebrew male babies. Should not we be repulsed by the action that would lead to every Egyptian household losing the male firstborn? There is no getting around the fact that Exod 12:29 says, "At midnight the LORD struck down all the firstborn in the land of Egypt." It is tempting to look for something in the story that might explain how the Egyptians had deaths in their families and the Israelites didn't. Perhaps we could invent an explanation that has some disease blamed for the death of newborns among the Egyptians but Israelites are protected because of the seven days in which they ate unleavened bread and roasted their lamb on the night of Passover. Ultimately, we have to accept that we don't know how to reconcile the cruelty depicted in our biblical stories that come to us from antiquity. We do know that it is not our place to be the avenging angel of God on any other person or groups of people.

It must take faith to carry out a ritual that is expected to save people's lives. What would we think if we were told that to be safe in our homes we should dash some blood on our doorways? We might compare it to someone superstitiously wearing garlic around their neck to protect them from a vampire coming at night to suck their blood. In the case of the Passover, the people's faith was rewarded with safety. Passover continues to be a reminder of God's redemption from enslavement.

Whatever God calls us to do, we must do in faith. It could mean the preservation of life or even the salvation of souls. We may not be able to see how what God calls us to do is going to work. That's the nature of faith: To do what God says even though you can't see what God does.

Moses: Faithful Leadership for the People of God (11:23–28)

Will we be people of faith? Will we do what's right in spite of retribution; choose reproach that brings rewards; withstand the rage of others for the sake of what's real; and do what's "rite" to provide release from bondage. For many people, their practice is just the opposite. They would have us keep a low profile, protect what's yours, look the other way when someone else is in danger.

When I rode the subway in DC, it seemed like most people who traveled alone either watched the scenery out the window, read something, or stared at the floor. Everyone seemed to avoid making eye contact. Even when a strange looking guy acted weird and menacing, people ignored him and left him alone. When another man at the back of the car talked loudly on his cell phone and continually swore at his girlfriend or wife, no one looked back there to see what was happening.

A cute little African-American girl noticed me and blew me a kiss. She tried to get away from her mother and even started to reach her arms out to me. I made the mistake of noticing her and responding with a smile. Then I met her father's eyes and something told me: look out the window, read a book, stare at the floor. The little girl didn't know any better. I didn't know any better than she. We both were innocently connecting as two humans. Society wants to teach us to behave like those who have been hardened by city life. Although we might encounter negative consequences for our interests in the well-being of others, let us be people who live by faith just like Moses.

Israelites, Joshua, and Rahab: Faith Brings Us Through (11:29–31)

WE OFTEN THINK THE obstacles we face in life are more than we are going to be able to handle. No one else has to do what we have to do. As big as our problems may seem, there are those who have faced tougher obstacles than we.

A common theme in superhero stories is for the superhero to hide from a mate what he or she does during the day. That evening, when the couple is sharing what happened that day, the spouse of the superhero goes on and on about the most mundane and petty problems. The superhero, being the kind and generous person he or she is, listens patiently while trying to move around without letting the spouse know that he or she has broken ribs and bullet wounds.

The people who appear next in Hebrews 11's list of heroes of faith are ones who experienced extreme tests of faith. From the story of Moses and the Passover experience in Egypt, Hebrews proceeds to the next event, the departure from Egypt and the crossing of the Red Sea. Hebrews then fast forwards to the end of the story of the wandering in the wilderness and the beginning of Joshua's leading of the Israelites into the Promised Land. The walls of Jericho stand in the way between them and their resettling of the land. Finally, Hebrews backs up to catch the story of Rahab who protected the spies who had been sent to scout out the land for General Joshua.

Through the example of these people of faith, Hebrews teaches us that faith can take us through obstacles (11:29), it can break down barriers (11:30), and it can preserve us from destruction (11:31).

FAITH CAN TAKE US THROUGH OBSTACLES (11:29)

The author of Hebrews continues the story from Exodus. After the tenth plague and the death of the firstborn of human and animal alike, Pharaoh

Israelites, Joshua, and Rahab: Faith Brings Us Through (11:29-31)

once again, and for the last time, relents and tells Moses to take the Israelites into the wilderness to worship.

> Rise up, go away from my people, both you and the Israelites! Go, worship the LORD, as you said. Take your flocks and your herds, as you said, and be gone. And bring a blessing on me too! (Exod 12:31-32)

The Egyptians welcome their departure and are even willing to pay them to go with gold, silver jewelry, and clothing (Exod 12:35-36). The Israelites head for home, so to speak. Get while the getting's good.

The first obstacle they encounter is the area that separates the African continent from the Arabian peninsula, what is known as the Great Rift Valley. This rift system is connected by several bodies of water. It extends from the Red Sea to the west through the Gulf of Suez, several small lakes, into the Suez Canal, and finally dumps into the Mediterranean Sea. No one really knows where the Israelites crossed to begin the journey to the Promised Land.

The Hebrew Bible's term for the large body of water we call the Red Sea is literally the "Sea of Reeds." It's only a coincidence that Reed Sea and Red Sea are similar in English. All of the Greek texts, from ancient Greek historians like Herodotus and Strabo to our ancient Greek Bibles containing the Greek translation of the Old Testament and the New Testament, call this the Red Sea. The name apparently arises from the reddish-brown color produced by algae blooming in the Red Sea during the summertime.

God tells Moses to put into action a maneuver intended to draw the attacking Egyptian army to them (Exod 14:1-2). The Israelites set up camp and wait for Pharaoh to fall into their trap (Exod 14:9). As Pharaoh and his infantry approach, the Israelites call out to God in fear. They are the ones who seem to be trapped between the looming threat of military action and a body of water blocking their escape (Exod 14:10). Upon the instructions from God, Moses stretches out his hand and a strong east wind blows all night long, driving back the water and creating a dry path for the people to cross (Exod 14:21-22). The Egyptians pursue the Israelites (Exod 14:23) only to have the water return and drown the entire army (Exod 14:28).

The author of Hebrews interprets this story as an act of faith on the part of the Israelites. They trusted God, believing that they could pass safely through the parted water. The counter-example is the Egyptians.

Section Six: Examples and Exhortations to Faithful Living

They did not believe in the God of the Israelites and, therefore, their attempt was not met with success.

Surmounting obstacles takes a vision for what might be possible. Physical obstacles like bodies of water have been crossed over and tunneled under. Those who have created those bridges and tunnels have been people of vision. Their efforts have connected people together allowing them to pass through that huge obstacle that has divided groups of people and prevented them from working together.

Many people live in an area where they rely on bridges and tunnels to get them where they're going each day. For several years I lived in southeastern Massachusetts and commuted to Middletown, Rhode Island near Newport. If it weren't for the bridges, I wouldn't have been able to make that trip. While living there, I learned about the Quakers who settled in the Newport area. One of the oldest Quaker meetinghouses still exists in Newport. George Fox describes how he and his companions waited "for a wind to carry us to Rhode Island."[1] Friends from Massachusetts had to travel by boat in order to attend the annual meeting in Newport, Rhode Island. It eventually led to a separation of those groups as more and more Quakers settled in southeastern Massachusetts.

There were some days that I wished the bridges weren't there, so I wouldn't have to go to work. But the connections that bridges make provide many more people with the opportunity to live their lives. There are many other types of bridges we try to build to enable us to overcome obstacles, obstacles not just of geography but also of culture.

In 2004 a footbridge was completed connecting Strasbourg, France with Kehl, Germany. Not only does the bridge cross the Rhine, it crosses the borders of nations which have often been at odds with each other. In the middle of the bridge, there is an area where people from the two nations can meet each other halfway to sit, talk, and relax.

I'm reminded of an example in which Quakers have sought to build a much larger bridge, metaphorically speaking. New England Yearly Meeting of Friends has organized what they call *Puente de Amigos* (Bridge of Friends). This bridge is intended to cross a huge obstacle that is much more than just a body of water—but it is that too. Quakers in Cuba have been isolated from the rest of the world and through this program Friends visit Cuba and Friends from Cuba are brought to the States.

1. Fox, "Journal," in *Works*, vol. 2, 125. Accessed April 15, 2008. Online: http://dqc.esr.earlham.edu/toc/E12877488B-000.

Israelites, Joshua, and Rahab: Faith Brings Us Through (11:29-31)

These are examples of the sorts of bridges we need to construct. But these bridges take a sense of vision of what we can do in our world to overcome the many obstacles we face. Many people live in fear around the world. They feel as though they are between the proverbial rock and a hard place. The evils of violence, poverty, famine, and disease are terrorizing people each day. They cry out to God for a way to make it through the obstacles that endanger their very existence. Our obstacles seem just as insurmountable and give us as great a cause for fear. Even though the obstacles seem impassable and survival seems impossible, God is able to rescue us and provide us with a way.

FAITH CAN BREAK DOWN THE BARRIERS (11:30)

For the author of Hebrews, who has been tracing the faith history of the Hebrew people, it is necessary to leap forward from the story of the Red Sea crossing to the events related to the entering of the Promised Land as told in the book of Joshua in order to continue to recite the examples of faith. Hebrews, in fact, jumps ahead to Joshua six, and then in verse 31 will move backward in the text of Joshua to recall the previous incident with Rahab.

Following the dismal disobedience that characterized the 40 years of wandering in the wilderness and ultimately the death of Moses preceding the entry of the Israelites into the Promised Land, the people are now on the verge of crossing the Jordan and settling back into the land that Jacob and his families had left over 450 years before (Exod 12:40; Josh 5:6). Joshua is now the new leader of the people, who await his instructions to cross the Jordan. God gives Joshua his marching orders and encourages him repeatedly to "be strong and courageous" (Josh 1:6, 7, 9). Joshua relays the orders to the people, and they respond with words that must have given Joshua cause for alarm, "Just as we obeyed Moses in all things, so we will obey you" (Josh 1:17). Frequently, the Israelites did not listen to Moses or obey him (Exod 16:20; Deut 8:20; Josh 5:6).

For the moment, we skip over the events preceding the crossing of the Jordan and entrance to the Promised Land. We will return to the story of Joshua sending scouts ahead to scope out the current inhabitants and the strength of their armies and fortifications.

After the Israelites miraculously pass through the parted waters of the Jordan River (Josh 3:1-17), Joshua leads the people to the walled city

Section Six: Examples and Exhortations to Faithful Living

of Jericho. The city of Jericho was completely shut up with no one entering and no one leaving (Josh 6:1). Yahweh tells Joshua that the city is to be conquered (Josh 6:2). Here's the plan: Joshua's army is to march around the city once a day with seven priests blasting on seven trumpets made of ram's horns (*shofar*). "Shofar" so good. Then on the seventh day march around the city seven times with the priests blasting on the ram's horns. Finally, the priests give a long blast, the people shout, and then look out. As the song says, "the walls come tumbling down."

What happens next is not a proud moment in biblical history. The Israelites execute every man, woman, and child in Jericho (Josh 6:21), everyone except for Rahab and her family (Josh 6:17, 22–23). The city was then sacked and burned (Josh 6:24). Hebrews summarizes the experience of the Israelites in simple terms. It was an act of their faith in God's leading that led to the walls of Jericho coming down.

Rather than breaking down walls in order to commit violence, let's think about how we tear down walls to bring about peace. In the mid to late 80s, I was trying to learn to read German. I remember reading about the reunification of eastern and western Germany. One of my sentences—and my favorite example of a long German word—was, "Das Wiedervereinigungsproblem steht hinter der ganzen Außenpolitik Europas."[2] This "reunification problem" was considered by most people to be unsolvable. The Berlin Wall stood as a barrier between East Berlin with the communist bloc and the freedom of the west.

I can remember hearing those now famous words in 1987 when Pres. Reagan at the Brandenburg Gate challenged the repression symbolized in the Berlin Wall, "General Secretary Gorbachev, if you seek peace, if you seek prosperity for the Soviet Union and Eastern Europe, if you seek liberalization: Come here to this gate! Mr. Gorbachev, open this gate! Mr. Gorbachev, tear down this wall."[3]

We now live in a period when no one holds much hope for peace in the Middle East. The Israelites tore down a wall to kill the local inhabitants, and now modern Israelis have built a wall—ostensibly for their protection—which is again leading to the destruction of the local inhabitants. There is no simple solution to this age-old problem. But if by faith the walls of Jericho fell, surely by faith we can break down the barrier that

2. Sandberg and Wendel, *German for Reading*, 24.

3. Rondald Reagan, "Tear Down This Wall," Accessed: April 15, 2008. Online: http://usinfo.state.gov/infousa/government/overview/reagan06_12_87.html.

Israelites, Joshua, and Rahab: Faith Brings Us Through (11:29-31)

now exists between the Israelis and Palestinians, between Jews, Muslims, and the Palestinian Christians.

Faith can break down the barriers that prevent us from fulfilling God's calling. Everyday barriers keep us from experiencing the best that God has for us. When we identify those seemingly impermeable walls of Jericho, we need to hear the voice of God that tells us the victory is already ours. It may take some time, maybe more than the week it did at Jericho. But God will break down the walls that defeat us and lead us on to the joy and peace that characterize the mature Christian life.

FAITH CAN PRESERVE US FROM DESTRUCTION (11:31)

Before the Israelites crossed the Jordan, entered the Promised Land, and attacked the city of Jericho, Joshua sends two young men to scout out the territory, especially the city of Jericho (Josh 2:1). These spies manage to infiltrate the city and locate the house of a prostitute named Rahab where they spend the night. Somehow the king of Jericho learns that spies are in the city (Josh 2:2). Why he assumes they are at Rahab's house, we aren't told. The king tells Rahab to turn over the men (Josh 2:3). She admits that they had been at her "best little whorehouse" in Jericho, but claims they had already gone (Josh 2:4-5). The truth is Rahab had hidden the men on her roof beneath stalks of flax. She comes to them and wants them to return the favor by protecting her and her relatives when Jericho is taken.

> I know that the LORD has given you the land, and that dread of you has fallen on us, and that all the inhabitants of the land melt in fear before you. For we have heard how the LORD dried up the water of the Red Sea before you when you came out of Egypt, and what you did to the two kings of the Amorites that were beyond the Jordan, to Sihon and Og, whom you utterly destroyed. As soon as we heard it, our hearts melted, and there was no courage left in any of us because of you. The LORD your God is indeed God in heaven above and on earth below. Now then, since I have dealt kindly with you, swear to me by the LORD that you in turn will deal kindly with my family. Give me a sign of good faith that you will spare my father and mother, my brothers and sisters, and all who belong to them, and deliver our lives from death. (Josh 2:9-13)

The spies reply to her, "We will deal kindly and faithfully with you when the LORD gives us the land" (Joshua 2:14). Rahab is to hang a crimson cord from the window of their home, which was part of the city wall

(Josh 2:15). As we have already seen, Rahab and her relatives are spared when Jericho is destroyed. The book of Joshua makes the statement, "Her family has lived in Israel ever since" (Josh 6:25).

Jewish legend says that Rahab was one of the four most beautiful women who have ever lived, became Joshua's wife, and from them descended eight of Israel's prophets (*b. Meg.* 14b–15a). In the New Testament Rahab is listed as married to Salmon, the father of Boaz and so she appears in the lineage of Jesus (Matt 1:5). The New Testament book of James says of her, "Likewise, was not Rahab the prostitute also justified by works when she welcomed the messengers and sent them out by another road?" (James 2:25).

In Heb 11, Rahab is possibly the only woman from the Old Testament who is designated as acting "by faith,"—the other being Sarah (some translations regard the subject of 11:11 to be Sarah rather than Abraham). Nothing is said in Hebrews regarding her designation as a prostitute. More significant than the fact that she was a woman and a prostitute is that she was not a Jew. This righteous Gentile was spared because of her actions, even though her actions involved her in a lie. Rahab acted in faith believing that God was behind the movement of this group of people to that land and she showed hospitality and safety to those whom she regarded as God's people.

The comparison is often made between Rahab's actions and those of Corrie ten Boom described in her book *The Hiding Place*. Corrie and the ten Boom family hid Jews from the Nazi's and lied about their presence in their home. God miraculously preserved their lives in spite of the great danger they were in. Her sister Betsy, however, did lose her life. That stands as a reminder that God may preserve us in times of difficulty, but God may also call us to the ultimate sacrifice on behalf of others.

The effect of the example of Rahab is to put us to shame. Surely if someone in her situation is bold enough and faithful enough to choose the side of God in a little matter of hiding someone under the covers, we can be brave enough to exhibit faith in our lives. As insignificant as we are, in the big scheme of things, God can use us in ways that can get our names listed in the Faith Hall of Fame.

Israelites, Joshua, and Rahab: Faith Brings Us Through (11:29-31)

What will be our experience? Will we discover that faith can take us through obstacles? Will we trust that doing God's will can result in the breaking down of barriers? Will we be so bold as to believe that faithful actions can preserve us from destruction?

Most of us are not superheroes and most of us don't encounter such tremendous obstacles, formidable barriers, and life-threatening decisions. But if faith can help those people in those situations, surely it can help us with our everyday hindrance, the typical thing that tries to trip us up, and the ordinary choices we have to make each day. Who knows what bridges we might be able to build, walls that we might tear down, and lives we might protect? The superhero costume we wear each day is emblazoned with the words "By Faith."

The Sordid and Unsorted
People of Faith (11:32–40)

FOR MANY AMERICANS, LIFE has been rather normal during the years that our country has been involved in Afghanistan and Iraq. If you let a few days pass without watching or reading the news, you might forget the millions of dollars being spent and the hundreds of lives being lost. While listening to old radio programs from the 40's, I've become more aware of the daily sacrifices people were making in their homes and places of work each day during a time of war. Women were collecting fat from cooking and bringing it to their local butcher for collection to be used for military purposes. People were asked not to be wasteful in their consumption of food and energy. Everyday, people were making everyday sorts of sacrifices for the national good to accomplish what they considered to be a noble purpose. Many Americans felt it a Christian duty to participate in the war effort in whatever way they could. Now these same people and the children who grew up in those households are confused, hurt, and angered by those who don't see our national interests being served through military action. Some religious people, however, can't imagine how anyone could be a committed Christian and be committed to the military.

This section of Hebrews reminds us that much of biblical history involved war, either in fighting for something or enduring the military attacks of others. After spending what amounts to about 30 verses in which Hebrews has traced the history of faithful people from the creation of the world to the conquest of the Promised Land—Genesis through Joshua—the author now seems to feel the need to summarize the rest. It's like a student writing a term paper, who suddenly concludes within a few paragraphs because he or she has almost reached the page limit. In the remaining verses of this section of Hebrews, the author shows two sides of faith. First, how faith is expressed through military action (11:32–34) and, second, how faith is experienced in response to military aggression

The Sordid and Unsorted People of Faith (11:32-40)

(11:35-38). The author concludes with the way in which the faithful enjoy the culmination of God's promise together (11:39-40).

FAITH EXPRESSED THROUGH MILITARY ACTION (11:32-34)

What is most notable about the group of people given in this section and the type of activities Hebrews lists is the military context. For instance, Barak, Gideon, Jephthah, and Samson are all military figures. These heroes of the faith are all too human: their failings are as much a part of the Biblical story as are their triumphs. Hebrews begins this closing section with, "And what more should I say? For time would fail me to tell . . ." (11:32). Today someone giving a speech might wrap up with, "What else can I say?" or "My time is running out; just let me add . . ." This is as much an understatement as the closing statement at the end of Hebrews, "For I have written to you briefly" (13:22).

First, the author lists a group of individuals by name. Why he chose these names and not others (Deborah or Eli, for example), there's no way to know. Why he put them in the order he did is also a mystery. Anyone who knows their Bible history can see that the names are not exactly in chronological order.

The historical sequence would be Barak (Judg 4-5), Gideon (Judg 6-8), Jephthah (Judg 11-12), Samson (Judg 13-16), Samuel (1 Sam 1), and then David (1 Sam 16). What we notice is, these names form pairs and each pair is switched from its chronological sequence.

TEXT	PAIR ONE		PAIR TWO		PAIR THREE	
Hebrews 11	Gideon	Barak	Samson	Jephthah	David	Samuel
Old Testament	Barak	Gideon	Jephthah	Samson	Samuel	David

The first two pairs are judges. Judges were leaders who functioned as arbiters in civil disputes and as commanders in military expeditions. The faithlessness of the Israelites was punished by God through oppressing nations. Israelite repentance was rewarded with the raising up of a judge who would lead them to victory and freedom. Hebrews skips over the first judges (Othniel, Ehud, and Shamgar) and begins with Gideon and Barak. We'll look at these individuals in their chronological order.

We begin then with the second person in the first pair, Barak (Judg 4-5). He was a military leader appointed by Deborah (Judg 4:6). Judges calls her a prophetess and describes her as also judging Israel (Judg 4:4–5). Barak was successful in battle against the Canaanites, but it's difficult to understand why Hebrews would choose him as a hero of faith. He agreed to go to battle, but only if Deborah would go with him (Judg 4:8). The defeat of the opposing force's general, Sisera, was accomplished at the hand of a woman, Jael. She was the wife of Heber, the leader of the Kenite clan, who were allies of the Canaanites (Judg 4:17). When Sisera sought sanctuary in her tent, Jael covertly attacked Sisera by nailing his head to the ground with a tent peg (Judg 4:21; 5:26). It was the ancient equivalent of a woman killing an intruder with a rolling pin. The Canaanites are subdued, but Barak's reputation is tarnished by his reluctance to fight and by the enemy having been killed by a female civilian.

The next person chronologically is Gideon (Judg 6–8). The angel of the Lord called Gideon to be a judge in answer to the outcry of the Israelites because of the seven years of oppression from the Midianites (Judg 6:1–6). Gideon, like Barak, was also a reluctant servant of God (Judg 6:11–15). He first needed a miraculous sign from the angel of the Lord before he volunteered to be a judge (Judg 6:17–22). Gideon did obey God's instructions about tearing down an altar and sacred pole dedicated to Baal worship (Judg 6:25–26). But the text says he was too afraid to do it during the day, so he did it under the cover of darkness (Judg 6:27). When the townspeople learned that Gideon had done this, they went to his house to get him (Judg 6:28–29). It was his father Joash who came out to defend his son (Judg 6:31). Gideon earned the name Jerubbaal because he had acted against the pagan deity Baal (Judg 6:32).

Before going into battle, Gideon insisted that God should give him a sign, not once, but twice. The first sign was a fleece of wool was wet in the morning and the ground dry (Judg 6:36–38), and the second sign was that the next morning the fleece was dry and the ground was wet (Judg 6:39–40). Gideon obeyed the unconventional military actions God instructed him to do. His army was reduced from an initial 32,000 to 300, so the victory would be credited to God rather than the size of the army (Judg 7:2-7). The enemy was routed when Gideon and his army terrorized them in the middle of the night by suddenly shouting and revealing the light from their torches (Judg 7:15–23). In spite of Gideon's religious failing (he set up his own religious icon, Judg 8:24–27) and moral failings (his harem produced seventy sons, Judg 8:30), the Israelites did have forty years of peace following his victories over the Midianites (Judg 8:28).

The Sordid and Unsorted People of Faith (11:32-40)

A few more judges are skipped to arrive at the next pair, Samson and Jephthah. Jephthah, the first of the two chronologically, was an illegitimate son from a prostitute (Judg 11:1) and a renegade leader of a mercenary group of outlaws (Judg 11:3). When Israel needed a military commander to liberate them from the encroachment of surrounding nations, they turned to the guy they thought could get the job done (Judg 11:6-10). Jephthah attempted to sue for peace, arguing that God had given them the land they occupied (Judg 11:12-23). He reasons, "Should you not possess what your god Chemosh gives you to possess? And should we not be the ones to possess everything that the LORD our God has conquered for our benefit?" (Judg 11:24).

Before going to battle, Jephthah vows to God that he will give to God as a burnt offering whoever comes out the door of his house when he returns victorious (Judg 11:30-31). He delivers a massive defeat to the enemy (Judg 11:32-33) and returns home only to see his only child, his daughter, coming to greet him (Judg 11:34). In the end, Jephthah fulfills his vow (Judg 11:39).

A few more judges rule over Israel before we get to Samson (Judg 12:8-15). Samson was born to a couple who had not been able to have children (Judg 13:2-3). The angel of the Lord told Manoah and his wife that this child was to be the deliverer of the Israelites from the Philistines (Judg 13:4-5). Samson was to be a nazirite—we might say a devotee—from birth, which meant that he should never cut his hair (Judg 13:5).

In spite of the domination of the Philistines against Israel (Judg 13:1), Samson had a thing for Philistine women. When his first Philistine dalliance led to him being tricked (Judg 14:1-18), he responded by killing thirty men (Judg 14:19), then setting fire to the Philistines crops by tying torches to the tails of foxes (Judg 15:4-5), and finally killing a thousand Philistines by wielding the jawbone of a donkey (Judg 15:14-16). His next reported tryst was with a prostitute (Judg 16:1). He tore apart the gates of the city to avoid an ambush (Judg 16:2-3). His final affair was with the Philistine woman Delilah (Judg 16:4). She cooperated with the Philistine commanders and nagged Samson into finally revealing the secret to his great strength (Judg 16:5-17). His hair was cut, the Lord left him, and he was then made a mockery in his weakness (Judg 16:18-26). In a final act of retribution, God gave Samson the strength to pull down the pillars holding up a building killing himself and his molesters (Judg 16:27-30).

Section Six: Examples and Exhortations to Faithful Living

In that act, Samson was said to have killed more than all those he had killed previously.

To get to the next individual chronologically, Hebrews passes over Eli (he judged Israel forty years, according to 1 Sam 4:18) and goes directly to the next pair, David and Samuel. In the words of Heb 11:34, "time would fail me" to list the significant events and personal qualities of Samuel and David. Samuel functions like another Moses in the history of Israel, whose place in history is a turning-point from the period of judges to that of kings and prophets. Although Saul is the first to be anointed king by Samuel, David is the king of Israel *par excellence*. Hebrews tacks on to the end of this initial list the prophets, but doesn't bother to mention any of them by name, such as Elijah and Elisha.

In verses 33 and 34 Hebrews alludes to the accomplishments of Israel's military heroes with what seems to be three sets of three phrases. Since the three sets of two individuals are each given in reverse order, might we not expect the three sets of three also to be reversed? It's impossible to know because these phrases could refer to multiple events in Biblical history. The table below shows how this might work.

	First Triad		**Second Triad**		**Third Triad**	
	conquered kingdoms, administered justice, obtained promises		shut the mouths of lions, quenched raging fire, escaped the edge of the sword		won strength out of weakness, became mighty in war, put foreign armies to flight	
#3	*obtained promises*	Patriarchs	*escaped the edge of the sword*	David	*put foreign armies to flight*	Gideon
#2	*administered justice*	Judges	*quenched raging fire*	Daniel	*became mighty in war*	Jephthah
#1	*conquered kingdoms*	Kings	*shut the mouths of lions*	Daniel	*won strength out of weakness*	Samson

The first set, for instance, could be understood this way in reverse order. Those who aided Israel in the journey and conquest of the Promised Land could be those who "obtained promises." The judges could be said to have "administered justice." David and the kings of Israel and Judah were those who "conquered kingdoms."

The Sordid and Unsorted People of Faith (11:32–40)

The second set might also be read this way. One who is said to have "escaped the edge of the sword" is David. The Greek of the Old Testament in 2 Sam 15:14 uses the same expression as in Hebrews (the verb form and the Hebraism "mouth of the sword"). If the next two phrases refer to Daniel, then the order in Hebrews is reversed, since Daniel first escapes the fire of the furnace (Dan 3) and then the mouths of lions are shut (Dan 6).

The third triad is more difficult. I suggest that the reverse order refers to Gideon, who "put foreign armies to flight." Then the phrase "became mighty in war" refers to the judge listed previous to Gideon but who came after Gideon, Jephthah, of whom it was said he "was a mighty warrior" (Judg 11:1). The first phrase in the triad then applies to the one who follows Jephthah, which is Samson; he is the one who "won strength out of weakness."

What is significant about this group of heroes of faith is the preponderance of military accomplishment. Nearly all of them are soldiers. Hebrews says they carried out their calling "through faith." Most of these people seem to have had great difficulty believing God and their lives were marked by brutality and immorality. In spite of their great weaknesses, God still used them to accomplish what God willed.

Christians have been divided over the issue of war and military involvement. A stereotype of the American soldier as a godless brute and maniacal murderer has been reinforced through multiple war movies. In recent years, the stories in the news about the Iraq coalition have perpetuated the image of soldiers as barbaric and sadistic. Churches all over the country want to dispel that myth. They put forward as models of the American military the faithful Christian men and women from their churches who see volunteering for the military as a religious duty. Stephen Mansfield in *The Faith of the American Soldier* (Tarcher, 2005) attempts to show that side of the U.S. armed forces.

At the very least, we must give these people credit for their faithfulness to the calling of God. We need to resist the temptation to stereotype soldiers based on the actions and character of those whose crimes become headlines. We should honor the valor of those who go into harm's way with a Bible in their pack and Christ in their heart. Nevertheless, the lives of those who have been warriors for God in biblical history should also be a caution. Although these Bible heroes may have acted in faith, their lives as a whole have little to be admired. Do we really want our sons to grow up and be like the reluctant Barak, the self-serving Gideon, the child-murderer Jephthah, or the womanizing, Hulk-like enraged Samson? Their military actions may have been enacted through faith, but the sins in their lives have made them less than adequate models for Christian living.

FAITH EXPERIENCED IN RESPONSE TO MILITARY AGGRESSION (11:35–38)

Verses 35–38 change the perspective. The Bible portrays the Israelites during the time of the judges and the kings as being at war with the surrounding nations. Beginning with the period of the Babylonian exile, the return to Judea under the domination of the Persians, and the subsequent Hellenistic control, the Jewish people are a subjugated people. These verses in Hebrews mainly reflect a period described in Jewish literature absent from Protestant Bibles (which are based on the text of the Hebrew Bible) but present in the Bibles of the Roman Catholic and Eastern Orthodox churches (which are influenced by the texts of the ancient Greek Bible translations). Since the author of Hebrews is clearly quoting from the Greek Bible throughout Hebrews, it makes sense that for him these apocryphal or deutero-canonical stories are part of biblical history. The phrase in verse 35, "Women received their dead by resurrection" is often taken to refer to the experiences of the widow of Zarephath whose son is resuscitated by Elijah (1 Kgs 17:8–24) and the Shunamite woman whose son is brought back to life by Elisha (2 Kgs 4:11–37). It's also possible that this phrase is the beginning of allusions in this section of Hebrews to the experience of the Jewish people during the time of the Maccabean revolt, a few hundred years before Jesus. In a famous story found in the Maccabean literature, a mother and her seven sons along with the high priest Eleazar are tortured and then executed in an attempt to get them to defile themselves with a pagan sacrifice. In 2 Macc 7:23 she says about her seven sons who have been put to death, "Therefore the Creator of the world, who shaped the beginning of humankind and devised the origin of all things, will in his mercy give life and breath back to you again, since you now forget yourselves for the sake of his laws." The next phrase in verse 35 continues the allusion to this story. The Greek word "tortured" is a term meaning to be stretched on a drum, what we would call the rack. We get our word "tympani" from this Greek word, because the skin of the drum is stretched across the opening. The elderly Eleazar is tortured in this way. 2 Macc 6:27–28 describes his refusal to accept release,

The Sordid and Unsorted People of Faith (11:32-40)

"'Therefore, by bravely giving up my life now, I will show myself worthy of my old age and leave to the young a noble example of how to die a good death willingly and nobly for the revered and holy laws.' When he had said this, he went at once to the rack."

The experience of "mocking and flogging" in verse 36 is also described in the Maccabean literature: "It happened also that seven brothers and their mother were arrested and were being compelled by the king, under torture with whips and thongs, to partake of unlawful swine's flesh" (2 Macc 7:1; 4 Macc 6:3, 6; 9:12). Verse 37 describes the various methods carried out to execute those who were God's faithful. Because of their faithfulness, these people often dressed in simple clothing and had little means of support. They were persecuted and tormented, Hebrews says. They experienced homelessness, having to live away from cities and villages, finding places to live in caves and holes in the ground. These are the people who experienced military aggression and endured for the sake of their commitment to God.

There is another side to the way in which we remember our national history. We go to great lengths to remember those who died in battle. We have special cemeteries and national monuments for the war dead. When we learn history, we tend to focus on the wars that were fought and the generals that led them. We talk about the number of those soldiers who died in battle. We have numerous holidays in which we show patriotism by remembering those who fought and those who died fighting.

We also need to remember those who have made sacrifices and even have given their lives but who were non-combatants. We might be able to name of few of those, but the vast number are unsung heroes. Heroes of faith are also those who help bring about times in which nations can live at peace. Most Americans learn history by focusing on the times of war. But what name do we call the time of peace that exists between the times of war? Why does that time become unrecognized in national history? There are other incongruities. Why is there a Nobel Peace Prize but not a Congressional Medal of Honor for Peace? Why a Secretary of War and not a Secretary of Peace?

Christians will continue to experience the division between those who see themselves in the previous section of Hebrews and those who value the second. Others will say that this whole section of Hebrews points to a pornographic fascination humans have with violence and its consequences. We must hold out a better hope for humans that will bring us away from violence, suffering, and destitution. Wherever we find ourselves responding to God, may we be faithful to our calling like those who have gone before us.

CONCLUSION: THE FAITHFUL ENJOY THE CULMINATION OF GOD'S PROMISE (11:39–40)

The conclusion to this section refers back to the complete list of those in the heroes of Faith's Hall of Fame. The author of Hebrews wants to recognize that the people we read about in biblical history are people of faith. Yet, these people did not reach the culmination of God's plan for humanity. God had something more in mind and in the view of Hebrews, something better.

It's not only something better, but it's also something later. God wanted to include "us." They didn't reach what God promised because it wasn't time yet. God provided something better and later so that together God's people would experience the culmination and completion of God's good work.

I don't know if this happens to you. At our house a few people might starting watching a movie and stop half-way through. Later, when we are all together, the first group wants to finish watching the movie. But they have to wait while the other group watches the beginning of the movie and catches up. Then we all finish watching the movie together. The faithful of biblical history weren't allowed to get to the end of the unfolding drama of redemption. They have had to wait for us. It may mean "us" in this time period. It might actually refer to "us" as the Gentiles who, according to Christian thinking, now have been included in the people of God. We're still waiting for more people to join us. Paul described this in Romans, "So that you may not claim to be wiser than you are, brothers and sisters, I want you to understand this mystery: a hardening has come upon part of Israel, until the full number of the Gentiles has come in. And so all Israel will be saved" (Rom 11:25–26). The end of the movie is still to be seen. We still wait to see what God will do in our world. Meanwhile, we are called upon to be faithful people of God.

⸻

The models of faith from biblical history have been those whose faith has been expressed through military action as well as those who have expe-

The Sordid and Unsorted People of Faith (11:32-40)

rienced faith in response to military aggression. Those who have gone before us have been waiting for us, so that together the faithful will enjoy the culmination of God's promise together.

Many of us today have life so easy. Our biggest complaints are slow internet connections and dropped cell phone calls. Instead of being concerned about the ravages of war, we fuss about our aches and pains. Young people think their life is over if they don't get to go to Hollywood and be the next American Idol. It's no wonder people have such a hard time being people of faith. We have it much too easy to know what true suffering and endurance is about, the kind of experiences that develop people of strong faith and values. Some Christians feel they are fighting for an American way of life, a vision of democracy that allows people to be faithful to God and live according to Christian values. They see the current war on terror as a noble cause in the world. The conditions we face in our world today, however, are more a result of wrong ways of living than they are a lack of democracy enforced by a superpower. We would do better as Christians if we, as people of faith, devote ourselves together to a war on error in our own lives and in our own society, rather than support a war on terror elsewhere in the world. Nowhere in the rest of Hebrews will people of faith be called upon to take up arms for the sake of the kingdom. Rather, the message of Hebrews will be, "Pursue peace with everyone" (12:14).

The Race Is On (12:1–4)

For some people, life is a walk in the park. For others, it's a race to the finish. As much as we might value the imagery of a life that has frequent moments of "smelling the roses," the Bible depicts life more as a struggle to endure or as a race that we are to run well.

Elizabeth Mahr tells of her first marathon. She trained for four months to be able to compete in a 42.2 km marathon in Toronto. She arrived at dawn to begin at the earliest start time. She writes,

> It was still cold out. "I HATE running in the cold." I had three layers of clothing on. I was famous for overdressing for my runs—and this marathon day would be no exception.[1]

Her coaches urged her to lighten the three layers of clothes so she could perform better, but she resisted. The gun went off and she began the race. She realized after awhile that she had been reading the wrong distance-markers, which had thrown off her timing. Frustrated with herself, she set a new goal, not just to finish but to finish well. It was about this time that the Kenyan runners, who had started at the later start time, were now passing her. She describes her feelings as she watched them run.

> Five of them moving in perfect unison. So silent were they that had I closed my eyes for just one second, I would have missed them entirely! They were things of beauty—grace united with speed, sinew bound by silence. Godly creations, perfectly built running machines. Yet, for all their athletic prowess, they seemed to me the most tranquil of creatures. Zen monks. Mystic men.[2]

Although they were soon past her, she was encouraged by their presence in the race. It was an honor just to be running with them in the same race.

---

1. Elizabeth Mahr, "The Start is the Finish," Marathon Guide.com, Accessed March 26, 2008. Online: http://www.marathonguide.com/features/FMStories/ElizabethMahr.cfm.
2. Ibid.

The Race Is On (12:1-4)

> These men changed my course. I was headed in a new direction. "They are running gods." I thought. "And they are here for ME! They have come to take away the defeatist—that cynical demon responsible for my lousy start."[3]

However, after a few more kilometers she began to tire and negative thoughts began to fill her head. Then she saw her family.

> They were screaming and taking pictures, frantically waving signs. And I thought about them. Family—they are the other ones that helped make this happen. My husband who took care of the kids while I was out chasing my dream, my children who took care of my husband while I was out chasing my dream. Everyone working together. All for me.[4]

More people in the crowd began cheering for her. But the fatigue was setting in.

> My legs were really tired—my quads burning, knees throbbing. I kept my head down and just tried to run through the pain. I knew I had less than an hour to go but wondered "Can I keep it up? Would I really give up now?" Negative thoughts. Fold them up. Put them in a jar. Throw the jar out![5]

The spectators continued to cheer her on and she continued to make progress. Then it happened. She began to feel like she couldn't go on.

> "This is it." I thought. "I have hit the proverbial wall." I wasn't sure I could go on. The pain was there but worse, I was really thirsty. Dehydrated. I had failed to fill my water bottle up at the last station. Big mistake. I stared at the pavement just ahead. Keep going, I thought. I remembered the task analysis my coach, Richard once gave me on running: "Right ... Left ... Repeat."[6]

Finally she saw the 40 km marker. Just 2.2 km left in the race. She thought to herself, "It's almost over! I am almost there!" People were calling out to her, encouraging her, urging her on to the finish line. It helped her to find the energy to make it to the end.

---

3. Ibid.
4. Ibid.
5. Ibid.
6. Ibid.

Section Six: Examples and Exhortations to Faithful Living

> They were invested in me and applauded me forward. I waved to them. I waved to EVERYBODY. I have to admit, as far as race finishes go, I had definitely gone Hollywood. Well at least I didn't stop to pose. But I wasn't sure I was running anymore. I had been lifted—floating across the pavement now. I felt no fatigue. I felt no pain. "I must be going to heaven!" I thought.[7]

And then she saw it. The finish line.

> I did it! I finished the race! All that self-doubt, all that second-guessing, all washed away in one single moment of glory. I ran to the right side entrance, stepped across the mat and made darn sure the sensor picked up my running chip. I shot my arms in the air and whipped my head back in joy.[8]

For the author of Hebrews, the life of those who are faithful to God is more like a race than it is a walk in the park. Having concluded the listing of the examples of those from the Bible who are models of faith, Hebrews goes on to encourage his audience to live the faithful life. He calls on imagery from Greek culture that portrays the contest for the moral life in terms of athletic games. What follows then from chapter 11 is the author's exhortations to live the kind of life that leads to spiritual and moral maturity. Those who would be followers of Jesus should run the race with perseverance (12:1–2), remember the example of Jesus' endurance (12:3), and resist a defeatist attitude (12:4).

RUN THE RACE (12:1–2)

Everything that has gone before in Hebrews 11 leads up to this moment. With a strong transition in 12:1, the author of Hebrews says, "therefore." Men and women in the Bible from the earliest characters in Genesis through the more recent history of the rebuilding of the second temple and the struggle for Judean independence lived their lives "by faith." Hebrews says, "Therefore, so can you."

We've talked before about how the author of Hebrews acts like a coach giving a pep talk. Metaphorically speaking, the pep talk has traced the past history of the stars who have played on the team. It's like a homecoming game, and the past all-stars are there in the stands watching. The

---

7. Ibid.
8. Ibid.

The Race Is On (12:1-4)

coach reviews the highlights of the season, what the team's strengths and weaknesses are. The coach wants the team to do their best in the contest.

Hebrews describes the spiritual and moral life of the person of faith to be like an athletic contest. It is common among Greek authors to describe living the philosophical life—the pursuit of moral progress and the prize of achieving maturity through endurance—with the metaphor of the athletic competition. The people of faith from chapter 11 of Hebrews are imagined to be the spectators, a "great cloud of witnesses." They have run their race, and it is as though they are watching the next heats in the competition.

The author encourages his audience to remove any burden (*ogkos*) that might weigh them down and impede their performance. Philo uses the same word within a similar context.

> Let us then, with reference to our gratitude to and honouring of the omnipotent God, be active and ready, deprecating all sluggishness and delay; for those who are passing over from obedience to the passions to the contemplation of virtue, are enjoined to keep the passover with their loins girded up, being ready to do service, and binding up the burden (*ogkos*) of the flesh, or, as it is expressed, their shoes, "standing upright, and firmly on their feet, and having in their hands a Staff," that is to say education, with the object of succeeding without any failure in all the affairs of life; and lastly, "to eat the passover in haste." For, by the passover, is signified the crossing over of the created and perishable being to God:—and very appropriately; for there is no single good thing which does not belong to God, and which is not divine. (Philo, *On Sacrifice*, 1.63)

We understand the metaphor of lightening our burden before walking and running. For instance, the runner who has a bad habit of flailing the arms too much needs to overcome that error. The runner who runs flat-footed must learn to roll the foot forward and push off with the balls of his or her feet. Running a race and living the life of faith both require a person to strip away excess baggage and avoid the errors that cause defeat.

The main verb clause in these verses is "let us run." We are to persevere in the race that stretches in front of us. It is a test of endurance to keep a steady pace until we reach the goal. This race is a struggle. The Greek word here translated as "race" (*agōn*) is the word from which we get our English word "agony." Of course, this is not a race in the sense

Section Six: Examples and Exhortations to Faithful Living

of a competition for who can finish first. This contest is about how we compete in the contest, how well we endure the agony of the struggle.

Hebrews introduces Jesus to the scene. It would be common for the various athletic games in Greek society to revere those divinities who best represent the values of strength and endurance. For example, the Pythian Games at Delphi were associated with the Greek god Apollo. Hebrews pictures Jesus as the one who is the founder of this contest of faith and it is as though Jesus is sitting on a throne observing the race of the faithful. In the words of Hebrews, Jesus is the "pioneer and perfecter of our faith" (12:2). Jesus has set the example of what faithfulness is, and he is able to bring our faithfulness to its ultimate goal of spiritual and moral maturity.

Hebrews goes on to explain what Jesus did to be that example. Jesus focused on the goal of his mission and saw it as joy. He endured the suffering and shame of the cross and for that reason was exalted to heaven to sit at the right hand of the throne of God. Hebrews puts this in very human terms and in keeping with the Greek way of thinking about how a hero attains a divine status.

We've talked before about the way in which this can be compared to the Hellenistic Jewish text called Fourth Maccabees. In this story, the Syrian king Antiochus Epiphanes wants the Judeans to defile their altar by making pagan sacrifices. The elderly woman and her seven sons are tortured to death but do not do what the tyrant wants. The high priest Eleazar also refuses and is finally executed. The end of Fourth Maccabees describes the epitaph commemorating the struggle they endured. The language here is filled with the same athletic imagery as in Hebrews.

> "Here lie buried an aged priest and an aged woman and seven sons, because of the violence of the tyrant who wished to destroy the way of life of the Hebrews. They vindicated their nation, looking to God and enduring torture even to death." Truly the contest in which they were engaged was divine, for on that day virtue gave the awards and tested them for their endurance. The prize was immortality in endless life. Eleazar was the first contestant, the mother of the seven sons entered the competition, and the brothers contended. The tyrant was the antagonist, and the world and the human race were the spectators. Reverence for God was victor and gave the crown to its own athletes. Who did not admire the athletes of the divine legislation? Who were not amazed? The tyrant himself and all his council marveled at their endurance,

The Race Is On (12:1-4)

because of which they now stand before the divine throne and live the life of eternal blessedness. (4 Macc 17:9-18)

This is the language of Hebrews 12. For the author of Hebrews, this is his pep talk that builds on all that he has said so far. The people of the Bible ran their race and many were considered faithful. It's now our turn to run the race in the way Jesus did.

I can't help using the opportunity to talk about my own athletic prowess. It was half my life ago at a time when I was half my current weight that I played sports in high school and enjoyed running and cycling. I remember one time during basketball season that I wanted to lose a few pounds. I had seen the wrestlers run around in sweat suits and knew they were good at losing weight for matches. So I dressed up like a wrestler for basketball practice. My coach thought I was nuts. After an hour I took the sweats off—along with all the sweat—and continued practice in the typical t-shirt and shorts. What a relief to get rid of that extra weight and the close fitting clothes! I could run faster and jump higher, with the added benefit of not dripping all over the basketball court or becoming dehydrated.

During those last years of high school, I loved to run near my home. I lived on the edge of a small town near a large hill where motorcycles had developed paths off into the countryside. I would run along those paths that led through pine groves and wooded areas, past ponds and fields, up and down hills. A gravel road led up a hill to a spot where the local canning company would dump cherry pits in the summer. I sometimes ran sprints up the hill. I made it into a spiritual practice. I imagined that Jesus was at the top encouraging me on and the devil was chasing me from behind. That wasn't too far from reality, since I was often attacked by little demons called deer flies which would chase me and bite my back.

The Christian life is a contest or struggle in which we as a team are trying to reach a goal before the time runs out. Our individual efforts are important but so is our work as a team. The mass of spectators are those who have had their chance to reach the goal during their lifetimes. According to Hebrews, the old team didn't make it to the goal and didn't enter God's rest (11:39-40). Jesus is the one who paved the way for the rest of us, and he is the one who will help us get to the goal. His endurance and perseverance are our example. But we need to remove the bad habits of life, put away the vices that prevent us from making progress to the goal of the completed person, to attain to the ideal human life, the spiritually and morally mature person. We must keep our eyes on Jesus, we must put everything we have into the task of life, and we must run the race to win the prize.

REMEMBER THE EXAMPLE (12:3)

The author of Hebrews encourages his hearers to think long and hard about the example of Jesus. Jesus endured the hostility from those who would have had him conform to the political and religious agenda of the Jewish leadership in Jerusalem (Mark 11:18; 14:1; Luke 13:31; John 5:18; 7:1). Jesus endured the hostility of the Roman military when they tried to get him to give in, to weaken, to take the easy way out (John 19:8–11). This example of Jesus should help us when we experience the fatigue that comes near the end of the race. Remembering what Jesus endured is supposed to motivate us when we begin to think about giving up. Notice that the context of Hebrews involves actions of faith. Faith is not simply an act of passive assent to a doctrine, but it is an active obedience. We are involved in a struggle which goes beyond simply adopting a Christian lifestyle to experiencing a transformation into people of character and virtue. It is a struggle that is not only a spiritual or mental activity but one that involves us in the world.

Long distance runners know what it's like to hit the wall. It's the time when you feel like you can't go any further. You want to give up. You imagine what it would feel like to stop. Your shins would stop aching, the cramps in your calves and thighs would cease, the burning sensation in the lungs would end. Experienced runners will focus their minds on what motivates them. Perhaps it is a positive image in which they picture themselves winning the race, or they imagine someone important to them congratulating them. Maybe the image that gives the extra perseverance is the negative one of not wanting to lose, thinking how bad a person feels if he or she gives up.

When we get tired of the work we are doing for God, both in the molding of our own character and in the mission we do in the world, we can use the same techniques to get us to think about what's most important to us in life. We can read the stories of Jesus in the Gospels and use them as inspiration. Meditating on the meaning of those stories can make them available to us when we experience difficulty and want to give up helping others and trying to be a force for good in the world. When we work through those times, we will find renewed energy and motivation to continue the race God has put us in.

RESIST THE DEFEATIST ATTITUDES (12:4)

Hebrews has given us small glimpses into the setting of his first-century audience. Remember what he says in chapter 10.

> But recall those earlier days when, after you had been enlightened, you endured a hard struggle with sufferings, sometimes being publicly exposed to abuse and persecution, and sometimes being partners with those so treated. For you had compassion for those who were in prison, and you cheerfully accepted the plundering of your possessions, knowing that you yourselves possessed something better and more lasting. (Heb 10:32-34)

The author reminds them, though they have suffered much, they have yet to experience physical attack and torture, a kind of violence causing them to bleed.

The Maccabean martyrs, who seem to be part of the narrative of faithful living at the end of chapter 11, endured such bloody conflict. Jesus suffered to the extent of being executed on a cross. But the struggle of the community to whom Hebrews is written has not been tested to its fullest yet. The models of faithfulness endured much more than these have yet to suffer. The agonistic contest has been tough, but the athletic competitors are still in the game. They might be bruised and battered, but it's not time yet for the sidelines.

Sports can be brutal. You've heard the things coaches say. Someone is in pain and the coach says, "Walk it off." A player gets hit and holds his injured limb. The coach yells, "It's not bleeding, get back in the game." Or if the player is bleeding, the coach chides, "It's just a little blood."

We Christians do a lot of moaning and groaning. It's good to be a sympathetic, caring, and compassionate people. But maybe some of us need to hear some tough love. When someone complains about some hurtful thing someone said, the pastor might need to say, "Walk it off, Mrs. Smith." When a church member can't participate in the soup kitchen because they're not feeling well, an elder could say, "Brother Jones, you're not dead yet, are you?" Maybe even if someone gets hit by a bottle at a peace rally, a friend might say, "Hey, sister, it's just a little blood." This Christian life is not for the faint-hearted, for people who want to give up, for people

Section Six: Examples and Exhortations to Faithful Living

who just want to sit on the sidelines. We're in the game, it's a contact sport, and we're in it to the end.

∽

If we expect to achieve the goal of the Christian life, we need to run the race with perseverance, to remember the example of Jesus' endurance, and to resist the defeatist attitude. Life is more than a walk in the park. It might be a race in the park or even a rally.

The famous "I have a Dream" speech of Martin Luther King, Jr. is the sort of pep talk that we find in Hebrews. King encouraged those in the civil rights movement to continue the fight. He said,

> We cannot turn back. There are those who are asking the devotees of civil rights, "When will you be satisfied?" We can never be satisfied as long as the Negro is the victim of the unspeakable horrors of police brutality. We can never be satisfied as long as our bodies, heavy with the fatigue of travel, cannot gain lodging in the motels of the highways and the hotels of the cities. We cannot be satisfied as long as the Negro's basic mobility is from a smaller ghetto to a larger one. We can never be satisfied as long as our children are stripped of their selfhood and robbed of their dignity by signs stating "for whites only." We cannot be satisfied as long as a Negro in Mississippi cannot vote and a Negro in New York believes he has nothing for which to vote. No, no we are not satisfied and we will not be satisfied until justice rolls down like waters and righteousness like a mighty stream.[9]

King went on to encourage them in their great suffering.

> I am not unmindful that some of you have come here out of great trials and tribulations. Some of you have come fresh from narrow jail cells. Some of you have come from areas where your quest for freedom left you battered by storms of persecution and staggered by the winds of police brutality. You have been the veterans of creative suffering. Continue to work with the faith that unearned suffering is redemptive.[10]

The civil rights movement was a work of faith, the kind of faith that Hebrews is talking about. In the concluding words of King,

---

9. Martin Luther King, Jr., "I Have a Dream," 1963. Accessed March 26, 2008. Online: http://usinfo.state.gov/infousa/government/overview/38.html.

10. Ibid.

The Race Is On (12:1–4)

With this faith we will be able to transform the jangling discords of our nation into a beautiful symphony of brotherhood. With this faith we will be able to work together, to pray together, to struggle together, to go to jail together, to stand up for freedom together, knowing that we will be free one day.[11]

The author of Hebrews tells us the race is set before us, we are in the struggle. With our eyes on Jesus we press ahead to the goal of being the people of faith God has called us to be.

---

11. Ibid.

The Discipline of God and Its Benefits (12:5–11)

In 1981 Rabbi Harold Kushner discussed the issue that has bothered people since the days of Job and before in his book, *When Bad Things Happen to Good People*. It's an important topic. We often say, "Why do bad things happen to good people?" I would rather put the question this way, "Why do bad things happen to people, and some become bitter, while others become better?"

The saying goes, "What doesn't hurt us, makes us stronger." We may feel that's a harsh attitude. But, if you think about it, that's the way life works. For instance, what would you tell someone who complains of being tired? Perhaps someone might suggest the person take a nap. Afterwards the person might feel refreshed, but chances are the person will still feel sluggish. The way our bodies seem to respond is the more we sleep the more our bodies want to sleep. Instead, we tell someone who's feeling tired to get some exercise. "But that's hard, and it can hurt." That's true, but it has the effect of making a person stronger. The stress on the muscles and tissue, for the most part, makes them grow and strengthen.

Take another example. We overcome ignorance and immaturity through tough experiences of study and encountering new ideas. Going to college or graduate school can be a difficult experience. We can become disoriented and our world become confused because education requires us to question assumptions and challenge firmly-held beliefs. In school, people are forced into a community of people with whom they must get along and to whose differing perspectives they must listen. Through the experience a student develops and matures. Their beliefs and values may change, but whatever they come to hold as valid and beneficial will have been strengthened by the discipline of education.

The person who does not want to change and improve, who wants to exist in the bliss of ignorance, apathy, and lethargy, will resent the stress of life and its effects. This sort of person becomes angry and resists the changes life brings. This person experiences frustration and disillusion-

The Discipline of God and Its Benefits (12:5-11)

ment by becoming aware of the conflict and tension between competing ideas and the complexity of religious and philosophical choices. Without spiritual grounding, the crises of life can lead a person to give up in what seems to be a world of meaninglessness and chaos.

Whether or not God is to be blamed as the direct cause of every calamity, crisis, or catastrophe is a theological conundrum. It's also a matter of interpretation whether any particular event has been brought about as God's vengeance against sinfulness. More to the point is the principle that difficult events and experiences happen to people, and wise people find ways to make themselves stronger as a result.

Clearly the intended audience of Hebrews had been experiencing some sort of persecution. We don't really know the historical setting of the book of Hebrews. We don't know when it was written, who wrote it, or to whom it was written. Therefore, we can't identify any one set of events as the historical context for the audience of Hebrews. We do know from the text of Hebrews that the author was aware of the persecution his audience was facing (10:32). There was confiscation, or at least loss, of property; some were being imprisoned (10:34); there was physical violence (10:33) but not to the extent of bloodshed or martyrdom, as far we know (12:4).

The message of Hebrews to those who suffer is to endure the experience and to go forward in faith. In the previous verses, which began chapter 12, the author applied the metaphor of athletic competition as a way of describing how people are to endure the toils of life. Hebrews now blends the metaphor of athletic struggle with educational discipline. The author picks up this imagery from a proverb (Prov 3:11-12) in the Old Testament, which includes in the Greek version the word *paideia*. In our English translations, the word is translated in Hebrews 12 with words like "discipline, chastening." It basically means, "education, instruction, correction."

For the Greeks, *paideia* referred to the foundation of culture, the educational development of young men into fully-formed adult citizens. An aspect of that education involved what we call negative reinforcement: discipline in the form of reproof, chastisement, and even punishment. *Paideia* can also relate metaphorically to divine instruction and discipline. In ancient times, when bad things happened, people assumed it was the result of a divine power punishing humans for their wrong-doing. Calamities occurred as part of the educational process. If we think of this as God hurting humans simply as punishment, then we miss the point. The goal of discipline is correction, which leads to improved behavior, which in turn results in the full maturity of character. In Greek thought, the more fully developed a person is as a human, the closer that person is to being like God.

The author of Hebrews does not want his audience to forget the nature of divine discipline (12:5-6) but to endure God's parental discipline (12:7-8), which by comparison to our biological parents is even better for us (12:9-11).

DON'T FORGET THE NATURE OF DIVINE DISCIPLINE (12:5-6)

The author of Hebrews introduces a saying from the book of Proverbs (Prov 3:11-12) as though it were a wise saying from a philosopher (12:5-6). In fact, those Jews who participated more fully in the dominate Greek culture around the time of the first century considered people like Moses and Solomon to have been philosophers. This proverb would have struck a chord with Greek-speakers because of its discussion of *paideia*.

Hebrews reminds the audience of what this proverb teaches. We are not to have a bad attitude about difficult experiences (12:5a) because they happen as a way of making us better. The wrong attitude would be to slough off a difficulty as being meaningless ("regard lightly"). The opposite extreme occurs when someone is devastated ("lose heart") by something that happens.

The "discipline of the Lord" is God's *paideia*. It is God taking us to school. In the second phrase (12:5b), the word "punish" is a word that emphasizes reproof or rebuke. In classical Greece, for example, to correct wrong ways of thinking and behaving Socrates was known for his method of rebuking people and persuading them of the right way to think and act. Philosophers, like the Cynics Diogenes and Crates, were known, in fact, for getting a little violent with their walking stick to make a point. Corrective measures, however, were not practiced out of contempt and hatred. Those whom God loves, according to the precept in Proverbs, he gives educative discipline (*paideia*).

If you were to read Proverbs 3:11-12 in your Bible and compare it to the quotation in Hebrews, you would notice a slight difference in the second sentence. The Hebrew Bible, on which our translation of Proverbs depends, reads, "the LORD reproves the one he loves, *as a father* the son in whom he delights" (italics mine). It seems the Greek translator of the

The Discipline of God and Its Benefits (12:5-11)

version from which Hebrews quotes understood the Hebrew not with the expression "as a father" but as a verb form meaning "to give pain." Therefore, the quotation in Hebrews 12:6 reads, the Lord "*chastises* every child whom he accepts." The Greek word for "chastise" means, "to whip." For instance, this is the word which appears in contexts describing the custom of "flogging" or "scourging" in the New Testament (Matt 10:17; 20:19; 23:34; Mark 10:34; Luke 18:33; John 19:1).

In my experience of growing up, we called it "getting a whipping" or perhaps "gettin' a whoopin.'" I can remember several instruments of discipline, and I can recall vividly the welts a whipping left. One of those devices may have been a wooden paddle. I remember the saying "apply the board of education to the seat of knowledge." I didn't think it was very funny then.

My oldest daughters think it unfair that I spanked them and not their younger three sisters. I wish I could say I stopped using corporal punishment later in life because of a philosophical objection. Truthfully, I probably became better able to handle my anger as I grew older and was no longer compelled to apply physical punishment. I have come to believe the experiences of life are a better teacher than a parent hurting a child. There are plenty of ways that children experience consequences for poor decisions and bad behavior. If they are wise, they will learn from the experience. They will learn in general that it's better to do what's right than wrong.

There are also other difficult times we experience as children that help to form us into mature adults. Relocating as family can be a hard thing to do for children. Yet, it has a way of strengthening a person's ability to handle change and to adapt to new situations. Having to go through tough financial times can place stress on a family. But it teaches us to value what we have and enjoy the simple things of life. The loss of a loved one can deeply wound a young person or an adult. When handled well, it can teach us to consider the meaning of life, take more time to show love to others, and realize how short and transient life is.

We tend to pray that bad things won't happen to us. That suggests that God is trying to decide whether to hit us with something or not, and we're trying to talk him out of it. We might as well acknowledge that bad things are going to happen, and they're not happening because of some wrong we've done like cheating on our taxes or watching a racy movie—unless the bad thing is an IRS audit or your spouse slapping you.

Section Six: Examples and Exhortations to Faithful Living

We have very difficult things happen to us. What we do with them will determine whether we experience the educative discipline that can make us stronger and more healthy humans.

ENDURE THE PARENTAL DISCIPLINE OF GOD (12:7–8)

The author of Hebrews urges his audience to endure whatever circumstance they encounter because endurance brings about educative discipline. Based on what Prov 3:11–12 teaches, God is treating a person as a parent would a son or daughter (12:7). In the ancient world, one could assume parents tried to teach their children right and wrong by applying some form of physical discipline. Hebrews reasons, if you don't experience discipline as all children do, you could then assume you're not one of the legitimate children (12:8).

Jewish teaching held God punished Israel for its sins, but Gentile nations were left alone. God was, in essence, storing up wrath against the Gentile nations until the end of the age. Although terrible events might come upon the people of God, we should see them as the way in which God perfects God's people, rather than the means of retribution. The Old Testament does contain some stories of retribution, like Noah's flood and the destruction of Sodom and Gomorrah. Those stories reflect the way the Jewish people have interpreted God's actions. It doesn't mean every time something bad happens it's a consequence of someone's sin. Notice there is almost no hint of wrong-doing on the part of Hebrew's audience (10:26 and 12:1 are not explicit). God disciplines not for retribution but for correction. Difficulties occur not to hurt us but to help us.

If a father only punishes a legitimate child, as Heb 12:8 says, then I'm sure I'm not adopted. I can't say I ever had a very good attitude about what I received. Before anyone could spank me, they had to catch me. I remember once when my mother came at me. We were living in a small, country house. The house was divided evenly in quadrants with doorways leading into the central hallway. On this occasion, my mother chased me around the house in circles for awhile until I escaped to the kitchen, where we then ran around the kitchen table. I remember her looking at me across the table saying, "I just want to talk to you."

Once I had a teacher try to paddle me. It was sixth grade, as I remember. I have no idea what I must have done. I probably said a bad word or talked back to him. He brought me to the front of the class near his desk.

The Discipline of God and Its Benefits (12:5-11)

He grabbed hold on my left arm with his left hand and tried to turn me around so he could give me a swat with a paddle. I just kept going around in circles. He was swinging me around, trying to get a good aim at my backside. Meanwhile, on one of the times swinging around, my other arm swiped everything off his desk. When he finally gave up, I told him, "I'm telling my mother when I get home." Nearly exhausted, he replied, "No, I'm telling your mother."

I'm sure I deserved what I got as a youngster and even more so as a teenager. One time I deserved much more. I think I had called my mother a bad word—something like that. My father confronted me in the kitchen. I don't know why I did it, but I slugged him. I then ran for my life upstairs to my room, and he caught up to me where I was standing by my bed. He gave me some kind of warning, then pushed me down and walked away. I felt awful. He didn't take out his anger and vengeance on me for the injury I caused him personally. The discipline was clearly focused on correction rather than punishment, or he would have had his belt off and wailed on me.

All we can know about crises in our lives is that our challenge is to endure them for the purpose of developing who we are as persons. There may be a direct link from an event to our bad behavior. For example, when I wrecked a car back in the early 90s, while living in Rhode Island and working in Massachusetts, I learned that I needed to be more careful driving, to slow down, leave for work earlier, and pay better attention to traffic—especially when the pavement is slick.

Difficulties can arise in life without any direct connection to what we have done. In the past year, three of our family members have been diagnosed with potentially debilitating diseases. Lauren was diagnosed with Fibromyalgia. Abby has been diagnosed with Rheumatoid Arthritis. Suann has been diagnosed with Multiple Sclerosis. Although we have commented on the coincidence, no one has said—out loud at least—what is God doing to us? Why is God punishing us? There are plenty of things I could think of if I were to assign blame. Is God doing this to my family because someone did such and such? It would be a mistake to think that way. But we are learning from the experience. More than feeling that God has done something bad to us, I think we are feeling God's care for us. Through these health problems of ours and the additional ones of our elderly parents, Suann and I are growing more as adults and taking the time to appreciate our family.

Section Six: Examples and Exhortations to Faithful Living

BY COMPARISON GOD'S DISCIPLINE IS EVEN BETTER FOR US (12:9-11)

Each of the next three verses contains a similar grammatical structure forming three comparisons. We've seen how the author of Hebrews has structured his speech as sections of comparison followed by sections of exhortation. Hebrews also contains minor comparisons as in these verses. Each of these three sentences, therefore, contain within them the same "on the one hand, on the other hand" construction we have seen occurs numerous times in the major comparisons. The translators of our Bibles have chosen to ignore the Greek particle *men* in each opening clause as being insignificant, but it in fact serves to mark the beginning of the comparison.

The first comparison in verse nine seeks to prove we should have an even better attitude to discipline from God than we do to our parents. On the one hand, our human parents have given us discipline, and, in most cases, children show the parents respect and deference. On the other hand, a much better case can be made for how we respond to God. Translated literally, our parents are "fathers of our flesh," but God is "the father of spirits." We should be even more willing to honor God's discipline over us and live our lives under God's care.

The second comparison occurs in verse 10. It argues God's discipline is not the temporary and haphazard kind we might experience from parents. Educative discipline benefits us in the way it develops us into people who share in God's character of holiness. On the one hand, parents have a few decades to do what seems best to them. On the other hand, God disciplines us, not for God's own sake, but for our advantage. The benefit we get from God's discipline improves our character. We then receive the divine quality of holiness or moral sanctity.

Verse 11 contains the third comparison. It focuses on the way discipline is experienced. When it occurs we don't enjoy it, but it has a way of training us, producing a positive outcome. On the one hand, educative discipline hurts; it's not a joyful experience. On the other hand, our character gets exercised. In agricultural terms, it produces in us a peaceable fruit of righteousness.

Here at the end of verse 11 occurs an interesting word in Greek. We talked about this in Heb 5:14, "But solid food is for the mature, for those whose faculties have been *trained* by practice to distinguish good

The Discipline of God and Its Benefits (12:5-11)

from evil" (italics mine). An integral part of education in Greek culture was physical exercise, and that's what this metaphor relates to. The literal meaning of this word and the related word from which we get our word "gymnasium" is "to be naked." There was no problem with students in ancient Greece forgetting their gym clothes for Phys. Ed. because they didn't wear any. They didn't pick teams and have "shirts and skins;" everyone was "skins." The exercise of the body became a metaphor for the training of the mind and soul. It was all *paideia*. It was education for life, intended to form the person into the best they could be, to have a character like God's.

How we respond to the hardships of life determines what effect they have on our behavior and character. Someone who resents life's challenges will become hardened, instead of becoming malleable and moldable. Those who blame God for problems in life tend to react against what's considered proper and acceptable behavior. Rather than progressing through the pain of loss, the person who holds on to the pain fails to learn from the experience and be at peace.

I'm reminded of the situation of a teenaged girl I'll call Leslie. Leslie's father died when she was a little girl. It was hard enough to grow up without a father. Now as a teenager, she has had to experience the protracted illness of her mother. What was already a difficult life was made worse by her mother's eventual death. We can sympathize with Leslie's loss but be further saddened by the effect it has had on her. She now smokes all the time. She keeps getting more tattoos. She's cutting herself. All self-destructive behaviors. The confusion of sexual identity Leslie grew up with has worsened now that she claims to be bisexual.

This response to a life crisis is not unique. I don't mention it for the purpose of judging it. I would reject any suggestion that she in some way caused the death of her mother because of her homosexuality. God isn't in the business of killing people to teach others a lesson. Similarly, I consider it poor theology to believe that 9/11 was God punishing anyone or that Hurricane Katrina was God's vengeance on New Orleans. But the death of a loved one is something that God allows and from that we should find life-lessons and grow from it.

God does bring difficulties into our lives and allows hardships to happen to us. The interpretation of those experiences is an intensely personal matter. Only by a close relationship with God may we know in what ways we are to interpret their meaning for our lives.

Section Six: Examples and Exhortations to Faithful Living

For instance, we joke in our family about Heidi's accident with her new car. Just at the moment she was asking me how I liked her new car, we were rear-ended. It would be wrong of me to think God was punishing her for it. It would even be wrong for her to think God was punishing her for valuing material possessions too highly. The right response is to ask oneself, what can I learn from the experience? In what ways can I become stronger, wiser, better.

~

If we value the teaching of Scripture, we will take to heart the message of Hebrews. We will not forget the educational aspect of hardships God allows to happen to us. We will seek to endure difficulties as a part of the process of divine, parental discipline. And we will view those times as an even better way for our divine parent to bring about our improvement than what our earthly parents could do.

Joseph John Gurney, an influential Quaker among Friends in some parts of the US, had this to say about the nature of God.

> Now, it is a singular proof of the goodness, as well as the wisdom of God, that the pains and afflictions of mortals, the direct or indirect consequences of sin, are so overruled for good, that they are often the means of curing that very evil out of which they originate. We learn from the Scriptures, that they are directed by an all-wise and beneficent Deity, to the great and good purpose of moral probation and discipline—that they are powerful instruments in his holy hands, for the reformation and restoration of his wandering children. Affliction, in its varied forms, is calculated above almost every other means, to humble the pride, and to soften the hardness, of the heart of man. It is affliction by which our faith is tried, and in the end confirmed. It is affliction which calls into exercise our patience, our forbearance, our submission, and our fortitude.[1]

The common cliché is to say, "When life hands you lemons, make lemonade." Hebrews teaches, when life hands you lemons, you make the lemonade and you drink it. You take in the vitamins and nutrients and become a stronger person. You take the seeds from the lemons and grow trees. And from those beautiful trees you produce luscious fruit. You then

---

1. Joseph John Gurney, "Essays On The Evidences, Doctrines, And Practical Operation, Of Christianity," in *Gurney's Works*, vol. 2, 137. Accessed: March 26, 2008. Online: http://dqc.esr.earlham.edu/toc/E21625179B-000.

The Discipline of God and Its Benefits (12:5–11)

share that fruit with others and nourish their lives as well. You might even come to the place where you thank God for all of the lemons that have come into your life to make you the better person you've become.

Getting There Safely (12:12–17)

Taking a trip with a group of people presents challenges. I've now taken two international trips with colleagues from Earlham School of Religion. The first was our trip to visit Quaker sites in England in 2001. The second trip in 2006 was to become acquainted with the culture of Central America by visiting Honduras. The trip to England was by far the easier journey. We traveled everywhere in a comfortable, private coach. Most places we visited were readily accessible to us and didn't require much walking, though I did anticipate a bit of a workout one day. But because of the hoof and mouth disease in England at the time, we were prevented from hiking up the famous Pendle Hill.

I didn't have it so easy when we were in the lovely village of Copán Ruinas, Honduras. Packing us all into vans was not so easy. To visit the Mayan ruins, for example, it was decided we would walk. It's not very far to get there, a few kilometers I suppose. But then we spent the rest of the afternoon walking around the ruins and sometimes climbing up and down stone structures. On the return journey, we walked the few kilometers back to the village, which required us to walk up a steep hill. By this time our group was all strewn out, some people stopping half-way up the hill, others already at the top, and a few struggling to make the end of the journey, wondering if they would make it. On trips like these, there's always the problem of keeping people together. There are usually a few who like to be on their own, who get lost, or who just can't seem to meet at the prearranged times. It's fitting to describe it as trying to herd cats.

As we know, not all journeys of this kind end with everyone arriving safely at the destination. In July 1996, sixteen members of a French Club along with five chaperones died in the crash of TWA Flight 800 on their way to visit France. On March 2, 2007, a bus transporting a baseball team from Bluffton University went off an overpass, killing five players, the driver, and the driver's wife. In spite of the troubles and the dangers, people still take the journey together with every intention of everyone

Getting There Safely (12:12-17)

getting to the destination and everyone experiencing the joys and blessings that come with new places and new opportunities.

The over-arching narrative of Hebrews is the journey from the place of bondage to the place of rest. The Israelites through the exodus and the wilderness journey of Sinai experienced a national journey of the covenant people of God toward the fulfillment of God's promises and blessings. For the first generation of exodus survivors, the wilderness meant failure, in spite of God's covenant with them and God's provision of ceremony and sacrifice to maintain their standing before God.

Through Jesus God has given people a second chance to remain faithful and arrive safely at the promised rest. In every way, this new covenant is better than the previous and should bring about the success of God's people. Hebrews encourages the people of God individually and collectively to progress toward the goal. There's also a dire warning that a greater provision from God carries with it a greater judgment for failure. We are on the journey together and together we must reach the fulfillment of God's promises and enter God's rest. Once again, Hebrews urges his audience to continue the journey: (1) to pull themselves together to finish the journey (12:12-13); (2) to pursue peace and holiness with others along the way (12:14); and (3) to protect those on the journey (12:15-17).

PULL YOURSELF TOGETHER TO FINISH THE JOURNEY (12:12-13)

The author of Hebrews realizes his audience has had a difficult time so far. They've had a hard struggle and have suffered (12:32). They've been abused and persecuted (12:33). They've even had their possessions taken from them (12:34). So far they seem to be doing rather well, even though the author of Hebrews thinks they should have made better progress in their leadership development (5:12). In this section Hebrews strings together allusions to Biblical texts as a way of encouraging his audience to pull themselves together for the last leg of their journey.

Verse 12 alludes to Isa 35:3, "Strengthen the weak hands, and make firm the feeble knees." The Greek of Hebrews approximates what we have in the ancient Greek biblical manuscripts. Rather than quoting a text, Hebrews takes the language of Isaiah and gives it a new context. We get the image of a person who is exhausted, injured, and dejected. We can picture someone who no longer holds the arms bent at the sides and who

Section Six: Examples and Exhortations to Faithful Living

is unable to straighten the knees when walking. These two expressions also occur together in an early Jewish text, one that appears in the Old Testament apocrypha and in the Catholic Bible. Notice the context of depression in this rather peculiar text: "Dejected mind, gloomy face, and wounded heart come from an evil wife. Drooping hands and weak knees come from the wife who does not make her husband happy" (Sir 25:23). The author of Hebrews tells his audience, "Pull yourself together! Renew your energy!"

In verse 13 Hebrews seems to be alluding to Prov 4:26, "Keep straight the path of your feet, and all your ways will be sure. Do not swerve to the right or to the left; turn your foot away from evil." The Greek text of Proverbs is slightly different, and Hebrews seems to be picking up on some of the phrases. If verse 12 instructs the travelers to straighten up the bodies, verse 13 tells them to pay attention to where they are walking, so that they do not injure themselves and what parts of their bodies do hurt might be able to heal. Together this imagery connotes a much needed infusion of new strength and vitality, a renewed sense of looking ahead to the journey, a reorientation to the path being followed.

I've done a fair amount of running and taking trips on a ten-speed bicycle, but I've never cared much for walking. Even when I walk to work or walk in a store, I don't really walk, I amble. I couldn't understand the appeal when a colleague, Stephen Spyker, in 2002 decided to spend his sabbatical hiking the Appalachian Trail (AT). He later wrote about it in his dissertation, "Spirituality and Technology on the Appalachian Trail: A Study in Frontiers." I can't comprehend the continuous rigor of walking mile after mile, day after day, week after week, even month after month. Even though there are many who hike the trail on any given day, it's possible to spend a great deal of time in solitude. Sometimes people meet up with each other at the end of a day, and sometimes they decide to keep together in a group the next day.

I remember him talking about how important it was to prevent injuries and to care for his feet. Sometimes the AT leads a person over obstacles, fallen trees, and boulders. Anyone who wants to make it to the end has to watch their step, or they run the danger of crippling themselves along the way. Signs along the way let the hiker know how much farther it is to the next stop. It's not hard to imagine someone, who is exhausted from the day's hike, with arms drooping and knees bent, walking up to the sign, maybe even ambling up. This intrepid traveler discovers that the destination is not too far ahead and then starts off to the journey's end a little straighter, a little more encouraged.

We might think about the metaphor of travel in terms of the movement of history. The Israelites traveled toward the Promised Land but did not finish the journey. The author of Hebrews portrays the people of God as traveling toward a spiritual Promised Land, a place of rest. God's people walk together and at the end of the age experience the completion of this journey of the ages.

In another sense, each of our lives is its own journey. Within the community of faith, we travel this journey together. Each step of our journey leads us up to greater heights of spiritual and moral maturity. Sometimes we tire along the path and we need encouragement. We must take a fresh, deep breath of God's Spirit and draw ourselves up to fully engage the trials on the path before us. Like hikers on the Appalachian Trail, we are at different places along the journey. Yet, we share the same path and are headed for a common destination.

PURSUE PEACE AND HOLINESS WITH OTHERS ALONG THE WAY (12:14)

Again the author of Hebrews gives an injunction to the audience as part of his exhortation to them. With words reflective of Ps 34:14 (LXX 33:15), he urges them to "pursue peace." Paul alludes to the same verse in Rom 14:19, "Let us then pursue what makes for peace and for mutual upbuilding." Also in 2 Tim 2:22 we find a similar idea, "So shun youthful passions and aim at righteousness, faith, love, and peace, along with those who call upon the Lord from a pure heart." 1 Pet 3:11 actually quotes the Psalm, "let them turn away from evil and do good; let them seek peace and pursue it."

If we think of peace as the absence of conflict, that might help us to understand it in its dual sense. On the one hand, there is the peace we have in relationship to other people. When we seek to get along with others and work out our differences, we are able to co-exist and be at peace. According to this verse in Hebrews, the pursuit of peace with others is not limited to one's own community, city, or even country.

There is another important quality of peace. It is the absence of conflict and turmoil within ourselves. We don't achieve that state of tranquility simply by not thinking about life but rather by training our minds to think properly about life. There is much about life that we cannot control.

Section Six: Examples and Exhortations to Faithful Living

Only by trusting in the goodness and providence of God are we able to accept whatever happens. When we focus our attention on seeking to possess wealth, pleasure, status, beauty, power, and a constancy of all these things, we set ourselves up for continual disappointment and worry. We have no real control over these things. We are, however, able to control our own thoughts and actions. By disciplining ourselves to pursue a virtuous life and a dependence only upon what God gives us each moment are we able to develop the good character and spiritual wholeness that will bring us to experience peace and happiness. Hebrews challenges his audience to pursue the peace and tranquility which bring about a divine quality of life.

Hebrews' audience is not only to pursue peace but also holiness. Holiness is often described in the Bible as the quality of being set apart. Something is holy because it is given a holy purpose. Someone or something that has been consecrated for a divine purpose should never be used for something profane or unclean. To be holy is to set oneself apart from the ordinary and profane, to be the exclusive instrument for divine purposes.

Hebrews describes this holiness or sanctification in a dual sense. First, it is something that Christ has done in the past for the people of God (13:12) in the sense of consecration (2:22). Secondly, it is something happening to God's people (10:14 "those being sanctified"). If it were simply a work done to someone, how could Hebrews instruct his audience to pursue holiness? This maturity of the soul, whether it is called perfection or holiness, is the goal for which we are to strive.

This condition of sanctification is not an option. It is not something reserved for the best of saints while the rest of us just try our best. If we want to see the Lord, if we expect to experience the presence of God, we must strive after holiness. The only chance we have to be in God's presence, according to Hebrews, is to reach a state of spiritual maturity in which we experience holiness. In this journey of faith, we travel together; we are to stick to the road that leads to peace and holiness.

The only thing I dislike more than walking is taking a city bus. Once, while visiting Providence, RI to try to find an apartment to rent for when we were to move there, I walked miles up and down the streets instead of taking the time to figure out where I needed to stand to get on the bus. On the last day of my visit, I finally decided to ride the bus. I had already walked a few miles that day and my legs were aching and the blisters on my feet were hurting. I saw the bus approaching and noticed a bus stop nearby. The bus stopped, I got on, paid the fare, and went to find a seat. No sooner had I sat down than I saw the street name I had been looking for. By the time I got off at the next stop and walked back to where I needed to go, I ended up walking about the same distance anyway.

I had terrible times riding the bus. One time the driver accused me of short-changing him, when I know I put the exact amount in because I had counted my money 50 times while I had been standing there waiting. Another time I missed getting off where I was supposed to so I could catch another bus, and I ended up going to the end of the route and waiting until the driver took a break and made the return trip.

The most embarrassing time was getting on the bus one morning to ride to campus at Brown University. I went to the usual bus stop, but it must have not been at the usual time. There happened to be an unusual number of kids at the bus stop that day. The city bus came, and I got on. I had to walk to the back because the bus was so crowded. After I sat down on the edge of a seat, I began noticing that there were also an unusual number of kids on the bus. In fact, they were all teenagers. I finally asked a kid—it took awhile to get one to make eye contact with me—where this bus was going. My heart sank when he said, "Classical High School." About then the bus turned away from the normal route, and I realized I not only had taken the wrong bus but I would end up far away from where I needed to go. Providence has a relatively small downtown, but Classical High School was on the opposite side of the downtown than Brown University. I made my way to the front of the bus and explained to the driver what had happened. At first he wasn't going to let me off since the rule is not to make any unscheduled stops. He finally relented, and I was able to get off and make my way back to where I needed to go.

Life has a way of taking us places we don't intend to go. We can get carried along by making wrong choices. We become a part of the wrong group of people. Before we know it, we are headed for the wrong destination. Life becomes a disappointment and with it comes anger and bitterness. Before it's too late, we need to get off the road that takes us to the wrong place in our lives. It's only the pursuit of peace and holiness that will get us to the proper destination, the life-long and life-fulfilling vision of the presence and character of God.

Section Six: Examples and Exhortations to Faithful Living

PROTECT THOSE ON THE JOURNEY (12:15–17)

The sentences in verses 15–17 continue on from the previous verse, which contains the main clause, "Pursue peace and holiness." The words "see to it" in this section translate an opening verb, which means "watch over." Quite literally, this is an episcopal function since we get the English word "episcopal" from the noun form of this Greek word. This action refers to a supervision of people's life and conduct. Later in chapter 12, we'll find the words "see to it" again, but there it will be from a different Greek word. Here we have a call for people in the community of faith to watch over others and guard their progress in faith. In chapter 13, Hebrews will refer twice to leaders among the people.

In 13:7 we read, "Remember your leaders, those who spoke the word of God to you; consider the outcome of their way of life, and imitate their faith." And then in 13:17, "Obey your leaders and submit to them, for they are keeping watch over your souls and will give an account. Let them do this with joy and not with sighing—for that would be harmful to you." The verb form at the beginning of verse 15, "watching over," is followed by a repeating grammatical construction we could translate as "not any." These three instances form one idea of what the people are supposed to watch out for. Hebrews is saying, "Watch out that (1) not anyone lacks God's graciousness; (2) not any source of bitterness causes problems; and (3) not any immoral and corrupt person misses out on God's blessing." In other words, pursue peace and holiness while seeing that everyone avoids making the wrong choices and missing God's gracious blessings. The expression in verse 15, "fails to obtain the grace of God," is more literally translated, "be bereft from God's graciousness." No one should be missing out on God's favor and experiencing despondency and dejection.

Hebrews says it another way. They should watch out for any roots of acrimony or animosity sprouting up like a bitter plant causing dissension and defilement among the community. Hebrews seems to be alluding to Deut 29:18 (LXX 29:17). Not only are the central terms found in this text but also the same repeating grammatical construction appears twice in this text of the ancient Greek Bible. In this warning passage regarding God's covenant with the Israelites, the people are told to remain faithful to God.

> I am making this covenant, sworn by an oath, not only with you who stand here with us today before the LORD our God, but also

Getting There Safely (12:12-17)

> with those who are not here with us today. You know how we lived in the land of Egypt, and how we came through the midst of the nations through which you passed. You have seen their detestable things, the filthy idols of wood and stone, of silver and gold, that were among them. It may be that there is among you a man or woman, or a family or tribe, whose heart is already turning away from the LORD our God to serve the gods of those nations. It may be that there is among you a root sprouting poisonous and bitter growth. All who hear the words of this oath and bless themselves, thinking in their hearts, "We are safe even though we go our own stubborn ways" (thus bringing disaster on moist and dry alike)—the LORD will be unwilling to pardon them, for the LORD's anger and passion will smoke against them. All the curses written in this book will descend on them, and the LORD will blot out their names from under heaven. (Deut 29:14-20)

In the Old Testament context, the graciousness of God is God's loving-kindness to God's people enacted through the covenant. "Know therefore that the LORD your God is God, the faithful God who maintains covenant loyalty with those who love him and keep his commandments, to a thousand generations" (Deut 7:9). Defilement occurs when God's people seek other ways and lose God's blessing and favor. The next section of Hebrews continues this theme of the giving of God's covenant and the warnings associated with breaking God's covenant.

The third object to watch out for is in verse 16. Translations may begin a new sentence here for readability, but it is a continuation of the repeating clauses. In fact, verse 16 lacks a verb completely, "not any immoral and corrupt person like Esau." The author of Hebrews comes down hard on Esau. When referring to Samson, for instance, Hebrews ignores his sexual immorality (11:32). Now, when describing someone who was not guilty of sexual impropriety according to the Genesis account, Hebrews calls Esau in literal terms a fornicator. In polite terms we might translate these terms, "immoral and corrupt," but that doesn't come close to the disgust implied by the Greek words the author of Hebrews chooses to describe what Esau did and the way it represents disloyalty to God.

The brief story of Esau, the firstborn of Isaac and Rebekah, and Esau's brother Jacob, occurs in Gen 25:29-34. At the end of Isaac's life, Rebekah helps Jacob fool Isaac into thinking that he is Esau, the eldest. Isaac unknowingly blesses Jacob with the blessing of the firstborn. When Esau realizes how he was tricked out of the blessing, having already lost the birthright in a moment of weakness, Esau despairs and turns against his family. To spite his father, Esau marries foreign wives from the Canaanites. He becomes a symbol of the Israelite nation's adultery with foreign gods through idolatry.

The fact that Esau chose to satiate his desire for food rather than maintain what was his right as the firstborn was seen by the Jewish philosopher, Philo of Alexandria, as moral corruption. He writes, "But the bad man thinks the things of the body the more important, while the good man assigns the preference to the things of the soul" (*Leg All* 3.191). Esau, therefore, epitomizes what should be prevented among the community of faith. In order to prevent people dropping out along the journey of faith, those who are more mature should keep an eye out for signs that people's faith might be wavering.

We can all probably think of people who have dropped out of church. People stop going to churches for many reasons, not always because of moral failings or a rejection of Christianity. But when those are the reasons, leaders in the church should have already been watching out for the flock and keeping people from going astray.

My first experience as a pastor was serving as the part-time pastoral minister of a small Quaker church in Massachusetts. I was working full-time elsewhere and really wanted to devote all my energies to the pastorate. I confided with Wallen, a member of my congregation, my desire to serve the church full-time. Wallen was a retired minister and an experienced pastoral counselor. What he said to me surprised and also disappointed me. He said to me, "Why would you want to do that? The worst thing in the church are pastors with too much time on their hands." I think now he was probably right. It wasn't long after that experience I heard about a former pastor of mine, who apparently had too much time on his hands at church and was having a liaison with the church secretary. What's the saying, "Idle hands are the devil's play things?" In the case of the ancient Israelites, the danger was idolatry. For some others, moral laxity develops from simple idleness. Whether you discover people in your church who have a case of the "idols" or the "idles," you should be on the look out. Find it where it begins and nip it in the bud, before its effects spread to others. We shouldn't let any of God's people fail to continue to experience God's graciousness and blessings.

Getting There Safely (12:12-17)

Throughout this journey we are making together, we should continually urge those who are beginning to fall to pull themselves together to finish the journey. On the journey, we are to pursue peace and holiness as a way to make it to the goal. Finally, we should keep an eye out for each other and protect those on the journey with us.

I remember one of the bicycle trips I took as a teenager with the area Campus Life organization. I was in good shape in those days—I'm in a good shape now, the shape of a circle—and I had no trouble riding the approximately seventy-five miles a day. We rode in small groups, and the groups were spaced out. In my group one day was a pudgy kid riding a big Schwinn ten-speed. Not only was he weighted down himself but so was the bike. As I remember the bike had a heavy frame, chrome fenders, a rack on the back, and a big headlight. It was hard enough for him to keep up, but this one day his back axle broke. The bike would still work, but it was difficult, and it would slip in and out of gear. We didn't want to just sit on the side of the road and wait for help to come, so we kept riding with him. To help him along, I would ride up next to him and then push him for a ways to give him some rest. We didn't lose him that day; we all arrived at that day's destination.

We all need each other. We need each other's encouragement. We need for everyone to do their part and work at this thing we call the Christian life. We need for each other to be on the look out for when someone's faith is lagging, when we are at risk of losing the experience of God's best for us in life. We need to say to each other, "Let's make it together."

Making It to the Top (12:18–24)

WHAT PEOPLE SEEM TO miss the most when they visit us in Indiana are mountains—or even some hills, for that matter. Traveling north on Route 27 from Richmond, passers-by can see a sign pointing toward the highest elevation in Indiana, 1,257 ft. above sea level. Those who have been curious enough to follow the signs say it leads to a pile of rocks in the woods. You won't need your climbing gear to reach the top of Hoosier Hill.

I can understand the appeal of mountains. The first time Suann and I visited Black Mountain, North Carolina, we decided to drive up the mountain to see the tourist attraction called Chimney Rock. Driving up to the mountain, you can watch the clouds enshroud the top. It's no wonder ancient peoples thought of mountain-tops as the abode of God. Mountains are where the earth meets the sky. I had fun driving the rental car up the mountain, cornering around hairpin turns. Then the joy was taken out of it when Suann became dizzy and car sick. No more powering through the curves. By the time we reached the top a storm was passing over. We drove into the entrance to the park and pulled into line. After a long wait, we finally reached the ticket booth. We discovered that the elevator to the top of chimney rock was not in service because of the lightning. We were also told we should have come prepared to walk. As I remember, we didn't even think to bring umbrellas to the top of the mountain. We had to turn back and wind our way back down the mountain. We failed to reach our destination that day, even though we were so close.

The Israelites received the law of God from the top of the mountain. The book of Hebrews compares this foundational moment in Israel's history to another mountain-top experience. The exodus journey ended at Mt. Sinai, where Moses ascended to meet Yahweh and receive the ten commandments and the civic and ceremonial law regulating life in the tribal confederation of the children of Israel. The wilderness journey from Sinai to the north was to bring the Israelites to another mountain, one

Making It to the Top (12:18–24)

called Zion. The generation who disobeyed God in the wilderness wanderings would not reach the Promised Land, the place of rest.

The new covenant, inaugurated by Jesus, holds out the hope that God's people will reach the mountain at the end of their journey. It is a Mt. Zion, God's city, the heavenly Jerusalem. In comparison, the former brought fear. The latter is a welcoming place. Because Jesus mediated a new covenant through sprinkled blood, the heavenly Jerusalem is a place where God's people can approach to the one who is judge of all. Rather than prevent anyone from even touching this mountain, God's people belong in the heavenly city with their names recorded as citizens. The mountain-top experience of God's people is not the place of reproach as it was at Sinai (12:18–21) but the place of approach on God's mountain-top city (12:22–24).

THE PLACE OF REPROACH: MT. SINAI (12:18–21)

Hebrews begins the first part of this comparison in Greek with the negative, "Not have you approached." His words are deeply evocative of the sensations imagined in the giving of the first covenant on Mt. Sinai. The words the author of Hebrews chooses come from the descriptions of the event in Exod 19 and Deut 4 and 5. Israel is camped at the foot of the mountain. Moses receives instructions concerning how they are to approach Yahweh.

> Then the LORD said to Moses, "I am going to come to you in a dense cloud, in order that the people may hear when I speak with you and so trust you ever after." When Moses had told the words of the people to the LORD, the LORD said to Moses: "Go to the people and consecrate them today and tomorrow. Have them wash their clothes and prepare for the third day, because on the third day the LORD will come down upon Mount Sinai in the sight of all the people. You shall set limits for the people all around, saying, "Be careful not to go up the mountain or to touch the edge of it. Any who touch the mountain shall be put to death. (Exod 19:9–12)

The people prepare for the day when Moses will meet Yahweh on the mountain. Sense the awesome dread evoked by this description.

> Now Mount Sinai was wrapped in smoke, because the LORD had descended upon it in fire; the smoke went up like the smoke of a kiln, while the whole mountain shook violently. As the blast of the trumpet grew louder and louder, Moses would speak and God would answer him in thunder. (Exod 19:18–19)

Section Six: Examples and Exhortations to Faithful Living

There on the mountain Moses received the laws of the Israelite nation. In the book of Deuteronomy, in essence a retelling of the institution of the national identity of Israel, this scene is again described. Moses is reminding the people.

> But take care and watch yourselves closely, so as neither to forget the things that your eyes have seen nor to let them slip from your mind all the days of your life; make them known to your children and your children's children—how you once stood before the LORD your God at Horeb, when the LORD said to me, "Assemble the people for me, and I will let them hear my words, so that they may learn to fear me as long as they live on the earth, and may teach their children so"; you approached and stood at the foot of the mountain while the mountain was blazing up to the very heavens, shrouded in dark clouds. Then the LORD spoke to you out of the fire. You heard the sound of words but saw no form; there was only a voice. He declared to you his covenant, which he charged you to observe, that is, the ten commandments; and he wrote them on two stone tablets. And the LORD charged me at that time to teach you statutes and ordinances for you to observe in the land that you are about to cross into and occupy. (Deut 4:9–14)

According to Deuteronomy 5, the people felt like they barely survived the experience. Again we read a description of the awesome event. Moses reminds them,

> These words the LORD spoke with a loud voice to your whole assembly at the mountain, out of the fire, the cloud, and the thick darkness, and he added no more. He wrote them on two stone tablets, and gave them to me. When you heard the voice out of the darkness, while the mountain was burning with fire, you approached me, all the heads of your tribes and your elders; and you said, "Look, the LORD our God has shown us his glory and greatness, and we have heard his voice out of the fire. Today we have seen that God may speak to someone and the person may still live. So now why should we die? For this great fire will consume us; if we hear the voice of the LORD our God any longer, we shall die. For who is there of all flesh that has heard the voice of the living God speaking out of fire, as we have, and remained alive?" (Deut 5:22–26)

With this in mind, Hebrews announces to his audience, this is not how you are approaching God. The present people of God do not experience something tangible like the fury and the sound of Mt. Sinai. At Sinai

Making It to the Top (12:18–24)

the people saw the fire on the mountain. They saw the cloud descend and the darkness and gloom blanket the mountain-top. The wind blew and they could hear the sound of a trumpet blast and a voice that they wished not to hear. The people were to keep their distance from the holy mountain. Not even an animal should approach the mountain, or it must be punished by stoning. The entire experience was so devastating that Moses himself exclaimed his great dread.

Do you know that feeling? Have you ever visited someone's home, maybe as a child, and felt an uneasiness about your presence there, as if you weren't really welcome? I can remember visiting a friend's home and always feeling like an intruder. The home was strictly regimented. There were rules about where you could wear shoes, where you could sit, what times were okay for you to visit. While playing basketball together on a Saturday, the father made my friend go do a chore and just left me there by myself. There was always a sense of not being allowed to touch certain things and go certain places. To me, a gloom hung over the household. It was not a place where I was comfortable.

The first covenant, the one God made at Sinai, symbolizes for the author of Hebrews what is unapproachable. We have not come to a home in which we are afraid to approach God. We do not experience the fire, the darkness, the gloom. We are not scared away by loud sounds and a voice we wish we didn't have to hear. There is not the fear that coming close to God in this home will cause us pain.

THE PLACE OF APPROACH: MT. ZION (12:22–24)

Now Hebrews comes to the positive side of the comparison. God's people do approach God, and it can be described as a mountain-top experience. But it is much different than the terrifying events of Mt. Sinai, when God made the first covenant with Israel. The people of God now approach a different mountain. Hebrews describes this intangible place with three designations.

The first epithet is Mount Zion. From 2 Sam 5:7 onwards, the name Zion is associated with Jerusalem, the city of David. In this passage of Hebrews it is most surprising to find no acknowledgment of the temple, which has also been associated with being on Mt. Zion. The focus, rather, is on the city itself.

The second epithet is "the city of the living God." Already in Hebrews we have come across a reference to this city. In Heb 11:10, Abraham is said to have "looked forward to the city that has foundations, whose architect and builder is God." In 11:16, Hebrews says God's people desire "a better country, that is, a heavenly one." That verse goes on to announce, God "has prepared a city for them."

The third epithet calls this mountain "the heavenly Jerusalem." No longer are we able to identify this second place as a physical locality. It is not Jerusalem but a heavenly Jerusalem. In a similar way, Galatians draws the parallel between these two locations. Paul describes the two sons of Abraham: Isaac, the son by Sarah, and Ishmael, the son by Hagar.

> Now this is an allegory: these women are two covenants. One woman, in fact, is Hagar, from Mount Sinai, bearing children for slavery. Now Hagar is Mount Sinai in Arabia and corresponds to the present Jerusalem, for she is in slavery with her children. But the other woman corresponds to the Jerusalem above; she is free, and she is our mother. (Gal 4:24–26)

Hebrews next describes the residents of this heavenly Jerusalem. An innumerable host of angels fills the city with the sounds of their celebration. God's people, the firstborn of God, whose names have been written down, make up the assembly of citizens. God resides in the heavenly city as the judge of all. The Psalms speak often of God as the judge (Pss 7:11; 50:6; 68:5; 75:7). Hebrews calls another group "the spirits of the righteous made perfect." By referring to these as "spirits," we are probably to infer these are the people who have died and have been judged to be righteous. We have seen that the expression "be made perfect" is most often used in Hebrews in reference to Jesus (2:10; 5:9; 7:28). Hebrews emphasizes that the old system did not bring anyone to the state of perfection (7:19; 9:9; 10:1; 11:40). According to Heb 10:14, Jesus "has perfected for all time those who are sanctified." This perfection and sanctification relates to the priestly consecration by which the individual is enabled to come into the presence of God. Through the work of Christ, the people of God come directly to God in the heavenly Jerusalem.

In this heavenly city, we also find Jesus. Hebrews highlights Jesus' role as the mediator of the new covenant. We discovered this in Heb 9:15, "For this reason he is the mediator of a new covenant, so that those who are called may receive the promised eternal inheritance, because a death has occurred that redeems them from the transgressions under the first covenant."

Making It to the Top (12:18–24)

The final feature of this heavenly city to which God's people approach is the sprinkled blood. This celestially sprinkled blood is said to speak something better than that message said to have been spoken by the blood of Abel, which Cain spilled on the ground through murder.

We get a different sense about this heavenly city. When you were young, was there a party house in your neighborhood? It's the house where people are expected just to walk in. There's always people there having fun. When you're told, "make yourself at home," you believed them. The parents didn't ignore you, get angry with you for being there, or insist on you calling them Mr. and Mrs. These were adults who acted like they genuinely cared about you. The atmosphere was warm and inviting. It made you feel like home. That's how we experience this heavenly city. We are able to walk up to the city gates of the heavenly Jerusalem and walk right in. We are not to fear but to experience the joy of a heavenly party. We are not only welcome into God's home, but we are to find our own home prepared for us.

The first covenant of God was established in a place of reproach, but the new covenant holds out the promise of a mountain-top experience, which beckons us to approach.

When my colleague spent months walking through the forests that lead north toward the end of the Appalachian Trail, he had a destination in mind. Some people who walk the trail just hike a certain portion. Through-walkers begin at the furthest point to the south and walk through to the other end of the trail in Maine.

As I recall, my colleague ran out of time to walk the whole distance. He did, however, walk the last stretch. His family waited for him there on the day he would finish the ascent of the trail that leads to the summit of Mt. Katahdin. Imagine the sense of accomplishment to walk that distance and finally one day to come to the end of the journey. There on the mountain, to look back on how far you've come and to celebrate with family and friends.

The pilgrimage of faith we are on together leads up toward the mountain. Even before we reach the summit, we begin to enjoy the closer sense of God's presence. We become increasingly aware of our complete-

Section Six: Examples and Exhortations to Faithful Living

ness in Christ. We come to realize the fulfillment of our deepest longings as we approach the place that is truly home.

Believing Is to "Be Living" at the Summit (12:25–29)

With all the natural disasters we experience in our world, we never know when the big one is going to hit. When I was a little kid, living in southern Illinois, I thought the big one had struck. My father had been called to be the pastor of a small church in the country a few miles from the village of Noble, Illinois. Because the church and the attached parsonage had suffered fire damage only weeks before our arrival, they would need to build a new church building and then a new parsonage.

I was visiting the new construction of the church one day. I was a curious little guy, I guess. In fact, there's a family joke about that. One day, after tagging along behind Fritz, the farmer on whose land we were living, I am reported to have come home beaming with pride. When I was asked why I looked so proud with myself, I said to my parents, "Fritz told me today that I was a nuisance."

I suspect I was being a nuisance at the church that day. My father was working on the front of the church building. They wanted there to be a cantilevered overhang at the front door to protect people from the rain when getting out of the car to go into church. It all looked very dangerous to me. So I had gone inside the cavernous, cement-block building and was looking around, just amusing myself. All of the sudden, I felt the floor begin to shake under my feet. The lights hanging from the ceiling began to dance in mid air. For some reason I thought that the front of the building was falling off and was going to bring the whole building down. I raced down the aisle toward the front door and after clearing the doorway kept going until I was well out into the gravel parking lot. My little feet slid to a stop in the gravel, and I turned back around expecting to see the church crumbling. Instead, my dad was staring at me, laughing at his crazy kid, bolting from church at the slightest tremor. At times I still imagine feeling the ground shaking and then thank God everything's stable.

In the previous passage, the author of Hebrews imagined the present people of God as approaching God's heavenly mountain. He contrasted it with the experience of the Israelites as recorded in Exodus and Deuteronomy. When the first covenant was given to Israel at Mt. Sinai, the scene was filled with terrifying sights, sounds, and shakings. The boundary between God and the people was defined carefully: The people were restricted from coming too close or they could suffer the death penalty for their intrusion. The voice of God was so powerful they begged not to hear anymore from God.

The new covenant inaugurated by Jesus' death and the symbolic sprinkling of his blood speaks a better message to God's people. The distance between God and the heavens has been surmounted through Jesus and by the effect his actions have had on God's people. The act of consecration, which had only allowed priests to approach God, has now become realized in God's people, "the righteous made perfect." They not only can approach God intermittently and temporarily like the priests did the Holy Place, but they actually reside in God's presence in a heavenly existence.

Just as God promised to the Israelites a rest at the end of their journey back to the land God gave to Abraham, so God promises a future rest for God's people in the heavenly city, a promise based on a better covenant. In the former case, the exodus generation failed God in the wilderness and experienced God's judgment. Regarding the latter, Hebrews warns of a more severe judgment, if the present people of God fail to remain faithful. In this concluding passage, Hebrews warns God's people to beware of rejecting God's purposes (12:25–27). Instead, they should be responsive to God with gratitude and worship (12:28–29).

BEWARE OF REJECTING GOD'S PURPOSES (12:25–27)

Hebrews warns his audience to be careful not to "refuse the one who is speaking." Within the context, it may refer to "the sprinkled blood that speaks a better word than the blood of Abel" (12:24), but it certainly alludes to God's thunderous speaking at Sinai (12:19). The same word "refuse" in verse 25 is translated in verse 19 as "beg": "a voice whose words made the hearers beg that not another word be spoken to them" (12:19). The author of Hebrews is saying, "Be careful that you do not beg off from hearing God's voice, who calls you to be faithful to the new covenant in Jesus."

The reason for this warning goes back to the very beginnings of the book of Hebrews. Remember the very first verse: "Long ago God spoke to our ancestors in many and various ways by the prophets, but

Believing Is to "Be Living" at the Summit (12:25–29)

in these last days he has spoken to us by a Son" (1:1–2). Near the end of Hebrews, the author warns not to refuse to listen to this one through whom God now speaks. The very first section of exhortation in Hebrews begins with this warning:

> Therefore we must pay greater attention to what we have heard, so that we do not drift away from it. For if the message declared through angels was valid, and every transgression or disobedience received a just penalty, how can we escape if we neglect so great a salvation? (2:1–3)

The author comes full circle to once again say, "If they did not escape when they refused the one who warned them on earth, how much less will we escape if we reject the one who warns from heaven" (12:25).

Again, earlier in Hebrews, the author began with the same word of warning, "Take care, brothers and sisters, that none of you may have an evil, unbelieving heart that turns away from the living God" (3:12). Hebrews uses a slightly different word in 12:25, but the warning is repeated not to turn away from, not to "reject the one who warns from heaven" (12:25).

Hebrews goes on in verse 26 to interpret the Sinai experience as described in the Torah with a verse from the prophets. Haggai 2:6 reads, "For thus says the LORD of hosts: Once again, in a little while, I will shake the heavens and the earth and the sea and the dry land." Hebrews seems to be quoting from the Greek translation and modifying it slightly to only refer to the heavens and the earth and to change the word order. What is important to Hebrews is that God "will shake not only the earth but also the heaven" (12:26).

The author of Hebrews seems to give some evidence in verse 27 of a view of the world similar to Platonism, what philosophers call Middle Platonism by the time of the writing of Hebrews. Hebrews thinks of this material world, "the created things," as a substance that can be shaken and thereby destroyed. What cannot be destroyed is the immaterial, the transcendent, heavenly sphere of existence. The eschatological quaking of earth and heaven removes the material world of creation, but what can't be destroyed remains. In the next verse Hebrews will call that the "unshakeable kingdom."

When we think of shaking mountains, we probably remember Mt. St. Helens in 1980. There were indications that something was happening deep inside the long-dormant volcano. According to one journalist, when he was hiking on the mountain in the autumn of 1979, he knew something was wrong. He writes, "I sat down to rest and the whole mountain started shaking."[1] Another person called in January of 1980 to report seeing "smoke and steam pouring out of the mountain."[2] Over the next several months "scientists detected a series of relatively small earthquakes around the mountain."[3] A reporter recalls what happened next.

> Rumbling to life after more than a century of inactivity, the volcano erupted May 18, 1980, with mind-boggling fury, blasting away its glorious Mount Fuji-like dome and north flank. The blast killed 57 people, flattened 230 square miles of forest land and flooded the valleys. An apocalyptic plume of ash and pumice shot 15 miles into the heavens and turned that brilliant May morning into nighttime for hundreds of miles.[4]

One of the people who died that day was an elderly man named Harry Truman. He refused to leave his home and business and died in the blast. The mountain continues to give warning signs that another eruption might take place. According to the news report, what is different now is the "circus atmosphere" around Mt. St. Helens and what the reporter calls an "utter lack of fear."[5]

The author of Hebrews is warning us not to ignore the time when once again God will shake the earth and the heavens, like God did on Mt. Sinai. We are warned not to refuse to listen to God's warning. We will not escape judgment, if we as the people of God fail to be obedient and faithful people in the twenty-first century. We share in the new covenant with God. We have no excuse for failing to hold up our end of the agreement and be the people of God in the world.

1. Erik Robinson, "Mt. St. Helens, Quiet Now," *The Columbian*, Jan. 4 2000, a1.
2. Ibid.
3. Ibid.
4. "1980 Mount St. Helens Eruption Remembered." *Associated Press*, Oct. 5 2004.
5. Ibid.

Believing Is to "Be Living" at the Summit (12:25–29)

BE RESPONSIVE WITH GRATITUDE
AND WORSHIP (12:28–29)

What the people of God receive, what they inherit, in other words, is an "unshakeable kingdom." It is that which is permanent in God's universe that God's people will receive as an inheritance. Not only can the heavenly kingdom not be destroyed, it also is not transient or temporary.

Rather than balking at God's message in the new covenant, we are to accept our role with gratitude and proper worship. We can't help but remember how God's people worshipped at the foot of Sinai before Moses returned. By forcing Aaron to make them a golden calf to worship, they violated the very command God was giving them. The worship of idols is the opposite of giving thanks to God. It is ascribing to material objects the credit for what God does in the world. It is ignoring a proper reverence and fear for the all-powerful deity. The response of God's people is to offer an acceptable worship. The language should remind us of what Paul writes in Rom 12:1–2, "I appeal to you therefore, brothers and sisters, by the mercies of God, to present your bodies as a living sacrifice, holy and acceptable to God, which is your spiritual worship."

As much as we might like to think of God as our buddy in the sky—our heavenly Daddy—Hebrews describes our attitude of worship in the strongest terms possible. Because of this warning not to refuse God because there is no escape from God's judgment, we are to worship with trembling and terror. Notice the context, "Our God is a consuming fire." As different as our experience may be in other ways, this phrase reverberates the nature of God as described in the giving of the first covenant, "the Lord thy God is a consuming fire, a jealous God" (Deut 4:24). An approachable God is still a God deserving of respect and reverence.

Indiana may not have any mountains I need to worry about erupting, but we do have tornadoes. When my family and I moved to Indiana, we left the hurricanes of the New England coast for the tornadoes of the Midwest. While in New England we experienced several hurricanes. By the time the second one occurred I was already getting more daring. The 50–75 mile-per-hour winds were exciting to watch. From the upstairs window I could see the neighborhood. Across the street, trees bowed to the power of the wind. Street signs trembled at the force of the hurricane. But our house could not be shaken, and for that we were grateful.

Section Six: Examples and Exhortations to Faithful Living

In recent years we've had some tornado warnings. From where we live in the city, we can barely hear the sound of the tornado siren. I remember a few years ago when my family went to our basement during a tornado warning. We huddled together in the corner, listening to the radio reports and to the intensity of the sound of the wind. Our kids seemed fearful of what to expect. We waited a long time before we ventured back upstairs. Then we went outside to see how the world looked after the storm had passed.

The last time we heard a warning, however, we were less afraid. In fact, we ignored the siren and watched out the front door; some of us tracked the storm on TV. Like many other people, we've stopped paying attention to the warnings. Isn't that when life is most dangerous?

The kingdom of God that we are to possess, that we even now participate in, cannot be blasted by an earthquake or blown away by a hurricane or tornado. When we listen to the warning God has given to us in the book of Hebrews and determine to remain faithful, by being a "people on the move" toward maturity in Christ, we are able to bow before God in worship and even tremble in awe before the all-powerful God who calls us to approach our heavenly home boldly. As the church of God in the twenty-first century, we need to take seriously God's warning. Our worship and the focus of our lives should not be diverted away from this God who has spoken to us in ancient times and who now speaks to us through a Son.

We have been warned to beware of rejecting God's purposes and encouraged to be responsive to God with gratitude and worship. The life of faith is a life lived at the unshakeable summit of God's holy mountain.

If I were going to choose where to live in the world, I would certainly pay attention to what might happen in that part of the world. For one, I have no desire to live in Florida and get hit with the full force of a hurricane. I wouldn't mind living along the waters of Lake Michigan, but you probably wouldn't find me moving close to the ocean's shore. It certainly wouldn't be California, where any day now the San Andreas fault might become our new west coast. I wouldn't want to move further west in the Midwest. In Indiana we are in sort of the next street over from Tornado Alley. I don't want to move to the center of the twisters' favorite place to dance. Washington state is out; Hawaii, forget about it.

Believing Is to "Be Living" at the Summit (12:25–29)

Maybe that's why I like the idea of heaven so much. I look forward to that peaceful and unshakeable existence. I just don't want to get there any time soon by being blasted, blown, or buried—let's throw in struck by lightning or hit by a meteorite or other falling objects. A healthy fear is one that keeps us alive and living faithfully for God as we anticipate the wonderful world God has for us.

The Christian Path Is a Lover's Lane (13:1–6)

CHRISTIANS MAKE THE BEST lovers—or so it should be. Instead, Christians are often vilified as self-centered, dispassionate, and anti-social. For many of us, our Christian upbringing included a training in a way of life that was set in opposition to what was perceived to be negative influences in society: To protect young Christian hearts and minds from the evil effects of the world, we must react strongly against it; to guard against absorbing society's values, we must insulate our community from outside influences; to counter-act a cultural movement focused on "sexual experimentation and free love," we should restrain our children and ourselves from pleasures of the body.

You've read the bumper stickers. Every morning for about a week I would see a bumper sticker on a car parked in front of my house. It was the one that reads, "Hate is not a family value." As with all bumper stickers, simplistic slogans exaggerate the message to achieve maximum impact. There are a minority of Christians with fundamentalist tendencies who express anger and hatred for aspects of society deemed evil. Sometimes that emotion gets directed at specific people, and it looks ugly. But for the majority of Christians, we have progressed in our faith and understand the guiding principle of Christianity to be love.

That's not just an internalized or spiritual love, a devotion to God, but love that involves how we think of ourselves as loved and lovable people, how we experience love for spouses and family, how we interact with our faith community, and how we relate to the world. In fact, the Bible, when read in its full context, teaches from beginning to end God's love. God's love expressed itself in creation, through covenant relationship with a people, and by giving an only child to die on a cross to redeem all peoples. One place where we learn about how to love is at the beginning of the 13th chapter of Hebrews.

Chapter 13 might seem like the author of Hebrews has finished the body of his speech and is now tacking on to the end some parting words.

The Christian Path Is a Lover's Lane (13:1-6)

We do this sometimes when we end a conversation. Even a phrase like "good bye" is a shortened form of "God be with you." We might also say something like, "Take it easy," "Keep looking up," "Hang in there," "Have a good one," or "Don't take any wooden nickels"—whatever that's supposed to mean. We find at the end of letters in the New Testament brief comments in the form of moral advice. These are called maxims. Through short, pithy sayings, the author provides general advice about the values and virtues congruent with the form of life advocated throughout the letter.

In this case, the author of Hebrews closes his thoughts in chapter 13 by bringing to a culmination the exhortation to his audience concerning their faithful endurance to God within times of stress and persecution. Rather than responding with discord amongst themselves, they are to strengthen their ties within the community and show their love to those around them. Rather than rebel against those in leadership, the author of Hebrews will tell them to follow their spiritual guides and submit to the guidance they offer. Hebrews focuses verses 1-6 of chapter 13 on the proper expression of love within the faith community. Hebrews exhorts the audience to promote mutual love in the community (13:1-3), to protect marital love among the couples (13:4), and to prevent material love from spoiling contentment with what God has given (13:5-6).

PROMOTE MUTUAL LOVE IN THE COMMUNITY (13:1-3)

Within the larger context of the first five verses of chapter 13, three times the author of Hebrews chooses compound words made up of the Greek word for affection. We are familiar with the first term, *philadelphia*, what we commonly refer to as "brotherly love." The NRSV translates it more broadly and inclusively as "mutual love."

Elsewhere, Hebrews has described the love his audience has shown to others. In 6:10, "For God is not unjust; he will not overlook your work and the love that you showed for his sake in serving the saints, as you still do." He has exhorted them to promote that love, "And let us consider how to provoke one another to love and good deeds" (10:24). In 13:1-3 the author connects the ways in which they are to express their love within the faith community.

First, they are to show their love for each other as siblings. They are to nurture that affection in order to have it continue to bind them together as if they are members of one family.

Secondly, in verse two, the author tells them to show love for those who come to them as strangers. The social custom of "southern hospitality" comes close to the ancient value in the eastern Mediterranean world of hospitality. In those cultures, you are socially and morally obligated to welcome a stranger into your home, provide for that person's needs, and protect the stranger at any cost. The term here in verse 2 is another compound word like *philadelphia*, but here the term translated as "hospitality to strangers" means "affection for the stranger or foreigner." While nurturing the sibling relationship within the family of faith, the community should also not forget to express that same affection for those from the outside who come as guests within the community. From what we know of the development of early Christianity, the center of Christian community was commonly a single household and involved a larger network of people, such as family, friends, and fellow-workers. This injunction would have had practical consequences as people sought rest and refuge from travel or were attracted to the group from observing their character and conduct. The author of Hebrews could have appealed to common moral teachings about hospitality, but he chooses to remind his audience about the way in which people in the Bible showed hospitality to strangers, only to discover they had unknowingly been entertaining angelic beings.

Thirdly, they are to show their solidarity for members of the community who have been imprisoned because of their faith. They are to remember them and sympathize with their condition. Rather than forget them and leave them to fend for themselves, they are to practice empathy and imagine themselves as though they were languishing with them in prison and experiencing the pain of torture. The author of Hebrews doesn't say this just to spread the pain around but as a way to motivate the community to care for its own when they are in trouble. In those days, someone in prison would get very little to eat and no creature comforts. They relied on family and friends to visit them and bring them food and whatever else they needed to survive. The penal system often forced those caring for someone in prison to pay bribes in order to give safety for prisoners and to secure their release. Someone without connections could easily die in prison of malnutrition if not maltreatment. The community of faith shows hospitality to everyone, treating everyone as though they belonged in the family.

What would it be like to live in a house in which the family members acted like people do at church. Imagine a member of the family walking in the door, proceeding to his chair, sitting down, and maybe only giv-

The Christian Path Is a Lover's Lane (13:1-6)

ing a nod to others in the room. Another family member enters and her brother greets her at the door, shakes her hand, and says, "Remind me of your name again." Two older family members happen to have a conversation. They've known each other for twenty years. They talk about the weather, their general health, their jobs (with phrases like, "Working hard, or hardly working?"), and maybe their golf game. Here's the clincher. They only see each other for an hour or so once a week and communicate with each other for only 10 minutes of that time. What kind of family would that be? And just because it sounds like your family, doesn't make it acceptable for how the family of God should relate to each other.

Somewhere in the distant past church meetings went from household gatherings to disparate people congregating to participate in a religious ceremony. There's nothing wrong with Christians spending time worshipping God together, but a dysfunctional church is one which only does that. Community cohesiveness is the foundation of the church. Our purpose flows out from the fellowship we have in church communities as individual microcosms of the worldwide family of God. That relationship must go deeper than the casual acquaintanceship Christians experience in most churches today. We start with the love we have for each other as brothers and sisters in Christ. From there we move our sphere of relationship to those who are new to our household of faith. And then we go further to remember those of God's family who are on the periphery of our fellowship for whatever reason. Love moves from the center toward the outside. If a church has no outreach, chances are the church is not reaching inside themselves and promoting mutual love within the community.

PROTECT MARITAL LOVE AMONG THE COUPLES (13:4)

The theme of love continues in verse four, but it moves beyond friendship to marriage. We find here the same type of language, the rhetoric of exhortation delivered by means of concise statements of moral advice. The sentences lack main verbs and are intended to be pregnant with meaning (pun intended).

There were voices within the first century which spoke harshly about the value of marriage. Some thought it better for people not to be bound in marriage. Some considered the sexual relationship within marriage to be a necessary evil for the purpose of reproduction only. The first phrase in verse four can be taken either as a statement "marriage is honorable," or as a warning, "everyone should value the social institution of marriage." Either way, the author of Hebrews supports marriage among couples in the church.

The next phrase reads, "let the marriage bed be kept undefiled." The author of Hebrews is not warning against crumbs in bed or advocating washing your feet before you get under the sheets. This second clause could also be taken either as a statement meaning, "sex is okay," or as a warning, "couples, keep it clean." How we interpret this depends on what follows.

It's the final clause in the verse which puts it all into context, "for God will judge fornicators and adulterers." In other words, cheating on your spouse dishonors and dirties the marriage relationship. You may think you've gotten away with an affair, but God will be the judge. Marriage is more than a wedding. God judges infidelity to a spouse in the same way God judges unfaithfulness on the part of God's people.

As a pastor I have performed my share of weddings. None of them have been marriages in which both people were active members of the church. Most often I've been called upon to perform a wedding just because someone wants a church wedding. One of the reasons couples go "church shopping" for a wedding is to find a cheap church they like and to find a cheap pastor, one who isn't going to make them go through weeks of pre-marital counseling. I can understand that. I don't want to talk with them about sex anymore than they want to hear me even say the word.

Can you imagine my situation as a young man about to be married? Our pastor was my father! It was back in the day when pastoral counseling was becoming popular. Christian attitudes about sex and marriage were opening up. Tim and Beverly LaHaye had published a book called, *The Act of Marriage*. My dad had us read it. I remember Suann and I sitting in my dad's study in the parsonage and listening to him talk about marriage. Fortunately, he didn't try to give us a summary of the book. I don't blame my father for trying to give us a good start to marriage. If anything, I should blame him for not making me take a test on the book.

Loving fellowship within God's family goes deeper than sibling affection. It's only natural that the household of faith honors the sanctity of the marriage relationship. It's only natural that the community support the covenant of marriage. The church must not only promote mutual love in the community and protect marital love among couples, it must also prevent material love from spoiling contentment.

The Christian Path Is a Lover's Lane (13:1-6)

PREVENT MATERIAL LOVE FROM SPOILING CONTENTMENT (13:5-6)

The author of Hebrews for the third time in this section makes use of a compound word constructed with the Greek term for affection. This time it is a rare word meaning literally, "not a lover of silver." God's people are not supposed to have an attraction for gaining wealth. One reason for this bit of moral advice stems from Greco-Roman popular philosophy, which taught that people should be self-sufficient—not dependent on circumstances external to themselves, those things outside of their control—if they want to experience happiness and contentment. This is what our author says, "be content with present goods."

He goes on to support this from the Bible, first from Deut 31:6 and then Ps 118:6. In other words, we should be content with what God provides us, since God will care for us and help us. Those who are "money-grubbers" (another way to translate the term) lack faith in God's provisions for the future. Rather than accepting what they have, they strive to store up against future times when God's blessing might not be as rich as they would like. As a result, they do not need to trust God, since they have amassed what they need to take care of themselves. The reality is, what has been stored up can be destroyed or taken away. Those who have devoted themselves to material goods have no ability to handle the loss and experience sorrow for their misfortune.

How are we to understand this? Let me make some suggestions. You know you're a money lover, if:

- the first thing you do when you get online is check your bank account and your stock activity. If your net worth has dropped from the previous day you are depressed.
- your outlook on the future is dependent on the condition of your investments and 401k plan.
- when you meet someone you judge them on whether they look like they are wealthy. You respect those wealthier than you and take pride in being wealthier than others.
- you consider all wealthy people like yourself to be rich because they're smart and industrious but all poor people are that way because they are stupid and lazy.

- the goals in your life are all related to obtaining bigger and better things, whether it's cars and houses, home furnishings and appliances, or vacations and retirement property.
- your friends and those you socialize with from your church have to be on the same or higher economic scale than you.

Attitudes about money often are the sorest points in church meetings. For many congregations, the business of the church is the finances. Those who hold the purse strings hold the power. And those who hold the wealth in the church are often those who hold the purse strings for the church. When our values get twisted within the church family, the fellowship of the church suffers. Let me put it frankly. At the point when a church becomes dependent on the rich for survival, the church ought to sell its buildings and property and meet together in homes and worship and fellowship in simplicity, equality, and integrity.

According to Hebrews, the revitalization of our churches should begin with promoting mutual love among the community, protecting marital love among the couples, and preventing material love from spoiling the contentment with what God has given each of us.

Hebrews' maxims are a good lesson for us. They're not what we often hear in our society. When it comes to hospitality, we quote Ben Franklin, who said, "Fish and visitors stink in three days." When it comes to marriage, we might agree with Mae West, who is reported to have said, "Marriage is a great institution, but I'm not ready for an institution yet." When it comes to wealth, we might sympathize with Alan Alda, who is quoted on the Internet as saying, "It isn't necessary to be rich and famous to be happy. It's only necessary to be rich." The same introduction to 1 Cor 13 could be made of Heb 13, "And I will show you a still more excellent way" (1 Cor 12:31). Love, properly expressed and experienced, is the family value most characteristic of God's children.

Follow the Leader on the Trail Leading to Life (13:7–9)

Children used to play the game Follow the Leader. As adults, we no longer want to follow anyone. We don't even like to have the responsibility of having anyone follow us. I notice it most often when driving. There are several places I travel frequently where streets or highways merge into one lane. Drivers will race to be in front of other cars before the merge. I'm not very nice in those circumstances. I tend to give them a little run for their money. One time I did that and the other vehicle went over the speed limit to get ahead of me before the merge. After doing all that to get ahead, the vehicle poked along at barely the speed limit the rest of the way. All I can imagine is that the driver did not want to have to be behind someone else.

There are situations where we have no choice but to follow the person ahead of us. When my oldest daughter, Abby, worked with AmeriCorps on trail repair in the Grand Canyon, she rode a horse on trails with her group each day. As you can imagine, the riders had to trust their horses to follow the others on the trail. It was not a time for people to go their own way. They had to play Follow the Leader. Someone trying to take a strange path would not only take himself in a wrong direction and those who are following him, but he could be in danger of going over the side, carried over the edge along with the horse. Abby knew to let the horse follow the others, and the horse got her where she needed to go. Unfortunately, the horse did one time decide to let her off before she was ready. He put his head down and dumped her off the front end.

There have been so many times people have been disappointed by leaders. It's hard to blame people for being reluctant to acknowledge the leadership of others. Not following leaders, however, leads to chaos. We can't solve the problem of failed leadership by choosing not to have leaders. What we will then have are leaders who have not been chosen because someone will take charge, whether anyone wants them to or not.

Section Six: Examples and Exhortations to Faithful Living

People don't want to follow others. They also don't want others to follow them. Celebrities can often be heard to say, "I'm not a role model." "I'm just an actor," one will say, or "I'm just an athlete." Where does it end? "I'm just a school teacher." "I'm just an elected official." "I'm just an elder in the church." "I'm just a pastor." The church desperately needs good leadership. It also desperately needs good followers.

The history of the early church seems to demonstrate the gradual development of hierarchy in church leadership. By the end of the writing of the New Testament texts, there were apostles, deacons, elders, and overseers (bishops). We have very little evidence that tells us how people were chosen and what kind of power they held. The further we go in the history of the church the more complex the structure of authority and the more power is given to certain people.

Periods of reformation and revival have often been accompanied or even sparked by grass roots movements to bring equality and equity to the common people. Quakers in seventeenth-century England were concerned about the failed leadership in the Church of England and the parishes served by men whose salaries were paid by onerous taxes squeezed from poor people.

We must not, however, project the failures of some on to all who would be leaders of the church in the twenty-first century. The need for good role models was present in the first century of the church and certainly is true today.

Besides the notable figures highlighted in the New Testament texts, we don't know much about those who functioned as leaders in the early Christian communities. For instance, we get glimpses of the identity of church leadership at the end of some of Paul's letters. It might surprise you to know Paul mentions about 10 women at the end of Romans, many of whom are described as leaders: Phoebe is a deacon (Rom 16:1) and Junia is an apostle (Rom 16:7). Many unnamed people rise to the ranks of leadership among the early churches, and once in awhile we encounter references to them and their work.

The apostolic leadership followed a pattern established by Jesus and practiced among various groups in that day. Scholars consider philosophical schools to be an important point of comparison. In those groups, people who are more mature become leaders or guides within the philosophical school. Students are expected to follow their leaders and imitate their example. The teacher sets before the pupils exemplary models for

Follow the Leader on the Trail Leading to Life (13:7-9)

virtuous living. Students become mature by following the examples of others. Similarly, throughout our New Testament texts, we find the language of imitation. Jesus is the primary model, but the apostolic leaders follow Jesus' example. They, in turn, encourage people to follow their example as they follow Jesus. Like looking in a reflection of a mirror in a mirror, the pattern continues into infinity. Leaders of today continue the pattern begun with Jesus 2,000 years ago.

Near the beginning of that process was the book of Hebrews. At the end of the author's speech, he brings to his audience's attention the need to follow their leaders. In Heb 13:7-9, the author takes them through three steps of leadership. First, the conduct of leaders presents a model for imitation (13:7). Secondly, the continuity of Jesus provides an ongoing example (13:8). Thirdly, the constancy of our own walk preserves us from error (13:9).

THE CONDUCT OF LEADERS PRESENTS A MODEL FOR IMITATION (13:7)

Twice in the closing verses of Hebrews the author will encourage his audience to pay attention to the leaders. Our English word hegemony derives from the Greek word related to the word in this verse, "leader." It refers to one who does something first for others to follow. Greek authors could designate governors and even emperors with this "hegemonic" title. It could also be applied to those in groups and communities who led the way. In 13:7 it describes those who first came and preached the gospel message to the community whom Hebrews addresses. They were leaders and founders of the community. Their role should not be forgotten.

A common method for encouraging proper behavior among philosophical groups was to remind them of the great models of virtue. The Epicureans would extol the virtues of Epicurus. The poet Lucretius describes him in adoring and even worshipful terms (*On the Nature of Things*, Book III). The Stoics might recall not only philosophers like the Cynics Crates, Diogenes, and Antisthenes, but most certainly the ultimate example, Socrates. Philosophers practiced the spiritual discipline of meditating on the examples of past greats as a means of strengthening their will against the vices brought about by the passions.

The next phrase in verse seven contains a second imperative. Not only should they call to mind those who have been their guides but they should also imitate their faith. What does that mean, "imitate their faith?" Does "faith" refer to the content of their beliefs or the conduct of their lives? But how could it refer to beliefs? How does one imitate someone's belief? Faith here should be understood in its normal connotation of faithfulness, loyalty, allegiance, obedience. That's what Hebrews is interested in. That's what the people are to imitate.

Preceding that main verb in the sentence is what gives us the context for imitating faithful obedience in leaders. Hebrews wants them to be considering the culmination of the leaders' conduct. Implicit in this is the recognition that proper leadership takes time to develop. Leaders are those who have stood the test of time. They have a track record of success. It's not that they never make mistakes but that the mistakes have become fewer and farther between as the years have gone on.

The philosophical life could be thought of as an early form of multi-level marketing. At the top of the pyramid is the ultimate example. Below are those who were close to the individual and who carry on the tradition. Below them are successive generations and levels of people who imitate the example of those who are their spiritual guides. They in turn follow the example of those above them and model that lifestyle for those below them.

Early Christianity followed the same pattern. Jesus was held up as the ultimate example. The closest disciples and the apostles followed Jesus and learned from him. They carried on the work by spreading the gospel to others. Those who became leaders of those communities imitated the example they had been given, and they themselves became models for Christian faith and practice. The church continued that practice throughout the world and throughout the centuries.

This model can be seen in the early history of the Religious Society of Friends (Quakers). Just as in early Christianity, the beginnings of Quakerism were formed in response to abuses of power and oppression of the lower classes of people. As the movement continued, however, there came to be a sense that organization and structure was needed to support the growing numbers. As early as 1657, a meeting wrote instructions for Friends in the North on how to structure their meetings and care for the needs of Friends. Near the end of the list, they wrote,

> That the Elders made by the Holy Ghost, feed the flock of God, taking the oversight thereof willingly, not by constraint, but of a willing mind; neither as lords over God's heritage, but as examples to the flock of Christ. That the younger submit themselves to the elder,—

Follow the Leader on the Trail Leading to Life (13:7–9)

yea all be subject one to another, and be clothed with humility; for God resisteth the proud, but giveth grace to the humble.[1]

I often hear people quote Elton Trueblood as saying something like, "The Quakers didn't do away with the clergy, they did away with the laity." Either way you look at it, whether we are all clergy or all laity, we cannot do away with leaders.

Leaders, however, must not only be those who have personal charisma and professional acumen, they must also be those who have experienced life and developed spiritually and morally, whose depth of wisdom and breadth of knowledge feed the souls of others and remain a witness to God's transforming grace as they become more reflective of the epitome of the divine life, which is Jesus.

THE CONTINUITY OF JESUS PROVIDES AN EXAMPLE (13:8)

Verse eight of chapter 13 is often quoted but always separate from its context. We recite it as a theological dictum concerning the immutability of Christ. The questions we have to ask ourselves are, "How does the verse fit in with what the author is saying? Does the author simply make a theological statement and then go on his merry way to continue encouraging the audience to faithful living modeled on the lives of leaders? Or does this verse actually function within the context?" My favorite adage about Bible study is, "Let your context be your guide." Notice that the previous verse concludes with, "imitate their faithfulness." Verse eight then seems to say, the kind of faithfulness to imitate is the kind Jesus models. His nature and character never fluctuate. Jesus is the same today as he was yesterday and will be forever. You can't get a better model than that.

Unfortunately, the leaders we have do not always demonstrate that continuity. Everyone has a past and for some people the past holds on to them into the future. Ted Haggard, the leader of the National Association of Evangelicals, was held as an outstanding example of Christian faithfulness. But inside he had a dark secret that came out of the closet and hurt

---

1. Abram Rawlinson Barclay,. *Letters, and c., of early Friends, illustrative of the history of the society from nearly its origin to about the period of George Fox's decease, with documents respecting its early discipline, also epistles of counsel and exhortation, and c.,* (London: Harvey and Darton, 1841), 281. Accessed: March 26, 2008. Online: http://dqc.esr.earlham.edu/toc/E11426601.

him, his wife, his family, his church, and millions of Christians. Another leader of a church, Pastor Matthew Winkler, allegedly had his own dark secret that led to his wife, Mary, in what her lawyers described as an act of self-defense for physical and sexual abuse, accidentally firing a shotgun at her pastor-husband and killing him.

We have imperfect examples in our churches, not only among clergy but also among elders, deacons, and others who are looked up to. That doesn't mean we shouldn't try to grow, try to improve, try to become models to lead others in the life Jesus has given us to follow.

The church's multi-marketing structure differs in that we are not in competition with each other. While we each function as the top of our pyramid of discipleship, we are to support and encourage each other for the good of the whole. If one of us fails, it's because we have failed. Our progress is corporate, our success is shared, our ultimate goal is the maturity of the body of Christ as a whole. Although we may fail—but hopefully less often as we mature—we know that Jesus, the epitome of human character and conduct, continues immutably to be our model.

THE CONSTANCY OF OUR WALK PRESERVES US FROM ERROR (13:9)

The final injunction in these verses continues the topic of remaining faithful. The end of verse nine contains a metaphorical usage of the verb "to walk." New Testament authors frequently describe the Christian life as "walking." The author of Hebrews claims those who are trying to walk the Christian life receive no spiritual or moral benefit from strict guidelines regarding what to eat on which days and under what conditions. Instead, what strengthens the soul is God's graciousness. Therefore, Hebrews tells them, they should not be misled by teachings foreign to what they've already learned.

Previously, the author of Hebrews had told them the tabernacle rituals "deal only with food and drink and various baptisms, regulations for the body imposed until the time comes to set things right" (Heb 9:10). In the ancient world, as in the modern world, there are never shortages of people who want to impose religious practices as a way to shorten the process to godliness and righteousness. Hebrews encourages his audience, as Paul did with his, not to be led astray from the path Christ set us upon but to continue to walk in God's Spirit rather than in human flesh.

Follow the Leader on the Trail Leading to Life (13:7–9)

Christians have been diverted from the primary purpose of strengthening the soul by all sorts of strange teaching about products that bring about wellness. Christians will sell you bread made the Bible way, an oil extracted from an Australian tree, jelly made by bees, or most recently a juice formulated with a berry from the Amazon. What they all have in common is the desire to find a secret ingredient God has hidden in nature to make us all well. Strangely enough, many of the products are distributed through multi-level marketing programs. Christians become involved and pretty soon a type of Christianity develops that has some kind of food as the thing the people share in common. Another group of Christians will market God's way to diet and be thin, so you can be more—or less—of what God intended you to be.

Yet over and over again, the New Testament points to the path of following in the steps of Jesus, doing the hard work of imitating the endurance and faithfulness of spiritual guides, and feeding the soul to become strong in God's grace. What benefits us are not plans to get healthy quickly—or get wealthy quickly—but the constancy of walking in God's Spirit.

That's what we learn from this text in Hebrews. The conduct of leaders presents a model for imitation, while the continuity of Jesus provides an ongoing example. The constancy of our own walk preserves us from error. We know how to walk because we have the straight path Jesus has given us. He has not altered his way, Hebrews has taught us. We have leaders who show us by their lives that we can follow them as they follow in the steps of Jesus.

In 1897 Charles M. Sheldon took the phrase "in his steps" and made a profound impact on American Christianity. His short novel by that title describes what happens to people when they guide their decisions by the question, "What would Jesus do?" The pastor in the story asks himself whether he is able to follow the path he sets before his congregation.

> But—am I myself ready to take this pledge? I ask the question honestly, and I dread to face an honest answer. I know well enough that I should have to change very much in my life if I undertook to follow His steps so closely. I have called myself a Christian for many years. For the past ten years I have enjoyed a life that has had comparatively little suffering in it. I am, honestly I say it, living at a long distance from municipal problems and the life of the poor,

Section Six: Examples and Exhortations to Faithful Living

the degraded and the abandoned. What would the obedience to this pledge demand of me? I hesitate to answer. My church is wealthy, full of well-to-do, satisfied people. The standard of their discipleship is, I am aware, not of a nature to respond to the call of suffering or personal loss. I say: 'I am aware.' I may be mistaken. I may have erred in not stirring their deeper life. Caxton, my friend, I have spoken my inmost thought to you. Shall I go back to my people next Sunday and stand up before them in my large city church and say, 'Let us follow Jesus closer. Let us walk in His steps where it will cost us something more than it is costing us now. Let us pledge not to do anything without first asking, 'What would Jesus do?' If I should go before them with that message, it would be a strange and startling one to them. But why? Are we not really to follow Him all the way? What is it to be a follower of Jesus? What does it mean to imitate Him? What does it mean to walk in His steps?"[2]

In Matthew 7:13–15 Jesus says, "Enter through the narrow gate; for the gate is wide and the road is easy that leads to destruction, and there are many who take it. For the gate is narrow and the road is hard that leads to life, and there are few who find it." We pass through that narrow gate, one by one. But we do it following each other, following our leaders, and we find the way together, the way marked by Jesus' steps.

---

2. Charles M. Sheldon, *In His Steps*, 1897. Accessed March 26, 2008. Online: http://www.ccel.org/ccel/sheldon/ihsteps.xxi.html.

The Outer Life of the Believer (13:10–16)

You can't earn your way to heaven, but you also can't learn your way to heaven. The church has had an uneasy tension between faith and good works, going all the way back to the book of Ephesians. On the one hand, there are those who think that the proper path in life is to follow some form of the Golden Rule, "to do good to others." On the other hand, there are Christians who think the only thing that counts is whether you've had a born again experience or not and how much you know about the Bible. No credit is given for any good you do. In fact, it would seem at times like doing good is detrimental to your being considered a true Christian. What counts is how often you say the name of Jesus and how much Scripture you have memorized.

The book of Hebrews has been in the middle of the debate over faith and works. For a long time, Hebrews has been considered to be a tract against Jewish believers lapsing back into the "dreaded legalism" of the Old Testament. In more recent years, Christian scholars of the Hebrew Bible have come to realize the Old Testament was not about Jews trying to obey God's laws in order to be considered righteous. God made a covenant with the Israelites for them to be God's people. To say Jews needed to obey Torah to be righteous before God is the equivalent of saying Americans need to obey the laws of the country to be considered U.S. citizens.

Another recent trend has been the way in which New Testament scholars have come to a consensus regarding the rhetoric of Paul's letter writing. Rather than treating the ending of his letters as miscellaneous advice simply tacked on to the end of theological arguments, they have realized the exhortations at the end of his letters function as the culmination of Paul's rhetoric from the very beginning of each letter. The message of the New Testament is more than thinking properly, it is also about the need for Christians to live moral and ethical lives. Christian spirituality is not just about thinking heavenly thoughts, it is about living and growing as mature humans. Rather than understanding Hebrews as a series of theological and scriptural arguments about why Jewish Christians should not abandon Christianity, we should appreciate the way in which Hebrews praises the life and character of Jesus as God's Son by comparison with the old covenant and exhorts us to take advantage of this second chance to be God's faithful people in the world.

Throughout his speech, the author of Hebrews has been comparing the Old Testament practices with the new reality of Jesus' sacrifice as God's son. One last time the author draws an analogy from that comparison to encourage his audience to put into practice what it means to be a follower of Jesus.

Hebrews calls to mind the image of the ancient Israelite encampment during the years of migration from Egypt to Palestine. At the center of their encampment was the enclosure within which was the tent they called the Holy Place. Near the entrance to that tent was the altar on which sacrifices were made. Hebrews alludes in this passage to the special sacrifice made on the Day of Atonement. After sacrifices have been made and the blood applied to the ark of the covenant within the Holy Place and to the four corners of the altar, there was an additional step for disposing of the sin offering. The book of Leviticus includes special instructions for what happens to the sacrifices. Normally priests had the right to take some of the roasted meat for their food but not in this case. According to Lev 16:27, "The bull of the sin offering and the goat of the sin offering, whose blood was brought in to make atonement in the Holy Place, shall be taken outside the camp; their skin and their flesh and their dung shall be consumed in fire."

The author of Hebrews builds on this language, making it a metaphor for Jesus' sacrifice. Remember that Jesus' execution took place outside of the city of Jerusalem. Just as the sacrifices for sin were disposed of outside the encampment of the ancient Israelites, so also were people executed outside the walls of the city. Jews considered both actions defiling and needing to be performed away from people.

Typically Christians talk about the inner life. Hebrews, however, calls for an outward view. For one, we should focus our worship outside of society's expectation (13:10–12). Secondly, we should follow Jesus outside of what the world considers the proper place (13:13–15). And thirdly, we should not forget the basic message of Jesus to do good (13:13–16).

The Outer Life of the Believer (13:10–16)

FOCUS OF WORSHIP IS BEYOND (13:10–12)

Hebrews presents the audience with allusions to the Day of Atonement as described in the book of Leviticus. How we interpret the metaphor will determine how we understand the overall message of these verses. For instance, what is the altar in verse 10? Is it a physical altar, as some might want to suggest? In that case, one could imagine it referring to a eucharistic or communion celebration in which only Christians have a right to eat at the altar. Early Christianity used that type of language, but it seems to be a later development than the book of Hebrews.

A less literal reading could take the altar to be a reference to the heavenly sanctuary, which has been a theme throughout Hebrews. Yet, the image of the heavenly sanctuary has been limited to the sanctuary itself and not to the altar outside the tabernacle. This type of reading would lead to the ridiculous interpretation that the phrase, "Let us then go to him outside the camp" is an encouragement to mass suicide!

Often in metaphorical language a part of something can refer to the whole. If I were to say, "You are welcome to come to my door anytime," I would not mean you are only welcome to stand in my doorway. "Door" represents entrance to my home. In the same way, the word "altar" may refer more broadly to the aspects of sacrifice which are a part of the actions performed on an altar. Verse 12 applies this to the action of Jesus, which took place outside of the normal location of social interaction.

We shouldn't try to force too much out of the metaphor. Ultimately, the analogy breaks down. Jesus' execution was not on the Day of Atonement. He was not offered on the altar in the temple. His body was not burned outside the city wall. Jesus' sacrifice was like the sin offerings on the Day of Atonement in the way in which both were connected to a location outside of the normal function of society. Sociologically speaking, a sacred shrine functions as the center of a social unit. Power and purity emanate from the center. The further out you go, the weaker the influence. That which is powerless and impure lives at the margins of society.

The author of Hebrews understood his congregants to be outsiders in their communities. Whether we think of a Jewish context or Roman, the followers of Jesus lived on the margins of society, no matter how much they functioned in any other way as a part of their own culture. The actions of Jesus were counter-cultural and so were the lives of those who followed him. Whether or not the temple still existed in Jerusalem at the time of the writing of Hebrews or not, those who followed Jesus could not be a part of the mainstream of Jewish life. In a Roman city, early Christians were ostracized for not participating in the religious aspects of city life. For life in a Roman city was a constant acknowledgement of the Roman gods and of the genius of the emperor. The focus of worship for followers of Jesus was outside of the normal function of society. Serving God did not mean engaging in the accepted means and place for worship within their society.

Down through the centuries, Christians, to one degree or another, have imagined the church building to be equivalent to the temple in Jewish life during biblical times. Some churches even have "temple" in their names, like Baptist Temple. Christian traditions include priests and altars with all of the symbolism and accoutrements associated with worship of God in the temple. This is not what we find in the language of the New Testament. How we came to have a piece of furniture in our modern churches called an altar baffles me. As the Church developed in the early centuries it began to view itself as a "spiritual Israel," a replacement of the Jewish people in the Old Testament. The customs and practices of the Old Testament were spiritualized and became symbolic of Christian beliefs and practices. The altar came to represent the place of Christ's atonement and the center of the practice of the eucharist. In Protestant churches the collection of money is called an offering and it has become a part of the altar table. It's supposed to symbolize the offering of money as a sacrificial gift to God, but it may say more about how we have come to worship our money in the church.

Since high school, I have been passionate about understanding and teaching Scripture in the church. I've devoted much of my life to studying the Scriptures as a ministry, only to discover that Scripture teaches the place of service is not within the walls of the church but outside. The place of meeting God is not at an altar inside of a sanctuary, according to this text in Hebrews. The place of holiness and sanctification is the endurance of suffering and temptation on the margins of society. As many Christians have learned through the years, the place of service is outside of the cloister walls.

The Christian focus, therefore, should not be one inward to the structures of institutions and organizations but outward to places where people live, where people have been abandoned by society. Where would Jesus be in our cities? We have only to drive to the outskirts of our city,

The Outer Life of the Believer (13:10–16)

to the place where our city dump is or the sewage treatment plant. There we find the ramshackle houses and trailer parks. There we would find the place Jesus would be.

FOLLOW JESUS (13:13–15)

The author of Hebrews beckons his audience to follow Jesus' example. He urges them to exit the confines of the encampment and go to Jesus, experiencing the reproaches of society for not conforming to accepted roles and behaviors. That seems to be the best way to understand this passage. An alternative approach takes this text to be reflective of a situation in Jerusalem in which the Christian inhabitants face some impending crisis. But it makes little sense to take this as a warning to Christians to flee Jerusalem. Hebrews' language in verse 13 is not about the city of Jerusalem but the ancient Israelite encampment. Verse 14 speaks of the hope for a heavenly city, not for an escape from violence about to come upon Jerusalem. It also does not make sense to take this as an encouragement to leave this world for the heavenly city. Death would also be an escape from any potential abuse Christians might share with Jesus. The author describes the heavenly city as one which is to come to us, not that we should hurry up and go to it. Rather, these verses invite us to move out from the center of society and identify with a different city, the heavenly city that is coming at the end of the age.

Recall Hebrews' language about this city. The author has said Abraham "looked forward to the city that has foundations, whose architect and builder is God" (11:10). The patriarchs and matriarchs of the Bible desired "a better country, that is, a heavenly one" and God "has prepared a city for them" (11:16). Hebrews announces in chapter 12, "But you have come to Mount Zion and to the city of the living God, the heavenly Jerusalem" (12:22).

In verse 15 Hebrews again reinterprets the language of worship in the tabernacle to the new experience of the reality of Jesus. The phrase in Greek rendered "continually" in English is reminiscent of language about sacrifice in the Greek Old Testament (1 Chron. 16:40; 23:31; 2 Chron 2:4; 24:14). The expression "sacrifice of praise" appears several times in Leviticus (7:12, 13, 15) and in the Psalms (50:14, 23; 107:22; 116:17).

We might expect to see the words from verse 15 "let us continually offer a sacrifice of praise to God" emblazoned across the stage of a contemporary worship setting as the praise team leads the people in yet another chorus. This phrase, however, functions as the first part of the analogy. Sacrifices were offered continually as praise to God and had almost nothing to do with singing. But what we are to offer, according to what the author writes in the application of the analogy, is the acknowledgement of our allegiance to God through Jesus. The "fruit" is the outcome based on what we confess to be true. As the saying goes, "The proof is in the doing."

What Hebrews says in verse 13, it seems to me, must also be what he is saying at the end of verse 15. To go outside the camp and bear Jesus' reproach is equivalent to acknowledging our commitment to God through Jesus. According to the way I'm reading this passage, this means we are to remove ourselves from the comfort zone of our social context, in spite of what it does to our personal status, and acknowledge our commitment to God's purposes in the world through Jesus.

In many communities, however, the church functions as part of the social structure. We might think of the way in which some governments have co-opted the institution of the Church as a tool for their own agenda. In our own society, the Church has also allowed itself to become a tool for the social elite. Hebrews, however, tells us that we should go outside the center of social structures and join with Jesus in his reproach. Our allegiance is not to any particular society. Our commitment is with God's city, the only one that will last, the one that is about to come. We are resident aliens in this world, in this society, in our cities. Find the center of this world's structures, then go outside, and there we will join Jesus.

In one church I attended for a number of years, I had a friend who was into Christian heavy-metal music. Even then he was an aging "Jesus people" guy, not someone you wanted to see dressed in spandex playing bass guitar in a heavy-metal Christian band. He always seemed to be something of a misfit in our sedate and proper Baptist church. He could be an irritant. Like when he would say, "We need to get out of our seats and go." I was never sure where he wanted us to go, he just wanted us to go somewhere. I didn't want to go. I enjoyed my seat in the church.

I'm reminded of a story people tell where I work. Some years ago during the Christmas season, a woman came into our building. She used to work in our building and now works for another department on campus. On her way out, the story is told, she noticed the crèche being displayed in the hallway. She recognized it as having been hers, which she had left in storage on her departure. She promptly picked up the nativity scene, an-

The Outer Life of the Believer (13:10-16)

nounced that it was hers, and walked out the door. One of the secretaries watched with amazement as this woman walked out with our Christmas decoration. In a priceless moment, the secretary remarked, "Jesus has left the building."

In essence, that's what this text is saying, "Jesus has left the building." Jesus left the conventional way of life expected of a good Jewish man and was executed by the Romans outside of town. Metaphorically speaking, we are to leave the city limits with Jesus and experience his reproach. By doing what Jesus would do, we are acknowledging our commitment to God's actions in the world through Jesus.

DON'T FORGET TO DO GOOD AND SHARE (13:16)

Verse 16 clinches the way in which we've been reading this passage. The author of Hebrews once again urges his audience not to neglect the appropriate response of helping people. In 13:2 he had said, "Do not neglect to show hospitality to strangers." Likewise, he tells them in this text not to neglect to do those things which function as the equivalent of sacrificing animals to God in the tabernacle system. There are two related things they are not to neglect.

The first thing not to neglect is "good action." This term is rare in Greek texts, but it represents a common theme for the way in which faithful people of God are to live their lives. The second term is one normally translated as "fellowship" in New Testament texts. Fellowship is far more, however, than just enjoying each other's company and having coffee and doughnuts after church. The way in which we are to perform our duties before God, like priests did continually in the tabernacle, is to do good for others and share what we have with others. That's the way we walk before God in a way which pleases God.

I haven't always been open to Christian service in this way. The Baptist church we attended years ago organized a men's group. I thought it would be great. I imagined men getting together and talking about their faith. Perhaps you would not be surprised to learn that no man opened up and shared his feelings about God. We didn't discuss the spiritual life of males. There was no conversation about how to be better Christian husbands and fathers. Instead, they talked about what projects needed to be done in the community: lawns raked, houses painted, gardens tilled. It was not the kind of group for me, though I was interested in how to get on the list to have those things done for me.

Believe it or not, I once did have a work group come to our apartment to help take care of some projects. Suann's parents and her sister and her husband came all the way from Michigan to Rhode Island just to work around our house. It was during a time when I was writing my dissertation—that's my only defense. It gives a whole new meaning to the concept of "dissertation defense." It's the defense you have to make for not having time to do anything else in your life. Anyway, I was extremely uneasy about having them come to do the work I was expected to do around the house. I was particularly anxious about the job my brother-in-law was given to do. You see, the heat in this house was the kind with baseboard radiated heat. The tiny bathroom in our duplex apartment had a white, metal, baseboard heating panel along the side right next to the commode. After a few years—for some unknown reason—the metal had begun to rust near the toilet. Everyone assumed it was my fault. My brother-in-law was given the task of sanding it down by hand and repainting it. I was so embarrassed I hid myself away in my study. As I remember, I made a great breakthrough that day working on my dissertation. I accomplished so much I wanted them to stay the whole week.

We had a different experience at another church more recently. On our first Sunday we were greeted warmly and our kids were introduced to Sunday School teachers. One Sunday School teacher made a comment about the way in which my daughter was dressed. In the churches in which I grew up you might expect an older woman to scold a young girl for not being dressed up enough. In this case, the woman remarked that my daughter was a little too dressed up for their activity that day. They were going to go and do a service project during Sunday School. I responded rather poorly, I'm afraid. To me it sounded like liberal, social gospel. Rather than study Scripture, sing gospel songs, and pray, they were going to do some work for elderly people in the church. For years I have felt justified in my attitude, until recently. The message of the early Christian writings is the best way to be like Jesus is to be and do good.

The message of Hebrews is, the best way to fulfill what God wants for God's people is to be like Jesus. When it comes down to it, Hebrews is not about theology and it's not about religious practice. The central message concerns living faithfully to God because of what God has done through

The Outer Life of the Believer (13:10–16)

God's Son, Jesus. The simple, kindergarten-level message of this verse is, be nice and share.

If we take seriously the message of Hebrews, we will focus our worship differently than society's values. We will follow Jesus out to the margins of society. We will also not forget the fundamentals of the faith, to do good and share with others.

I give my father a lot of credit for my successes in life. I achieved what I have in biblical studies and in church work because of his example. As I grew older, I came to appreciate my dad's desire to study Scripture, to craft expository sermons, to lead people in deep and meaningful worship. Growing up as a preacher's kid, however, gave me a distorted view of the work of ministry. I only saw the work my father did when he was at home in his study or behind the pulpit. I came to think that was what being a pastor was all about: studying in the office and preaching in the pulpit. But that's not only what my father did as a pastor. Now that I think about it, I can remember him objecting to the words "worship service." He would say, "Service is what happens when you leave church." I never quite understood why he said that. Now I get it.

The irony is, I never learned from my father any of his skills by which I could be of service to anyone. If I had learned his skills of carpentry and house painting, I could volunteer with Habitat for Humanity. If I had learned gardening from him, I could help others in their garden or grow my own vegetables to share with others. If I had learned how to cook from my mother, come to think of it, I could be of use at a soup kitchen. As it is, I have a Ph.D. but no practical skills to be of use to anyone! It's like the Greek anecdote about a slave. While working, the slave fell out of a tree and broke his leg. The comment was made, "That slave has now become a teacher." The old adage is, "Those who can, do. Those who can't, teach." Let me change that to say, "Those who can, do good deeds. Those who can't should at least teach others to do good deeds."

An "Apple"cation a Day
Keeps the Soul Doctor Away (13:17–25)

BEING A PASTOR IS one of the most difficult and one of the most rewarding things I do. I've been extremely fortunate in the two pastorates I've served. Most of my experience has been very positive. But having grown up as a preacher's kid and having attended many different churches, I'm quite aware of how difficult and even devastating churchwork can be. One of my all-time favorite jokes, and one that can be found all over the Internet, expresses the feeling many clergy have about ministering as a pastor of a church.

> A husband and his wife arose one Sunday morning and the wife dressed for church. It was just about time for the service when she noticed her husband hadn't moved a finger toward getting dressed. Perplexed, she asked, "Why aren't you getting dressed for church?" He said, "Cause I don't want to go." She asked, "Do you have any reason?" He said, "Yes, I have three good reasons. First, the congregation is cold. Second, no one likes me. And third, I just don't want to go." The wife replied, wisely, "Well, honey, I have three reasons why you should go. First, the congregation is warm. Second, there are a few people there who like you. And third, you're the pastor! Get dressed!"[1]

There are many pastors who struggle with their vocation. Actually, it's not so much the vocation itself. "Being a pastor would be great," we can imagine some burned-out pastor saying, "if it weren't for the people." But a pastor without people is like a shepherd without any sheep. We commonly refer to church people as sheep. The language of shepherd and sheep seems so idyllic, so pastoral. The reality is many pastors feel like a shepherd who's trying to guide a pack of wolves. Wolves, as you know, not only eat sheep, but they are just as happy devouring a shepherd once in awhile.

---

1. Case Studies by Dan Case—"Pastor Appreciation . . . Month?" Accessed: May 3, 2007. Online: http://www.case-studies.com/articles/pastor_appreciation_month.htm.

An "Apple"cation a Day Keeps the Soul Doctor Away (13:17-25)

There are churches who consume pastors one right after another. The back of a pastor is a favorite place from which to take a bite. Parishioners can take small bites, little nips of callous remarks, cynical expressions, and sarcastic jibes. Or they can tear off large chunks of self-worth, confidence, and even dignity. Pastors would rather their congregations changed their eating habits to become less "clergivorous" and be committed "wordivores." Instead of parishioners wanting to shove the preacher's words back down his or her throat, pastors would desire their congregations to want to devour the words of a message: to think about the sermon, remember it, and to apply it to their lives.

The author of Hebrews composed a sermon to be delivered to a group of people as a way of exhorting them to continue to be faithful people of God, in spite of the repercussions they had been experiencing. He reminds them of what God had done for the Israelites by tracing their story through the books of Moses, most likely in a Greek translation not too dissimilar from the manuscripts which have come down to us. In spite of all God did, the story of the wilderness journey tells how the people of God ultimately failed to live up to their potential. The defining moment was their failure to remain faithful to God and to God's leaders in the desert of Sinai.

As the author of Hebrews looks back at what had happened more recently, he interprets the death of Jesus as instituting a second chance for God's people. It is a new covenant, that which Jeremiah had prophesied. Hebrews believes this new covenant will have a better result for God's people.

Throughout the book of Hebrews the author compares aspects of what one reads in the ancient scriptures with what God has done now through the Son. In this way the author praises Jesus by showing how Jesus compares with the angels (1:1—2:18), with Moses (3:1—4:16), with the priesthood of Aaron (5:1—6:20), with the priesthood of the Levites (7:1—8:13), and with the tabernacle (9:1—10:39). In each case that which God has done through a Son has been considered more excellent than what God previously did in antiquity.

Along with that praise of Jesus through the use of comparison comes exhortations to his audience to make the best of this second chance. The author also warns that punishment for failure will be even greater (2:1-3; 3:12; 4:1, 11; 10:29; 12:25), and there is no third chance (6:4-6; 9:24-26; 10:26-27). The message was foremost an encouragement to God's people

Section Six: Examples and Exhortations to Faithful Living

to work together as God's faithful people. This requires each person to accept the responsibility for him- or herself to mature as faithful people of God. That work is not done alone, however, but within the community of faith.

This closing passage of Hebrews reminds the community of faith to be responsive to those who are leaders in the church. The author of Hebrews concludes by telling his congregation, first of all, to acquiesce to their spiritual guides (13:17–19). The closing benediction urges them to allow God to make them complete (13:20–21). Finally, in sentences appended as the closing of a letter, the author makes a last appeal that they apply the message to the way they live their lives (13:22–25).

ACQUIESCE TO YOUR SPIRITUAL GUIDES (13:17–19)

Previously Hebrews mentioned those who are leaders in the community: "Remember your leaders, those who spoke the word of God to you; consider the outcome of their way of life, and imitate their faith" (13:7). He again calls on the audience to pay attention to those who are their leaders or guides. I prefer the language of spiritual guides rather than the language of leadership, which might imply a hierarchical structure and authoritarianism. The phrase "keeping watch over your souls" implies moral and spiritual guidance rather than control over how people act and think.

Hebrews does have strong language in verse 17 regarding people's attitudes toward their leaders. "Obedience" indicates an attitude which allows oneself to be persuaded by those who guide them. To "submit" in this context is to yield to another's guidance.

The reason for acquiescing to those who are spiritual guides in the community of faith is because of the accountability they have for the souls of those under their care. The Apostle Paul often wrote about the responsibility he felt for those communities with which he had been associated. He expected to appear before God in heaven and be judged on the basis of the work he had accomplished with those people (Rom 15:15–17; 1 Cor 3:10–15; 2 Cor 1:12–14; 11:1–3; Phil 2:16; 1 Thess 2:19–20).

The author of Hebrews hoped the people would respond to their spiritual guides in a way allowing them to view this task as joyful rather than grievous. Not only would it be better for the guides but it would also be advantageous for the people.

An "Apple"cation a Day Keeps the Soul Doctor Away (13:17–25)

The author, in verse 18, states his confidence that he and the other spiritual guides have done what was expected of them and done it honorably. They have tried to do everything in the best way possible. In spite of his confidence, he still asks them to pray for him and the spiritual guides.

Again in verse 19 he appeals to them to live up to this goal. In some way he connects this with his ability to return to them for another visit some time soon. He will tell them within a few verses about his desire to see them along with a person named Timothy. The same Greek word in verse 19 translated "very soon" appears again in verse 23 where it is there translated "in time." Verse 23 reads, "I want you to know that our brother Timothy has been set free; and if he comes in time, he will be with me when I see you." The author of Hebrews hopes to be able to be brought back to visit these people some time in the near future.

The sort of guidance Hebrews advocates includes imitating the example the guides set forth, listening to the advice given to them about how to live a good life, and accepting criticism as a corrective to improper behavior. Most of us don't like to be evaluated. We don't like anyone judging us. If we were asked what is our favorite metaphor for God, I'm sure none of us would say, Judge. If we were asked to give our favorite verse from the Bible, no one would say, "The LORD shall judge the people: judge me, O LORD, according to my righteousness, and according to mine integrity that is in me" (KJV Ps 7:8).

I don't know of any denomination other than the Religious Society of Friends in which each church is expected to write an annual evaluation of their spiritual condition. Meetings are expected to spend time in open worship and have individuals speak from their heart about their own condition. A state of the society report reflects the condition of members individually and corporately. In Quaker meetings with pastors, as in any other church, the spiritual condition of the church reflects on the pastor—and hopefully on the elders as well. Those who are in leadership positions have a responsibility, not only for themselves, but for those whom God has given them as their charge.

Teachers not only evaluate how their students are doing, but the progress of their students reflect directly on their own evaluations as teachers. If a student fails, a good teacher will think about what he or she might have done better to help that student achieve and be successful.

Leaders in the church not only give an account of themselves, but, perhaps even more importantly, they are accountable for the progress of their church members. When pastors and elders show concern for what's going on in someone's life, it's not because they're nosy and want to interfere in the life of their people—well, maybe sometimes. But the reason the leaders in the church need to be active in the lives of parishioners is to help sustain the spiritual health of each one and collectively the health of the church. As soul doctors, they need to give people regular checkups and at times prescribe treatments to regain vitality and warn against dangerous behaviors. Spiritual health, therefore, depends on how well the patients take the advice of the soul doctor.

ALLOW GOD TO MAKE YOU COMPLETE (13:20–21)

What most people probably remember about this benediction in verses 20–21 is what it says about God and what God did through God's Son, the Lord Jesus, the one called, "the great shepherd of the sheep." Those introductory words to the benediction are certainly packed with theological meaning.

At the beginning of verse 20, God is said to be the God of peace. God is characterized by peace, whether through the wholeness and reconciliation God brings or the tranquility and blessedness brought about by a right relationship with God.

According to the second phrase of verse 20, God led Jesus back from the realm of the dead. We find this idea in the early Jewish text, Wisdom of Solomon 16:13, "For you have power over life and death; you lead mortals down to the gates of Hades and back again." Paul uses this same word when he wrote, "'Who will descend into the abyss?' (that is, to bring Christ up from the dead)" (Rom 10:7). God leads up from the abyss the shepherd who will lead the sheep.

The expression "shepherd of the sheep" alludes to Moses, who lived as a shepherd in Midian before leading the sheep of Israel back home to their land. In the Gospels, particularly in the Gospel of John, Jesus is called a "shepherd of the sheep." 1 Peter also uses this language, "For you were going astray like sheep, but now you have returned to the shepherd and guardian of your souls" (2:25).

The word order in Greek makes clear that the action of God resurrecting Jesus was by means of the "blood of the eternal covenant." The covenant God made with Israel was to be an eternal covenant (Exod 31:16; Lev 24:8; Ps 105:10). The prophets understood that Israel had broken God's covenant. They looked forward to a time when God would once

An "Apple"cation a Day Keeps the Soul Doctor Away (13:17-25)

again establish an eternal covenant with God's people (Isa 24:5; 55:3; 61:8; Jer 27:5; 31:32; 32:40; Ezek 15:20; 37:26). The death of Jesus enacted the new covenant in Jesus' blood and with the raising of Jesus from the dead made possible the restoration of new life in the world.

The main verb in the sentence appears in the beginning of verse 21. Hebrews focuses this benediction on the desire that God will "complete" God's work in their souls. We can understand better what this implies by looking at ways in which this term is used elsewhere.

Within a military context, the Roman historian Polybius applies this term to the training the Macedonian soldiers received in rowing a ship (Polybius, *Histories*, 5.2.11). The Stoic philosopher Epictetus uses the word within athletic imagery to describe the development of strength and endurance. Epictetus then applies the metaphor to the training humans have through trials to progress in the development of their character and disposition (Epictetus, *Diss.*, 3.20). We also find this term in a context of education in Luke 6:40: "A disciple is not above the teacher, but everyone who is *fully qualified* will be like the teacher" (italics mine).

The author of Hebrews wants them to be completely prepared for the work God has for them. It can take training and discipline to achieve a mature state, but it is the work God is doing in God's people. It is a work which ultimately fulfills God's purpose in the world made possible through Christ Jesus.

My second to the youngest daughter Lauren plays trombone in her high school marching band. What do you imagine they do to prepare for performances and competitions? Do you think they sit in a room and just listen to someone talk to them about how important marching band is and how hard they should try to perform well? Do they recite in unison lines from the ancient marching band manual? Do they break into small groups to discuss how they feel about marching band? Do they gather together in a circle and sing praises to John Philip Sousa?

You know that's ridiculous. Each member of the marching band has to spend years learning to play their own instrument. Some have private lessons but all have to practice to get better. They have to learn and memorize the music as well as the intricate movements of the performance. When they all get together, they have to learn to play the music in harmony. All it takes is one person to play wrong notes or play at the wrong time to hurt the whole band. If one person trips up or is out of step, it can mean disaster as all those around fall over each other. Band directors and section leaders discipline those who make mistakes and show them the right way to do it. It's a grueling ordeal physically and emotionally to spend intense weeks getting into shape, learning the music, getting the steps down perfectly. And then there are months of honing the performance and playing at football games and competitions. But it's a thrilling sight to see. You can feel the percussion in your body, sense the pleasure of hearing beautiful and exciting music, watch the intricate patterns of movement and the precision of each person working in concert with the group.

This is the way in which we should function in the church. We are all responsible to work on ourselves. Each one develops as a whole person, mind, body, and spirit. Members get together in smaller groups during the week to help each other grow and give each other support. We all gather for mutual encouragement and to learn more and better ways to achieve the goals of the Christian life. The performance comes not on Sunday but throughout the week as we all are doing our part in the world. God watches us along with the great "cloud of witnesses" (12:1). A bird's eye—or rather a God's eye—view of the world shows not only members of our congregation but the faithful everywhere working in concert in the world. And God is pleased with God's people in the world.

APPLY THE MESSAGE TO LIFE (13:22–25)

In a final exhortation, the author of Hebrews urges his audience not to dismiss his message too quickly. We might expect such an appeal to appear at the beginning of a speech or even in the middle. But it seems out of place at the end of the document. It could be that this is a message to those who would carry this speech and read it to the intended audience.

The expression "word of exhortation" could be a formal designation for a hortatory speech in the same way an *epitaphios logos* was the technical term for a funeral oration. But then the author uses a Greek verb meaning "to write a letter": we could translate it as "I have 'epistled' to you." Is it a letter or is it a speech? Perhaps it is a written speech with an appended letter-closing for means of delivery of the document.

The most shocking part of the verse is the author's contention that he has written with brevity. Compared to letters written on papyrus we have from around the first century, Hebrews is anything but brief.

Does Hebrews 13:22 simply mean what many preachers would like to say at the beginning of every sermon, "I hope you'll put up with what

An "Apple"cation a Day Keeps the Soul Doctor Away (13:17–25)

I have to say." Perhaps this verse is his concluding appeal to his sermon. Like every preacher would like to say at the end of a sermon, "I've put a lot of thought and work into what I have to say, so I hope you'll think about what I've said and let it make a difference in your life."

The final verses read like a postscript to a letter: "Tim's coming to see you soon. Say Hello to everyone. Friends from Italy say, 'Hey.' Peace out." The closing reminds us this was a real person writing about real events, engaging with others for the purpose of making their lives better.

We've all heard thousands of sermons and read scores of books about how to live in the world. But how many of them do we really remember? How many have we taken to heart? How many have we let seep into our consciousness and change how we live?

One of our family jokes has to do with Suann watching movies and reading books. She enjoys movies and novels, but she uses them for entertainment and relaxation. She doesn't care for movies with symbolism and complex story lines. She likes feel-good stories that make you laugh or make you cry. For whatever reason, she has trouble remembering the movies and books she's read. It gives her the advantage of being able to watch a movie two or three times and still be surprised by the ending. She doesn't remember the plot, but she does remember whether she liked it or not.

I'm afraid most of us treat the church in the same way. After hearing a sermon or experiencing corporate worship, we can say whether we enjoyed it or not. Too often we wouldn't be able to pass a test on it a week later. I know what the key is to preaching a sermon people will like. Just like a feel-good movie, you have to make them laugh and make them cry. Most people then are sure to feel it was a good sermon even though they won't remember what the point was.

You might ask, "Why would we need to listen so intently? It's not as if we were going to be given a test? We don't take tests on sermons." And that's the point. We are tested in life all the time on what we learn in church and in our own training as Christians. If we are not paying attention to what we are being taught through sermons, lessons, and our own reading, we are wasting our time and doing a disservice to the rest of the church. The church has to stop entertaining itself and get serious about the work God has given us to do in ourselves and together in the world. It's a life-changing and world-changing business we are in. God has given us a second chance to be the faithful people of God. Woe to us if we fail.

Section Six: Examples and Exhortations to Faithful Living

In some ways, this last section serves a fitting conclusion to the entire book of Hebrews. The need to acquiesce to spiritual guides and teachers in the church was a focal point in the middle of Hebrews. Remember how the author chided them, "For though by this time you ought to be teachers, you need someone to teach you again the basic elements of the oracles of God. You need milk, not solid food; for everyone who lives on milk, being still an infant, is unskilled in the word of righteousness" (5:12–13).

The closing benediction urges us to allow God to make us complete. Jesus was made complete by what he experienced (5:8–10). That completion is the goal of each one of us. It was not something Torah was able to do (7:19; 9:9; 10:1), but through Jesus we are able to reach the goal of completion (10:14; 11:40; 12:23).

Then, in something of a postscript, the author implores us to apply the message to the way we live our lives. That's been the author's appeal and even warning throughout the speech. Remember the beginning of the first section of exhortation.

> Therefore we must pay greater attention to what we have heard, so that we do not drift away from it. For if the message declared through angels was valid, and every transgression or disobedience received a just penalty, how can we escape if we neglect so great a salvation? (2:1–3)

While attending Grace College in Winona Lake, Indiana, I went to hear a panel of professors from Grace Theological Seminary talk about the Christian life. Each one was introduced by citing the books they had written. After a few had been introduced, one professor interrupted the proceedings to tell a story. In a similar situation, after theologians and Bible scholars had been introduced and their writing credits established, someone led the group in prayer. He opened with, "Oh God, thou who didst also write a book."

Hebrews began by citing God's work in "writing a book" through the prophets. But what was more important was the work God did through God's Son, Jesus. It was a work that changed the course of history. It was a work that ultimately gave God's people a second chance to live faithfully to God. With that work has come the assurance that God will bring God's people to the ultimate destination, the Sabbath rest, the heavenly Jerusalem. But the focus is not just on the destination, rather it is the way in which we make the journey toward completion together.

An "Apple"cation a Day Keeps the Soul Doctor Away (13:17-25)

The praise of Jesus as better than what God did in ancient times has not been meant to detract from the example of faithfulness found by those living under God's covenant with Israel. It has been meant to give us hope and encouragement to live better, grow to be mature adults in the faith, endure hardships, be obedient to God's work in us, and together become all God would have us be.

I share the sentiment of the author of Hebrews in his conclusion. I hope you have put up with my messages of exhortation. I pray that it has meant something in your life. Unlike the author of Hebrews, I will not pretend that my messages have been brief.

www.ingramcontent.com/pod-product-compliance
Lightning Source LLC
Chambersburg PA
CBHW050618300426
44112CB00012B/1555